A TIME OF BIRDS

A Time of Birds is dedicated to the memory of my parents,

who gave me their unconditional love.

To them I am eternally grateful.

How could the drops of water know themselves to be a river?
Yet the river flows on.

Antoine de Saint-Exupéry

Contents

Prologue – Horizons *1*

PART ONE: WESTERN EUROPE

Netherlands

1. Waterways *11*
2. Miri and the Israeli Immigrant *16*
3. From Holland to Hollywood *23*
4. *Vaarwel Nederland, Hallo Deutschland* *29*

Germany and Switzerland

1. Storms, Bread and Bombs on the Lower Rhine *39*
2. Petra *49*
3. Looking for Marcella *53*
4. Monika and the Chilean Seaman *58*
5. Ghosts from the Past *61*
6. Hitler's Birdsong *67*
7. Romance and Death on the Middle Rhine *72*
8. Cycling through Vineyards *78*
9. Cuckoos and Storks on the Upper Rhine *86*
10. Ingrid's Redstart *90*

11. Manuela *93*

12. Back and Forth *98*

Germany and Austria

1. Starting Out on the Danube *107*

2. In the Wars with Klaus *114*

3. Blah-blah with Kat *118*

4. *Auf Wiedersehen Deutschland* *126*

5. A Detour along the Inn and Salzach Rivers *129*

6. Cycling with Coffins *137*

7. Mary Poppins and the Lock Keeper *145*

8. Sabine and Sisi in Vienna *151*

PART TWO: EASTERN EUROPE

Slovakia, Hungary and the Western Balkans

1. Slovakia *161*

2. Into Hungary *172*

3. Budapest Reunion *178*

4. A Tale of Two Teachers *182*

5. Croatia – Bullets, Landmines and Deadly Mosquitoes *189*

6. A Place Broken *194*

7. Into Serbia – *Cheers* in Bačka Palanka *199*

8. From Belgrade to Bela Crkva *205*

9. Tarzan on the Serbian Border *211*

Romania and Bulgaria

1. Into Romania *219*

2. Spokes and Spirits *225*

3. Troubles in Dolj County *231*

4. High-fives, Horse Carts and Touring Cyclists *238*

5. To the Black Sea *245*

6. Into Bulgaria *253*

7. House Martins *260*

8. Stranded in the Balkan Mountains *268*

9. Birthday Blues *278*

Turkey

1. Into Turkey *287*

2. The Turkish Twins *292*

3. The Sea of Marmara *296*

4. Into the Megalopolis *304*

5. Between Sea and Sky *312*

Epilogue – What if? *319*

Prologue – Horizons

There is a beach, and beyond that, islands. There are dune grasses that buckle in the wind and a cold sea frothing on the shore. There is the call of the gull, a volley of rasping cries above the ocean. I am standing on the edge of the sandbank. Squinting in the sunlight, I look across to the basalt rocks of the Farnes, and remember from school how Grace Darling had rowed from her lighthouse to look for the shipwrecked. I imagine Grace tossed and spun by the storm in her little coble boat as she searched for survivors from the *Forfarshire*. Darling, Slessor, Nightingale and Ferrier: all were house names at my school. But it was Grace I was drawn to – her fierceness and grit out there in the North Sea.

An idea begins to take shape.

I watch the clouds scud across the sky and the light playing off the ocean – slate grey to petrol blue, olive green to steel – then follow the path down through the dunes to the shore. Beyond the islands, there is the thread of horizon between ocean and sky. I feel the pull of the line between the visible and invisible. And I think, *What if?*

This is the beginning. As I remember it.

*

'Have you got a hat?' the boatman asked as he flung a rope over the mooring on Inner Farne, screwing his eyes up against the sea-misted sunlight. I laughed, not understanding, until the boys and I climbed the path lined with Arctic terns – a littering of white, like windblown paper-bags on the verges. The terns fluttered up, snow-pale wings feathered out to their full span, and hovered over us with lashing wingbeats before dropping down to our heads. Blood-red beaks jabbed at our skulls.

'Watch out. We're under attack.'

'The birds!' Jamie said.

'Run for it!' Patrick crouched down beneath the screeching terns, clutching his head, and hurled himself forward.

We ran, ducking and tripping on the path, our hearts drumming with each new attack. I thought, then, of the electric shock treatment they'd given my father all those years ago: the bit in his mouth and cattle prods to his temples. What had that felt like? The short, sharp shocks of electrons ripping through his brain? The convulsion of his body? The aftermath?

Once, my bird-loving father would have adored the Farnes, brimming over with Arctic terns, stubby-winged puffins, kittiwakes, guillemots and cormorants – and the punk-tufted, yellow-beaked shags lording it over the islands from their twiggy thrones. Before the depression and the electric shocks, that is.

The Arctic terns gave me a gentler shock, attacking the numbness in my own head. As we came out of St Cuthbert's Chapel, there was a fresh ambush, the terns swooping low and coming in from all sides, angry, screeching, clacking. I gulped air and my head was spinning with the birds. *I'm alive!* How had I got to this place where I'd stopped feeling? Was it the school where I taught, or was that just the trigger? Or did it go further back to some place I'd buried away?

Back on the mainland, the boys ran along the beach, ill-fitting wellies threatening to pull them down into the fluid sand, their cries lost in the roar of the ocean as they thudded along. Jamie, lanky and dark, awkwardly lolled along the shoreline. Patrick, smaller and paler, a stock of russet hair against the dark sea, turned in circles, arms outstretched. I watched them and felt a motherly love, which was almost immediately followed by an urge to be something more than mother, wife and teacher. Something beyond the horizon.

Gusts of North Sea wind snatched my breath and smacked at my cheeks. Sea spume dampened my skin. I pulled off socks and shoes and ran into the water, jumping over the surf as I'd done as a child. The sea was singing in my ears and the tide's rhythm was a pulse in my brain. On the hillside behind us, in our rented cottage, stacks of school books, test papers and progress sheets lay waiting for me on the kitchen table. *To hell with them.* As I ran through the water, I thought of the soulless school where I worked – where numbers on paper had become more important than children. I thought of my blunted soul and the dullness in my brain, and I feared I had inherited my father's depression. I looked again at the horizon. *What if?*

I ran after the boys and grabbed Jamie.

'How about we cycle to Istanbul? When you've finished school. Would you come with me?'

Jamie shrugged with the nonchalance of a fifteen-year-old and said, 'Yeah, why not.'

Patrick laughed and danced around us, kicking up sand. 'If you two cycle to Istanbul together, I'll eat my hat, I'll eat my hat, I'll eat my hat!'

Maybe Patrick was right: long-distance cyclists were usually bearded, lean and muscle-bound. I was a fifty-year-old woman, definitely not lean and definitely not muscle-bound, and, thank goodness, not yet sporting a beard. Long-distance cyclists were young and single and free of responsibilities. I had a husband and two children – and a job that helped pay the bills. Would Jamie even consider cycling with his mother when he was eighteen? But the idea of cycling to Istanbul had taken hold and wouldn't let go.

*

It wasn't just a fear of depression that came from my father – it was his restlessness too.

He sat in the care home, body slumped in the armchair, white hair thinning, face and hands covered in liver spots. 'Helen, Helen,' he said with a small smile as I greeted him. 'You were always wandering off.'

He took me off-guard in that moment, for he'd closed down years ago, decades even. Like a beach-hut shored up for winter, he'd battened down the hatches and stopped communicating beyond the smallest of small talk that tailed off into silence after minutes. Mostly his eyes were closed, his mind somewhere out of reach. Now this echo from the past.

'You were an awful wee girl.'

My father always said contentment was the most desirable state of mind, and though he could sit for hours staring peacefully out at a world filled with his birds, he also possessed a restiveness. He would drive us children across the cracked and pot-holed roads of Ireland, sometimes for two or three hours, all for a soggy sandwich on a rainy beach and a quick run-around before we did the long journey home again. It should have dampened my own wanderlust. But it didn't.

The dunes that backed so many of the beaches we drove to were a miniature landscape in my childish imagination: where sandy paths between grasses became roads that rose to mountaintops or dipped down to the great spaces of desert plains. I'd stand at the crest of dunes, holding my breath, then launch myself off, a landslide of sand giving beneath my feet, stick-thin limbs out of control, reeds pricking my calves.

My father offered me coastal adventures. And birds. The herring gulls were my first: brutish, in-your-face and as hungry as a seaside slot machine. I couldn't fail to notice them. They dived down for my fallen chips, their cries coarser than trawler rope. I'd make up stories for everything: the gulls, the rocks and the dune systems. I lived in the inner world of my imagination, filled with eerie and fantastic fairy-tales.

In the care home, he was speaking again. 'We couldn't keep track of you. You were always getting lost.'

I wanted to say, *I was never lost,* but this was his narrative and the storyline had been fixed a long time ago. In his mind. I thought of telling him about my plan to cycle to Istanbul, then didn't.

When did we start to walk out of step? I had wandered woodland, meadow and shoreline with him, struggling to learn the names of more elusive birds, my small hand folded into his larger stubby one; my hand growing in his, over the years of my childhood. Had I not learned the call of the road from him?

Daughter, Mother – I'd never felt entirely at ease in my roles. Wife too. Tom held me close the night before Jamie and I left.

'I don't want you to go,' he said, placing his cheek on mine. 'You know I've always supported you in whatever you want to do, but now the time is here . . . well, I'm afraid.'

I was afraid, too, but the panniers were packed and the ferry booked. And my mind was elsewhere, out of reach . . .

. . . on the North Sea.

The Rhine.

The Danube.

The Black Sea.

The Sea of Marmara.

Asia.

PART ONE

WESTERN EUROPE

NETHERLANDS

NORTH SEA

The Hague

Utrecht

50 km

N

Arnhem

Rotterdam

Europoort

Oude Maas

Dordrecht

Waal

Nijmegen

Beek

Berg en Dal

Meuse

Oss

's-Hertogenbosch

NETHERLANDS

Roosendaal

Tilburg

Meuse

Helmond

1. Waterways

From deep within the bowels of the ferry, I thought I heard the thrum of the engine spluttering and dying away. I strained my ears, wondering why the engines would cut out, then relief as I heard the low throb again. I turned over to sleep, but now my mind birled in tune with the rhythmic turning of the ship's engine.

What if my sit-up-and-beg bicycle was too heavy to ride across Europe? What if the panniers were too cumbersome? And beyond the Germanic countries where I'd lived and studied the language, how would I manage in the Balkans, where I would understand little or nothing? How would we ward off the packs of dogs that supposedly roamed the roads beyond Vienna? And what about the Gypsies everyone warned against? How would I manage the hills after Hungary? What if we got lost? What if one of us became ill, or had an accident? What if one of the bicycles broke down far from anywhere? How would I sustain a long-distance cycle over three and a half months? And how would I manage without Tom? He organised us all: took my dreams and gave them shape, made them reality, sorted out the practical details. And how would Tom and Patrick, both hot-headed Celts, manage without me – the go-between in their heated arguments? And what about my ninety-two-year-old father? What if he took ill? What would I do then?

Jamie's breathing was quiet and even, unperturbed by the imagined stumbling heartbeat of the ship, or the cycle ahead. He'd told his friends he was going to cycle across Europe, though failed to tell them he was travelling with his mother. But he'd made a promise so he would keep it.

*

Back in Hull, we'd struggled up the spiral roadway leading to the boat, laughing at our lack of fitness as we pushed down on the pedals. 'Luckily, this is the only hill we're going to see for quite a while,' I grimaced.

That evening on the ferry, we talked late into the night, giddy from cider and the idea of the 3,000-mile journey ahead. Jamie talked more to me that evening than he had in the previous year – prised away from his online world and computer games. I listened to his voice above the hum of the ship. *So, this is what my son's voice sounds like. This is what he thinks.* I smiled. Jamie took life head-on as it came to him. He was the 'even keel' in our passionate household, cutting through the noise with his level-headedness. He was our calming influence.

We emerged from the fume-filled belly of the ferry on the first day of May into the man-made world of Rotterdam's Europoort, eyes blinking in the milky light of spring. It felt as if we'd wheeled our bikes into a virtual gameshow: the grass too green, surfaces too smooth, lines too straight and buildings too angular. The Netherlands seemed devoid of texture and curve, or the worn scruffiness that characterised my own islands. I liked it just the same.

Centuries ago, it had been different. Flat-bottomed Dutch boats with their billowing sails and chubby paddles had been forced to sail through the wild salt marshes of South Holland for days, even weeks, before reaching the North Sea. By the nineteenth century, the engineering-obsessed Dutch had fashioned the Nieuwe Waterweg, or New Waterway, a large canal that connected the Rhine and the Meuse with the sea. The meandering rivulets and wetlands gave way to dredged, dammed and channelled waterways.

At the dock, the border guard glanced at our passports and waved us on into a Europe of endless horizons and open borders. I wobbled off on Gertrude, my Dutch-style bike. The weight of my panniers felt strange, as did the knowledge that I was pedalling into the unknown. I was a temporary migrant, forging a path across Europe against the rising tide of refugees coming in the opposite direction. I felt a lightness of head at odds with the heavy weight of my bike.

Cycling away from Europoort, we sailed into the geometry of manicured meadows, ruler-straight canals and intercepting roadways. There was still a feeling of being at sea on this reclaimed land, in the flatness of the topography and its watery veins, and in the sensation that something was shifting beneath us. There was something shifting in me too. I just couldn't say what exactly, except it was a feeling of coming to after a long sleep.

We continued alongside the A15, past concrete factories, chimney stacks and pale storage towers arranged in orderly rows like cheese wedges. Beyond, pylons, wind turbines and petro-chemical refineries claimed the horizon, along with the city tower blocks of Greater Rotterdam. But there was also the smell of freshly baked bread wafting through the air, reminding me that a semi-organic world still existed between the factories and geometrical lines. On the lawn-short strip of grassy peninsula between the Voedingskanaal and the Breise, we scattered sheep, goats, geese and ducks as we rode along. Mute swans drifted down the canal in ballerina gracefulness, fast-pedalling feet beneath the surface belying the effortless glide above the water.

It seemed I couldn't escape my father. I sensed his presence in the songbirds and waterbirds that claimed the Dutch canals and rivers. Like me, he was drawn to water: the Irish Sea, the Atlantic, Lough Neagh and the Bann and Lagan rivers. As Jamie and I cycled on into the Dutch day, he flittered in and out of my vision – a flash of memory, a burst of song. Before his depression, whistling and snatches of hymns – or the teasing mimicry of pets and birds – had filled our house. And, occasionally, a frost of voice or silence that stopped you in your tracks.

My early life with him had been filled with walks through farmland close to our home on Wood Lane or down at the bird-filled lough. This wild place of bog and water, just two miles away from my house, was a hostile place of reedbeds and midges, but migrant birds happily wheeled in from Africa in summer, while overwintering birds flew down from Canada, Iceland, Greenland and the Russian Arctic. It was a place my birdwatching father returned to again and again.

As I cycled along, I wondered what it was about birds that drew us to them, even subconsciously. Was it their music of the sky? The freedom of wing that allows them to travel thousands of miles over oceans? Their disregard for borders? Seeing the bent wing of the snow-white whooper swan, like Japanese origami against the slate-grey of Irish sky on Lough Neagh, had made my heart flutter. I imagined as a child that if I dared to touch those great white wings, I'd feel the exotic iciness of a far-flung North. If I hung on to its long, muscled neck and commanded it to take me to the icecaps and snowfields of its Icelandic home, I would see the Northern Lights. I envied its freedom in the air – its strong, downward beat of wing across the ocean. My father was warier of the swans on Lough Neagh as one had attacked him when he was younger. He felt happier among the beige greylag geese, with their orange-bright beaks and feet, another winter visitor at Oxford Island on our lough.

Now on the Dutch lowlands, I watched the familiar fawn and white of geese reach for the sky above the pylons, their harsh honks echoing in the chilled May air. And for a moment I was that child again on the lough with my father, when life was sweet and uncomplicated and full of love.

Here, teetering on the edge of my cross-continent journey, I felt disorientated – partly because our ship had tipped us out at the wrong starting point for the Rhine Cycle Route that we had wanted to follow, along the Nieuwe Maas river that joined the Lek and then the Nederrijn, the Lower Rhine. Instead, we were riding beside the Brielse Meer, or Lake Den Briel, to the Oude Maas river and on to the Waal. When planning the trip, I'd been confused by the strands of waterways veining across the map south of Rotterdam, and I'd missed the Lower Rhine path and unwittingly organised our third night in Nijmegen on the Waal. It would take three days of cycling before we'd cross the Waal to the Rhine upstream at Emmerich in Germany – and back on track. In truth, it hardly mattered that we weren't being faithful to the Rhine Cycle Route: the Maas and Waal are also distributaries of the Rhine.

But for now, we were spinning our wheels into the unknown, cycling away from the 'Gateway to Europe'. We hadn't pedalled far when Jamie stopped, unsure we were on the right path. He stood astride his bike, puzzling over the pile of crumpled pages I'd printed out from Google, trying to locate the right one. If we were confused this early into our journey, how would we make it to Istanbul? But at last, we made it through the threads of cycle paths that criss-crossed the landscape to reach the banks of the Oude Maas, or Old Meuse. Here, the river obligingly provided us with a foolproof map: all we had to do was follow its banks to Dordrecht. By mid-afternoon, we were cycling into South Holland's oldest city, an island of tall, narrow buildings surrounded by waterways and waders.

2. Miri and the Israeli Immigrant

My father would have loved Asher, drawn as he was to characters and misfits. He also liked a man or woman who gifted him a story – and Asher had stories to tell and tales galore to spin. He would have appreciated Asher's adopted home, too, at least in earlier times when the marshes were occupied only by waders and shorebirds, not unlike our lough. But over time Dordrecht rose from the wetlands to become a thriving trading centre surrounded by the four rivers of Merwede, Maas, Hollandschdiep and Dordtsche Kil. As we cycled into the old town, there was little evidence of the marshes, or the birds; instead there were tall, thin terraced houses that were more glass than brick, furnished with antiques and designer furniture, and backed by marine harbours and canals lined with pleasure cruisers and sailing vessels.

My father would have enjoyed the daft story behind the residents' nickname too. In the seventeenth century, when

Dordrecht was still a sleepy backwater, two men came up with a cunning plan of Baldrick-esque proportions in order to avoid paying the town import tax on meat and cattle: they dressed their sheep as a human, hoping to pass through the town gates unnoticed. Even if the officials had been taken in by a four-legged hooved animal disguised as *Homo sapiens*, the hapless tradesmen's cover was blown when the sheep began to bleat. The town became known as *Ooi-en Ramsgat*, or 'Ewe's and Ram's Hole', and its residents as *schapenkoppen* – sheepheads.

It seems appropriate then that the equally hapless Asher ended his European wanderings in Dordrecht several centuries later. The down-in-his-luck Israeli arrived in town with no money and nowhere to sleep, but Asher's quick thinking turned his misfortune around, in an unlikely story of love that should have had little chance of surviving.

I'd never met Asher before, but I found him on the Couch-Surfing hospitality website and he'd responded to my request for a bed (or sofa) in Dordrecht with the message: *Why don't you stay for the whole weekend and we'll show you around town?*

Jamie and I headed over a pedestrian bridge into a newer part of town, where historic elegance gave way to featureless redbrick housing. We cycled down a brick-laid road and on past a boy flicking and spinning his football. The street was alive with the sound of children – on bikes and scooters, or idling in corners – and their laughter and shrieks echoed in the spring air. I knocked on Asher's door, feeling a sense of displacement in this Dordrecht suburb, having propelled myself into someone else's world. Asher's wife, Miri, answered with a smile, leading us down a long back-alley to a handkerchief garden stitched with spring flowers where we stored our bikes.

Asher arrived late in the evening after a day of lorry driving. He sank into the chair and called for coffee, chin sagging into tired folds, his skin sallow and eyes hollow. He didn't look like a man who liked to dance, as his online profile stated, but when the caffeine kicked in he came to life, teasing Jamie and me.

He looked at Gertrude, my 'classic' bike, and shook his head: 'Helen, this is a bike to cross town, not Europe.'

I laughed. He was right.

Asher seemed determined to fill the house with travellers. More CouchSurfers arrived the following evening, and I helped Miri make *bourekas* – a combination of the Jewish *empanadas* and the Turkish *börek* invented by the Sephardic Jews who'd settled in Turkey. Earlier, I'd asked Miri if she would cook us a Dutch meal. She wrinkled her nose.

'Dutch food is boring. Just potatoes, vegetables and a lump of meat!'

It was difficult to counter her argument as we filled filo pastry triangles with Israeli feta cheese and minced lamb, the scent of cinnamon, cardamom, ginger, coriander spices and toasted sesame seeds permeating the whole house – a taste of our final destination at the start of our journey.

When the *bourekas* were ready, seven of us squeezed together around the small table. Asher looked around, ready to hold court.

'So how did you and Miri meet?' I asked him.

'On the boat from Israel to Europe.'

'How romantic.'

'Oh, no – not romantic!'

*

Asher had met two Dutch girls on the boat from Haifa. On disembarking, the women gave him their Dordrecht addresses. Miri wrote on one side of a card, her friend on the other.

Asher set off across France alone. At his first lodgings he helped himself to the bowl of 'complimentary' croissants on his table, then those from other tables. When he went to check out, he was presented with a bill for all the croissants he had eaten: the total amounted to his entire travel savings. Penniless, Asher hitch-hiked to Paris, taking up residence behind a railway station locker. Eventually, he scraped together enough money to travel to Amsterdam, where a friend had promised to get him work. But when he arrived in the city, he could find neither his friend nor a job. Winter had arrived and a biting cold wind swept over the lowlands. Somehow, Asher found himself in a country lane near Dordrecht on Christmas Eve. Snow began to fall and the temperature plummeted even further. Then through the darkness, he saw headlights. Asher flagged the car down.

'Where do you want to go?' the driver asked.

Asher had no idea, then remembered the girls from the boat. He pulled the card out of his wallet and handed it to the driver. The man read the side with Miri's address on and drove him there. She took him in, but Asher still couldn't find a job. His dream of settling in Europe was unravelling and he realised he'd have to return to Israel. Miri accompanied him to the station, but when they reached the platform, the train was pulling out. It was then Asher had an idea: he turned to Miri and asked if she would marry him.

'No strings attached,' he said. 'Once I have my green card, you can divorce me. I'll give you to midnight on Wednesday night to decide. If I don't hear from you, I'll take the train on Thursday morning and return to Israel.'

Asher went to stay with some friends and waited for Miri's call. By late Wednesday night, Asher still hadn't heard from her. Three minutes before midnight, the phone rang. It was Miri.

'All right, I'll marry you.'

It was a marriage of convenience that became a love affair. But just as Asher's life seemed to be coming together, the relationship fell apart. The couple went to the council office to file for divorce, only to be told that a cooling-off period was compulsory in Dutch law. All they could do was register their intention and come back in two weeks. The day before they were due to return to the council office, Miri phoned Asher.

'I'm pregnant,' she said. The divorce was off.

In 1995, Asher and Miri welcomed a daughter to the world. On Asher's birthday in 1997, Miri gave birth to their second child, a son. Twenty years later, they were still together.

*

Asher was a natural raconteur and joker. It was difficult to know when he was serious and when he was jesting.

'Noah's Ark is right here in Dordrecht,' he said. 'Not in Turkey, not on Mount Arafat, but just behind the house on the river – one minute away. Yes, really. Come, I show you.'

Asher was already on his feet and heading out the back gate. I followed, no time to gather my shoes, running down the path after him in my socks. He turned a corner onto the river promenade and stopped abruptly.

'It's not here! Where have they put Noah's Ark?' He looked up and down the river, shaking his head in disbelief.

Later, around the dinner table, Asher still looked as if he was reeling from the missing ark.

'Don't believe him,' their son said. 'There is no Noah's Ark. He's making it up.'

'No, no,' said Asher. 'It really does exist. Look, I show you a picture in the newspaper.'

He rummaged through a stack of newspapers, but to no avail: the article was missing. We continued eating, but just as it seemed Asher had forgotten the ark, he jumped up and beckoned us to follow him.

'Come, I know where Noah's Ark is. We go there in my car. It's not far.'

Asher drove us through the back streets of Dordrecht to the edge of town and took an unmade road down to the river. And there was a wooden vessel moored on its bank, so chunky and simple in outline it looked like a child's drawing. This was Noah's Ark: 300 cubits in length, fifty cubits wide and thirty cubits tall – built to the exact biblical dimensions.

I'd sung the Noah's Ark chorus in my tin-hut Sunday school decades earlier. My father led the Sunday school, gathering the 'scholars', as he called them, on the way there until the car was crammed with writhing children. I pumped the organ for the choruses we sang – unusually, as many Brethren halls excluded instruments from their meeting places. The choruses retold the Bible stories in song: *Mr Noah Built an Ark*; *The Wise Man Built His House*; even a rendition of the books of the Bible. Then we gathered in groups to listen to our Sunday school teacher teach us the Gospel, pairs of hard benches turned to face each other so that we could huddle in groups according to our age. I was fascinated by the story of the animal pairs entering the ark, two by two, and the dove who flew down to the ark with a fresh olive twig, an indication that the flood was receding.

And here, on this Dutch river, was a real-life ark looming out of the darkness. It looked too heavy to float as it towered over us, two plastic giraffes standing guard at either end of the boat.

'The ark was built by a rich man from Dordrecht,' Asher said. 'He began with half-size, then his friends and family say how good it is, so he builds a full-size one. Like the Bible.'

'What's inside?'

'Two of all animals. No! Really, he makes a café, two cinemas and has some plastic animals – but real living chickens!'

It was a strange mix of Bible and kitsch.

*

Early on the Sunday morning, Jamie and I, back on the road again, slipped past the ark silhouetted against the half-light – its name, *Ark van Noach*, lit up in neon lights – and I wondered if I was cycling away from the past or into it. As light filled the sky, the song of the thrush echoed through the branches of woodland on the edge of a housing estate.

Listen, Helen. Can you hear the thrush?

My father's voice was still with me, following me along the Waal.

*

3. From Holland to Hollywood

There was a single blue guitar on the edge of the Dutch village – a plywood cut-out secured to a post. No words beneath it. No advertisement, or name. Nothing to say why it was there.

We swung our bikes off the main road and cycled past the guitar. We were not in search of music, just coffee. Ahead were pairs of notes, swinging from frames and bolted to the walls and gables of houses. We rounded a corner to see a saxophone and more guitars. What was this? A music convention? A village festival? Towards the centre of the village, names began to appear: Frank Sinatra, The Andrews Sisters, Vera Lynn. It was still early Sunday morning and the village was devoid of life despite the musical decorations.

Asher and Miri's house in Dordrecht seemed far away now, although our musical village was just a short car journey away. In the dawning, we'd headed out of the Dordrecht suburbs and crossed the river, following the line of the railway. There had been no one around so early in the morning except for a couple with their children, walking the path. Father and son were dressed in Sunday suits and ties, and buffed shoes that reflected the cloud-splattered sky; mother and daughter in long skirts and headscarves, all carrying Bibles. They were on their way to church.

Growing up in Northern Ireland, my own Sundays were filled with meetings, hymns, sermons and formal dress. We were Plymouth Brethren, our meeting house lost in the folds of fields, narrow lanes and high hedgerows. Our church was a simple whitewashed building – although the Brethren saw the church as people, not buildings, and preferred to talk about assemblies or meeting halls. There was no soaring spire, stained-glass window or wood-carved pulpit, just plain austerity. Inside, the Brothers sat on hard benches around a cast-iron wood burner, constantly fed in winter by one of the elders. There were long *words* (sermons) from the scriptures – filled with 'thee' and 'thou' – readings and prayers, and lengthy pauses that amplified the loud ticking of the old clock while the Brothers waited for the Spirit to move them to speak. By their sides, the women sat demurely in tailored suits and smart hats. There were sober hymns, too, sung *a cappella*.

I was always glad when the one-and-a-half-hour meetings came to an end. It was a long time to sit in such sobriety and not wriggle. When I finally stepped out through that low doorway and blinked in the daylight, I inhaled the fresh air deeply, the natural world stirring me more than the sermons and prayers and hymns in the shadowy hall ever could. On summer days, my brothers and sisters and I started out on foot towards home along country lanes, while my father stayed behind to meet with the other elders. Cow parsley, brambles, dog rose and bindweed tangled the verges. I gathered wild flowers and picked blackberries. I preferred the songbirds that accompanied us on our way – the tits and finches that threaded through the hedgerows – to the sombre hymns. Sometimes, we'd walk nearly two miles, almost to the main road before our father picked us up. I didn't mind. I liked the freedom of the country lanes.

Here in twenty-first-century Netherlands I was also glad

to be out in the fresh air again, cycling along to the sound of warbler, wren and wood pigeon, as well as church bells. The darkened sky looked ominous – a threatening iron bar above our heads.

As we'd pedalled deeper into the Dutch countryside towards Germany, there had been a slow realisation that I was cycling further and further away from home. I was a vagrant, a traveller of no fixed abode. A sense of loneliness, mixed with excitement, settled in as we rode on. In England, I would have walked into the kitchen by this time and plugged in the kettle, sunk into the sofa, cradling a hot mug of coffee. Here, I didn't know where I could find a coffee – or even hot water. There was no sofa – just my saddle. At best, we'd find a riverside bench. I thought of the refugees coming in the opposite direction, with their leaky boats and makeshift tents. My journey didn't compare. But, like them, I was moving through a landscape of unfamiliar faces and we were invisible to them. At the same time, there was also a tug, pulling me eastwards and southwards towards the thrill of the unknown. My temporary migration was an indulgence. Theirs was one of survival.

At the end of the musical village's main street, a banner arched over the road with the words 'Land of Hope and Glory'. I'd hoped to find a café but there was none to be seen, so Jamie and I dropped our bikes and set down on a low wall beside a corner house, resigning ourselves to sharing a bar of chocolate Tom had slipped into my panniers. We sat in companionable silence, contenting ourselves with a swig of water. Jamie leaned against the wall, sooty hair dishevelled, his thick black eyebrows knitted together in thought. He stretched out long, thin legs. On his second birthday, we'd measured his height. We'd read that if you doubled a two-year-old's height, you could calculate how tall it would be in adulthood. We worked out he would be six foot eight. Six foot eight!

'Can't be very accurate,' I'd said to Tom.

But Jamie continued to grow at a pace. When he was three, a stranger stopped me in the street to ask why he wasn't at school. In his infant school, they'd drawn round Jamie's body to create a giant for a display. By eighteen, he hadn't quite reached six foot eight, just six foot five. But still his height drew attention, exaggerated by his skinny frame.

As we shivered in the sun-starved air, a man came out of the house, speaking to us in Dutch. We shifted uneasily on his wall, hoping he wasn't scolding us for loitering outside his home. Then, noting our blank looks, he switched to German.

'Where have you cycled from?'

'Dordrecht.'

He looked impressed. 'And where are you going?'

'Istanbul.' The word felt ridiculous as it left my lips.

'Istanbul!'

It seemed absurd to mention a place so far away, so I changed the subject and asked him about the musical decorations.

'We commemorate the liberation of the Netherlands by the Allies every five years in the Netherlands. This year, each house in the village will have their choice of wartime music played over speakers. There'll be dancing and fireworks. It's a big event here.'

Now it made sense.

'I've got an old American jeep there in the garage. I'm taking it on parade with invited veterans from Britain, Canada and the US this evening. Go and have a look.'

As I peered into the garage, I tried to imagine what occupation felt like, or the exuberance of liberation. My own grandparents and parents had also lived under the threat of occupation – but it remained just that. More pertinent to my grandmother was the threat of conscription. Her greatest fear was that her son would be called up, so she persuaded my father to volunteer as an ambulance driver in Belfast. Whether she feared for his life or whether she felt he was needed in his father's greengrocer's shop was never clear – nor how he felt about the experience. He never spoke about his time as a volunteer, and I could only guess he'd witnessed horrific injuries, even death. The silence around the subject was palpable. Could his experiences have contributed to the deep depression that settled like dust towards the end of his life – the suppressed anger that at times threatened to surface? The futility of my grandmother's endeavours was not lost on me: conscription never came to Northern Ireland.

At home, in one of our albums containing photographs stuck in with browning Sellotape, there's a rare black-and-white picture of my father from 1939. He's gazing clear-eyed and solemn into the camera, his mouth slightly open in an expression of both uncertainty and anticipation. To one side, there's a purple ink mark that made me wonder if this picture was his wartime ID. My father is wearing a suit and tie – the uniform of his life – but also a Fair Isle jumper. It must have been winter. Europe, to be followed by much of the world, was just starting out on a path of devastation and no one had any idea where it would all end.

There's another photograph of my parents, not dated, but probably taken just after the war. My parents look happy: the world is at peace; their life is full of promise and they are in love. My mother is standing close beside my father, wearing a smart dress, a pearl necklace and a gaudy brooch. Her hair's tied up and her eyes cast down to one side, looking demure and rather pleased with the world at the same time. My father's wearing goofy, Lennon-round sunglasses with what looks like white frames, and has a chequered tank-top on, his tie flopping outside of it. He's grinning at the camera, looking pleased with the world too. They have a look of survivors. Later, their love will be challenged, but they will cling to the flotsam of their marriage – and I will feel that I am being swept along with their wreckage – until the storms subside. War takes its toll long after a peace agreement has been reached.

As the Dutchman started to go back inside his house, I asked him where I could find a café.

'You won't get anywhere open around here today as it's Sunday – and a holiday as well.'

He hesitated, then spoke to his wife who'd just appeared. Turning back to me, he said, 'Look, we have to go to my nephew's birthday celebrations now, but my wife is going to make some coffee for you. Leave the cups on the wall. No one will steal them here.'

His wife arrived with a tray of hot coffee and brownies and the pair climbed into their car, waving cheerfully as they drove off. I had not counted on this – this random act of kindness from strangers. My depression, I realised, had distorted my world. I had focused on the negatives throughout my youth and adulthood. I needed to rewrite my own narrative with all its light and shade. There was light, wasn't there? Dappled and shadowy, warm and fiery in the fields where I played, and in my own home.

And so, warmed by the coffee and the generosity of the jeep owner and his wife, we mounted our bikes again and headed on into the next village, along 'Route 66'. We passed makeshift Burger King and McDonald's signs; 'Sunset Boulevard' with its plastic palm trees; a plywood cut-out of Mount Rushmore (the heads of local politicians rather than the presidents of the United States 'chiselled' into the rock); and a miniature White House with its neoclassical columns. I was learning that journeys were never what you expected.

4. *Vaarwel Nederland, Hallo Deutschland*

The Netherlands looked as if it had been pressed out by a rolling pin, the flattened land a thin strip beneath the wheel. It was the sky that filled our vision – shifting firmament rather than solid land, more water than grass and clod. Our colour palette was dominated by blues and greys and bursts of luminous light, not the solid greens and yellows and browns of earth. And the traffic that filled our eyeline was not of car, van, lorry or even bicycle, but bird. Geese flew above us, an orderly dart, while waders and small, indiscernible brown birds flittered in and out of the grey-blue. I wished I had paid more attention to my father. Which of these birds were overwintering? Which were flying in from the Mediterranean, West or North Africa for the breeding season? Which were heading northwards to Iceland or Scandanavia? And which were merely stopping off to fuel up before continuing on the long journey? I was almost as ignorant about this traffic of the sky as my ancestors who believed migratory birds hibernated, disappearing into holes and crevices for the winter.

When we headed out of Nijmegen, near the border with Germany, the next morning, the rise ahead took us by surprise. I expected the ascent to be short, but the road out of town continued to climb with no sign of a summit. On reaching Berg en Dal, I had to smile. The suburb of Nijmegen was hardly a *berg* – a mountain – but after the flatness of South Holland and Gelderland, I could hardly blame the Dutch for a little hyperbole.

Then our first free-wheel down into Beek – a one-in-ten gradient. We flew past lycra-clad cyclists grinding upwards through the woodland in the opposite direction. There was something else that was different, something that had been missing the entire way across the Netherlands: the road that dropped to Beek was thick with undergrowth and trees.

We plunged into inky darkness.

And lost the sky.

*

At Beek, we stopped for coffee and cake, the border town lined with elegant hotels and cafés, clearly popular with the incline-starved Dutch. We sat in the window of a Victorian hotel full of dark wood and shiny surfaces, and savoured our last Dutch apple cake. The crumble of the pastry, the crunch of tart apple, the sticky sweetness of sultana and the delicate spice of cinnamon had sustained Jamie and I across the lowlands, along with dark, aromatic Dutch coffee.

It wasn't only the *appeltaart* I would miss about the Netherlands. There was the friendly, straight-talking Dutch; the tall, thin buildings, with their 'out-of-proportion' windows; the geometric line of dyke, canal and road; the manicured countryside; the scrubbed homes; the unexpected quirkiness and the sharp Dutch humour. They made me think of my mother's family – the Poots. These Northern Irish farmers claimed their Dutch ancestors were granted land in County Down by William of Orange, who'd arrived in Ireland to protect it against Catholicism in the 1690 Battle of the Boyne, an ancient battle that Unionists still commemorate every year on 12 July. It was a romantic story that my Protestant relatives had latched on to, and I wondered if it was more wish than reality.

Later, I discovered there were indeed a few hundred Poots living in the Netherlands, particularly around Rotterdam. I knew there had been a strong linen industry in County Down, and that the Dutch and British had always exchanged trade and skills – perhaps the Poots had come from the Netherlands to rural Ulster to sew flax and to build weaving machines and linen factories. My mother's family had become farmers and business people, with a Protestant work ethic akin to the Dutch. It would explain why I felt at ease in this foreign land of waterway and polder. Everywhere I cycled in the Netherlands, I saw my grandfather and my aunts and uncles in determined jawlines and square faces; in sharp, shrewd eyes, straw-blond hair, weathered skin and high brows. There was an intent of gait and a toughness of demeanour that was familiar to me, perhaps imagined, perhaps not.

I thought of the Dutchman with his American jeep, celebrating the liberation of the Netherlands. Then the hardship, wars and persecutions that forced individuals and families to travel hundreds and thousands of miles for a better life or for survival: the Jewish Dutch escaping death to seek out a promised land; Asher making the return journey to Europe, to the Netherlands for a promise of something better; my Dutch ancestors seeking out a far-flung island of drumlin and bog where flax thrived. There were those other ancestors of mine who had crossed to Scotland from Ireland, only to return again during the Plantation (or colonisation) of Ulster in the seventeenth century. I was also of Ulster-Scots descent, with family names such as Wilson and McCullough. Who else was in my mix? Normans? Vikings? Saxons? Something even more exotic? I thought about the restlessness of the human race, criss-crossing the planet, undeterred by seas or walls or borders; the Syrian and North African refugees and migrants who were crossing the Mediterranean as I wobbled off across the Netherlands to Istanbul. Each day I saw fresh pictures of them on my newsfeed, sea-salted men and women and children rescued from boats that looked as flimsy as a child's bath-time tug. Others had been less fortunate, but still they came. Many of them felt they had no choice: to stay was to die; in leaving they had a chance.

Knowing the Rhine was now close at hand, I pushed down hard on the pedals towards the river marshes of the Düffel. These lowlands between Nijmegen and Kleve were once a primeval landscape of marsh and forest: a hostile environment of rubble, gravel banks and tidal pools caught in a tangle of willow, oak and elm, frequently washed over by the flood waters of the Rhine. There were remnants of this watery landscape on the edge of Beek – a world of ponds, wetlands and water channels.

In the remaining preserved ponds, sand banks, ditches, reeds and grasses, overwintering geese rested and fed here, along with shore and meadow birds.

It was an enchanting place that reminded me of trips with my father to the bird hides on Oxford Island at Lough Neagh, where we'd perched on thin wooden posts like the waders out on the water. The countryside around the lough was a place of enchantment too. In the school holidays, my father took me out in his green grocery van along narrow lanes, tooting the horn on every corner. I'd sit on the meal bags at the back. Sometimes, if I pleaded, he'd let me sit on the metal engine cover that rattled and vibrated beneath me, my father, next to me, smelling of Brylcreem, earthy potatoes, meal bags and the leather of his money bag. He dropped off boxes of groceries at farmsteads and cottages and left with armfuls of daffodils, crocuses and garden fruits for jam. Often, he'd pull the van over to listen and watch for birds.

*

'Kann ich Ihnen hilfen?'

On the edge of the Düffel village of Zyfflich, a small sign unceremoniously told us we were in Germany. We'd stopped to check one of the Dutch numbered cycle maps that had some-how spilled beyond the Netherlands border.

I turned to the villager who'd stopped to ask if we were okay. *'Schon gut, danke.'*

I grinned, pleased to hear a language I could understand; happy that a German had stopped to help us moments into Germany. It boded well. I'd studied German at university and was fascinated by the country's history and culture – even the darker elements of its recent past – and I was confident I'd feel more at home here, especially as I would be meeting old friends along the way. On a journey full of unknowns, it was comforting to be in a land that I was familiar with in some way.

On the edge of Zyfflich we found a bench for our packed lunch. Looking across the village, the change in buildings and their surroundings was already marked by a more natural look, a managed scruffiness that was not quite as pristine as the scrubbed Dutch towns and villages. We followed country lanes across the Düffel to the village of Mehr.

'More?' I joked with Jamie. 'Villagers of Mehr, don't be greedy!'

Jamie wrinkled up his nose at my silly joke. I wondered how long it would be before our relationship would fray, enduring each other's company virtually twenty-four hours a day.

Soon we reached the Oraniendeich, flying along the road on top of the dyke that was leading us ever closer to the Rhine. For a moment, the sun came out and warmed my skin. The air was fresh and gentle. I felt my pulse slow and the tightness in my chest loosen. A long-forgotten sense of peace stirred.

I remembered the Friday I'd walked out of my teaching job, fully intending to go back on the Monday. I never returned. The politics of a broken education system and the cold head teacher had made me sick. The days and months that followed were black. I couldn't sleep at night and couldn't stay awake in the day. I had yearned to leave teaching, but now that I was gone I didn't know what I was or what I could be. I went for long walks with Tom, but the Peak District countryside I loved did nothing for me. The birds' songs seemed hollow, the dales and moorlands dull. Once, we travelled for six hours to Scotland and I never spoke the whole journey. It was as if I had been pulled down into a blanket of shadows and couldn't find the way out. But I started to write a guidebook on the Peak District and my passion for my adopted home slowly returned. The depression receded, but would creep up on me when I felt I was getting better. How had I ended up in the same place as my father? And what if I never fully recovered – like him? I'd felt afraid. But here, on this German dyke, I now felt hope.

We crossed the bridge into Emmerich. The birds were in full throttle on this early May day. The air was filled with the scent of damp leaf and fresh bud. I would follow my newfound and burgeoning hope along the Rhine through Germany to Schaff-hausen in Switzerland. And beyond.

GERMANY AND SWITZERLAND

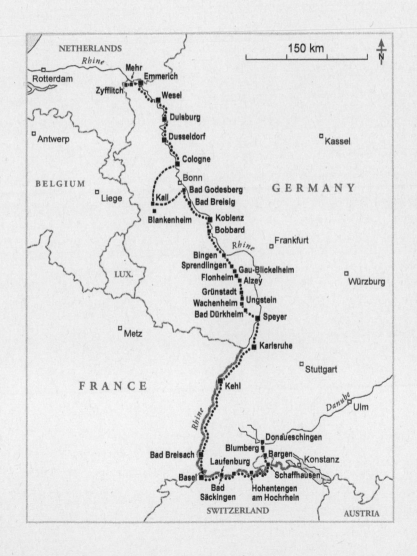

1. Storms, Bread and Bombs on the Lower Rhine

There was a storm coming. The sky hung low, pressing us into our saddles. From Wesel, we crossed the bridge and followed the west bank of the Rhine. The wind snapped at our wheels and the sky began to leak slow, fat drops on our heads; a slow beat, then a sharp drumroll. *Largo* to *vivace*. The journey still felt strange and uncertain. It was like trying on a new outfit and working out if it fitted, if it felt comfortable. If it felt right.

Hunger and rain drove us into a riverside hotel.

'*Ruhetag*,' the hotelier said without looking up from brushing the floor. I sighed, wondering why Germany still insisted on random weekday closures.

Turning our bikes, we dropped down into the village of Winkeling below the Rhine path and found a bakery, warm light radiating from its window. Peering through the glass, I could see the counter stacked high with bread: brown and white, rye and wheat, seeded, herbed and spiced, loaves and rolls. So much choice heaped in front of us. Inside, the aroma and warmth were comforting.

Bread – the essence of life and memory, woven in and through the passing years. My father supplied my mother with flour, cream of tartar, bicarbonate of soda, butter, eggs and sugar from the shop; the milkman brought buttermilk. I didn't like my mother's solid yellow-beige wheaten with its dry, nutty texture, but devoured her soda and potato bread. She'd sieve flour with salt and cream of tartar into a beige mixing bowl, decorated with a raised diamond pattern around its edge, the pattern broken by a chip on the lip. It's strange the random detail those memories serve up. All my memories of my mother's bread-making are in summer time, as if she'd never baked in winter; the soporific coo of the neighbour's homing pigeons drifting through the open kitchen window.

While my father was a dreamer, his head filled with birdsong, my mother baked and cooked and scrubbed and cleaned, bathing children and washing clothes. She had no time for nature. Her life was rooted in dusters and hoovers, the knitting needle and sewing kit.

I rushed home from school to scavenge from her baking session – licking out the mixing bowl, stealing a handful of raisins. I sat on the stepped kitchen stool and waited patiently for the soda farls, watching her make a well in the middle of the flour and pour in the buttermilk, inhaling its sour smell as my mother folded it into the soft dough. She'd rub the flour off her face with the back of her hand – year after year, across the decades: the sixties, seventies and eighties. Until I left home. She sprinkled flour onto the old Formica board and kneaded the dough with long thin fingers, shaping the dough into a half-inch circle with the palms of her hands before cutting it into four farls, which she placed on the griddle until they started to blacken. When cool enough, she cut one open, smeared it with salted butter and handed it down to me.

If I close my eyes, I can still hear that crunch of crust in my mouth and taste the melted butter on my tongue. I can still see her face – the landscape of her skin changing over time from smoothness to ridge and furrow.

My sister started to tell my mother, in her last days, about my plans to cycle to Istanbul. I remember squeezing Audrey's hand in warning, but my quite deaf mother did not catch what she'd said anyway. I was afraid my mother wouldn't approve, worried she would fret. No good wife left their husband for over three months. No good mother abandoned one of their sons. And I didn't bake bread.

Jamie grinned beside me at the counter of the German bakery and mouthed, 'Croissants.' We'd cycled for nearly an hour from Wesel on empty bellies and were now hungry, cold and damp. I mouthed back, 'Coffee.' He grinned again and gave me a thumbs up. He and I were doing okay together; I didn't bake bread, but I made sure our bellies were full and we had somewhere to sleep.

Jamie's job was to read the maps. Mostly we rode in silence, one behind the other. Now and again, Jamie would come to a sudden stop to have a quick look at our Rhine guidebook before taking off again without a word. My earlier fears of getting lost had been needless: Jamie seemed to have an innate ability to read maps. He was able to internalise a series of complicated manoeuvres – numerous rights and lefts over several miles – before checking again. His memory was impressive. (I should've realised – even as a two-year-old, Jamie could find his way through the complicated maze of Chatsworth House, a nearby stately home, never once failing to take a correct left or right.) When not reading the map, or lost in some inner world, Jamie would listen to podcasts. Sometimes, when he'd finished, he'd pull out his earbuds and tease me – sitting bolt upright on his touring bike to mimic me on Gertrude.

'Jealousy will get you nowhere, mate,' I laughed. 'Too bad you have to sit on a razor.'

'At least I don't have a tank for a bicycle,' he shot back. So Gertrude was rechristened 'The Tank'.

I was grateful for these moments, and that Jamie had honoured a three-year-old promise to accompany me on this trip – my dream, not his.

Early in the journey, he'd overshot a turning and slammed on the brakes. I was close behind him and didn't hit my brakes quickly enough and ended up in a ditch. The bike fell on top of me, metal slicing my little finger. Blood oozed from the finger and smeared the bike. Jamie bent over me in concern, angry at himself for causing my accident.

'Hey, I'm fine.' I got up feeling wobbly, worried I'd done serious damage so early in the ride. Jamie hauled the bike off me, and I shook my legs. They were working – just a grazed knee. My arms were fine too. We laughed, but realised we'd have to be more careful and keep a bigger distance between us if we were ever going to reach Istanbul in one piece. Jamie found a plaster and helped me cover the cut.

Maybe I'd done okay as a mother. Jamie would often retreat to somewhere inside his head, but he was also considerate and thoughtful, easy-going and cool-headed. In many ways, he was the perfect cycling companion – if only he would talk a little more.

Maybe I'd done okay as a daughter too. My dreams were not my mother's dreams, but I had a drive that came from her: a drive to challenge myself – to follow my own path – one that now led up the Rhine, down the Danube and across the hills to the Black Sea and Sea of Marmara. I was curious to know what lay out there, to see how other people lived.

She made bread; I made journeys. And I carried her with me along the Rhine.

'*Was darf es sein?*' The shop assistant was asking me what I wanted. We picked out *Brötchen* for our lunch along with meat and cheese, then took our croissants and coffee and settled at a corner table – thankful that the hotel had chosen today for its *Ruhetag*; thankful for the strong, aromatic coffee and steaming croissants; thankful for German bakeries.

Afterwards, we mounted the bikes again and made our way back to the Rhine. I was beginning to settle into the cycle, no longer worrying about flat tyres or mechanical problems with every push of the pedal. There was little point in mithering about what might not ever happen. I saw that there was already a shift in my thinking. I was living in the present, and the knot of pain in my chest slackened a little more.

*

Two men shot past on charcoal bikes, clad in black. They sat squat and square on solid frames and thick tyres. The word 'Bosch' flashed by in blurry letters. The wheels turned with the *Vorsprung durch Technik* precision of a German washing machine on an energy-efficient spin. The men were certainly advancing at an impressive pace. And their technique was faultless – they were forging ahead with minimal effort, easing along the riverbank, deep in conversation.

The air was still damp from the rainstorm and low cloud clung to the river. The Rhine sulked in grey. Vegetation dripped rainwater onto our numb hands and the odour of rotten vegetation permeated the air. Sodden leaves mulched the cycle path and deadened the sound of our tyres to a faint squelch. Winter clung on although it was early May.

I spotted the men were carrying panniers – our first touring cyclists! I pedalled faster, hoping to catch them, but they moved further and further ahead of us and into the distance. We finally caught up with them at a railway crossing. It was then I spotted the electric motors. My Formula 1 cyclists were cheats.

'*Ja, e-velos – Moustache Samedi 28 Titanium. Sie sind wun-der-bar. Su-perb.*'

They reeled off their bikes' credentials: cruising speed, 25kmh; top performance speed, 45kmh; hydroformed alloy chassis; hydraulic disk brakes; state-of-the-art crank drive motor. I took in the men's matching lycra, expensive cycling shoes, identical handlebar bags with plastic folders, neatly stacked with map printouts – and felt inadequate.

They asked where we were going, speaking German with thick Alsace accents. I felt embarrassed to admit I was cycling across a continent. The Alsatians frowned at my scratched town-bike laden down with my found-in-the-sale Raleigh panniers, now sagging under the weight of Rhineland showers – and hiding Tesco bags that kept my belongings dry. Their eyes dropped to my scuffed trainers and up again to my old hiking waterproofs. I was a model of make-do British improvisation, not German precision. My steed was a sit-up-and-beg bike, and at that moment I felt like the bag lady.

I blushed. 'Istanbul.' Again, that ridiculous word.

'Is-tan-bul!'

But the men seemed less concerned with my inadequate mode of transport and cheap equipment than the destination:

'Eastern Europe . . . Turkey. A risk. It's a question of your safety. It's not like here, not like western Europe . . .'

The words stayed with me as we continued up the Rhine. The warnings I'd heard before I set out filled my head once again – of murderous lorry drivers, vicious dogs, thieving Gypsies, scammers and unscrupulous opportunists. A place of monsters and dark shadows; a hinterland of Eastern Europe that few western Europeans actually knew but still had an opinion on.

*

But there were more immediate challenges. Just outside Rheinberg we came to our first obstacle: the building of a new flood defence. Our path was lost in the mounds of dug-up land. We slipped through a gap in the fence and crossed the wetlands toward Orsoy along the dyke, praying there wouldn't be another impenetrable barrier at the other end.

The wind dropped and we stopped by a pond of mute swans and tufted ducks to eat our *Brötchen* and hold our wind-battered faces to the weak sun. Home and all its comforting familiarity seemed far away now. Still, Duisburg was very close now and another stranger had invited us into *her* home for the night: a language teacher called Petra. As we drew closer to the city, I wondered how Tom and Patrick were managing on their own: I imagined Tom in the kitchen, chopping vegetables; Patrick surrounded by school books at the table. I felt a yearning for the other half of my divided family, my far-flung island, my home. But curiosity about the unknown drove me on, enticing me.

Ever southwards.

Upstream, the Duisburg Bridge delivered us to the district

of Ruhrort, an ugly echo of the larger Duisburg – a thrown-together muddle of mostly post-war buildings. No sooner had we reached the banks of the Ruhr than the wind and rain lashed down with the ferocity of a trapped animal, forcing us off our bikes. We sheltered behind a lorry, pushing our bodies against its overhang while gripping our bicycles with white-knuckled fingers to stop the wind from ripping them off us. It was a strange day, the weather a moody mess. And indeed, the wind died away as quickly as it had arrived. We cycled along the tree-lined Ruhr river, dodging drips and willing Duisburg to show us its kinder side.

The harshness of Duisburg lay in its industrial, then political history – the town cradled strategically in the crook of the Rhine and Ruhr rivers. Along with Essen and Dortmund, it sat in Germany's industrial heartland, the Ruhrgebiet, an area once so rich in coal and iron that it became a powerhouse of blast furnaces, factories, mines and mills connected by an extensive network of railway lines. By 1870, it was the largest industrial region in Europe, with an urban population of three million people.

During World War One, attention turned to the war effort and the entire Ruhr valley became one big weapons factory – a stockpile of ammunition rather than coal heaps. But by the end of the Great War, Germany was on its knees. In 1923, a bankrupt and disgruntled German government encouraged its Ruhr workers to sabotage production at the industrial assets that had been seized by the French and Belgian troops in lieu of unpaid war reparations. Then in 1936, in an act of sheer provocation, Adolf Hitler sent 30,000 troops into the demilitarised Rhineland. The French acted as if nothing had happened – *et alors*?

– while the British shrugged their shoulders and made mutterings to the effect that Germany had a right to its own backyard. Hitler interpreted this as a *carte blanche* to go on the march, and it was only after he had marched right into Poland that Britain decided enough was enough and declared war. Too late, Hitler's ambition was insatiable and soon the world was at war.

Germany's industrial and ammunitions heartland was an obvious target for the Allied bombers. In June 1941, the British dropped 400-odd tons of bombs on Duisburg alone and then went on to obliterate the old town in 1943 with another 1,500 tons, give or take. But this was nothing in comparison to a raid in 1944, when 9,000 tons of incendiaries were dropped in a raid that lasted all day and night. By the end of the war, little remained of Duisburg, arguably the most heavily bombed city in western Germany in World War II.

As the British carried out the ruthless and relentless onslaught on Duisburg in 1941, the Germans made a surprise first attack on Belfast that same year. It must have been a shock for my father: everyone believed our city was safe from the Luftwaffe. Even after the Nazis invaded the Cherbourg region of France, extending their reach, the city continued in its complacency to the point of carelessness, not even complying properly with blackout regulations. The Germans, realising Belfast was the most poorly defended city in the United Kingdom – despite the fact that shipbuilders Harland and Wolff, and Shorts the aircraft company, were busily tasked with building destroyers, aircraft carriers, mine sweepers and bombers – made the city a priority target.

At the beginning of April 1941, the Luftwaffe tested the ground, dropping 800 incendiary bombs on the docks area before returning a week later to widen their target. Some 1,000 people were killed in the Easter raids and another 1,500 injured. Two hospitals were targeted, placing my father's ambulance service under immense pressure. Was my father there when they took the bodies to St George's Market and laid them out for identification? Had he known the unidentified were buried in mass graves? Was my father there in the following May raid, when a further 200 corpses were dug out from bomb sites? I asked myself why I hadn't known this history of my own city, and I wished I had questioned my father about it before he had shut down. Would he have answered anyway? Had he put a lid on something that was too painful to resurrect? Probably. But I felt ashamed that I had not been interested enough to ask.

As Jamie and I pedalled along the Ruhr river, the city did little to endear itself to us, its buildings flung up after the war with no thought for planning or aesthetics – until we reached Duisburg's Inner Harbour, near our CouchSurfing host's home. We cycled along Philosophenweg, over canal bridges and on past cafés, restaurants, museums, offices and apartments. They stood in stark contrast to the scruffy town fringe we'd just passed through. Shiny architecture stood side by side with traditional wharfs, mills and pieces of industrial machinery on the harbour's banks. By the time Jamie and I had reached the end of Philosophenweg, the sun was shining primrose over the water and my view of Duisburg had changed.

We turned a corner and came to a halt outside Petra's townhouse. In front of the elegant façade, boxes of lettuce, carrots and leeks spilled from the front drive.

*

2. Petra

Petra opened the door to our knock, her hair swept back in a wave. She had a smoothness of skin, curvature of body and an economy of movement reminiscent of a ship's figurehead cutting water. Her containment of body didn't match her flow of chatter.

'Lucky you were coming on a Wednesday. My evenings are so busy. The apartment is rented out at the moment, but there's plenty of sleeping space in the living room. Chain the bicycles to the railing here. I've got a stew in the pot. You must be hungry. I'll get it ready straightaway. Don't worry about shoes. Leave your bags in the corner. Come on in.'

My brain worked hard to keep up with the rapid flow of information. We followed Petra to the kitchen where she busied herself with the stew. Above her head, shelves bulged with foodstuffs: containers of herbs and spices; jars of jams, jellies, chutneys and coffee; packets of tea and an assortment of dried foods and staples.

Petra served Jamie and I the perfect antidote to wind, rain and cold: a hot, spicy *Eintopf*, a one-pot full of flavour. The stew steamed and the smell of spice filled the ground floor of the house, mixed with the peppery aroma of savory herb. I took a taste of the sweet chilli sausage and its warmth coursed through my body. *Gemütlichkeit*: German comfort.

'I salvaged the beans and potatoes from the market,' Petra said. 'They would have been thrown away otherwise. My local market and some of the smaller supermarkets and shops have signed up to the food-sharing project.'

'So, what's food-sharing exactly?' I asked.

'Well, it's an internet community of people who don't want to see unsold or uneaten food go to waste. Members create a "basket" of food they want to give away – if they're going on holiday or they've had a party with lots of leftovers. Then it can be collected from the member's home or one of the pick-up points around town. A lot of the food I eat comes from the food-sharing community and is free.'

'Sounds like a great idea.'

'It is, especially when you think about how much food is thrown out. And I save a lot of money.'

There was little wastage for us growing up. With a house full of children, it was rare for food to find its way to the bin – and anything left over was given to the dog – potato skins, gristle and bones mixed in with lard and anything else that was left on a plate. It was a canine diet that would make a vet shudder.

In fact, nothing was thrown away – whether fabric or metal, or any general household item. The rag-and-bone man and travelling door-callers made sure of that. The Gypsy woman knocked on our door regularly – an exotic creature dressed in long flowing skirts and carrying a baby that was wrapped across her chest in a piece of cloth. I was fascinated by this traveller as she was unlike anyone else I knew. Nobody carried their babies in cloths in my town or spoke with a thick-as-broth southern Irish brogue that was almost impossible for me to decipher.

My mother rummaged around, looking for some small thing she could donate: a too-small dress or an old knitted jumper. Goodness knows what she hoped to find, for our own clothes were passed down from one to another until hems and cuffs were frayed and small holes appeared in elbows and knees, patched and re-patched.

My mother dug deep.

While the Gypsy tramped the town door-to-door on foot, the rag-and-bone man came with his horse and cart, a rickety construction of wood piled high with junk: scraps of bicycles, rusting buckets and bundles of rags, tied together with strips of fabric. And once again my mother would cast her eye around to find some scrap of something. Our house was filled with broken things since my mother had grown up in the War and couldn't bear to throw anything out, whether it was a defunct hairdryer or a broken vacuum cleaner. *The parts could be useful for something else, so please Helen, keep it.*

Petra was a modern version of my mother. Not a moment was wasted; her life filled to bursting point. I wondered how she found time to sleep. Gardening, crafting, sewing and knitting, cooking, baking, jelly and jam-making crammed her days. She hosted strangers from hospitality websites, rented out her children's old rooms as an Airbnb apartment and cooked for everyone who entered her home while chattering non-stop. She organised music events in her living room, which was filled with art and sofas and throws – and what looked like a row of bus seats.

Petra embodied the sharing philosophy. Her home, her car, even her camping equipment and gardening implements were all available for loan or rent. A leader, organiser and ambassador for all sorts of local community and international organisations, she spoke English, French and Dutch with fluency and was getting to grips with Spanish and Italian. Not content with all of that, she was delving into Turkish and Polish too. In between she worked as a French teacher. And when not knee-deep in her own community, Petra travelled all around Europe, throwing herself into other lives and cultures.

A child of Duisburg; a child of the world.

My mother had Petra's energy and organisational skills – although most of her time was taken up with children and her own home, not strangers. She sewed dresses for us girls, matching floral frocks with little bows and puffed sleeves, crocheted ponchos and knitted thick woollen jumpers for all of us. My father set parsley, celery, leek and lettuce and tomatoes in the greenhouse, and grew rhubarb and scallions (spring onions) and other root vegetables, along with lobelia, sweet pea, dahlias, chrysanthemums, geraniums, gladiolas and begonias for my mother's table arrangements. She cooked flavourless, salted root vegetables (no herbs or spices) and potatoes from my father's vegetable plot. But when it came to baking, she delighted our taste buds. Homemade bread, tarts and cakes emptied out of the stacked tins as quickly as they were filled up. Her children were as greedy as they were skinny. My mother swore we all had tapeworms.

The smell of homemade bread, the syrupy aroma of cooking jam or fruit tarts, the dust of snipped fabric and paper patterns, and the gentle fragrance of freshly cut sweet pea – all were the scents of my childhood.

Petra reminded me of my mother, but Petra was an eco-warrior, a hipster and progressive, kicking against the consumerism and wastefulness of modern life. They were labels that didn't exist in the sixties, yet my mother could match Petra action for action. No weekly shops to the supermarket for her.

She bought fresh, seasonal food from the fruit and vegetable man (who also delivered his goods in a horse-drawn cart) and the best joints from the local butcher, a man who punctuated every sentence with a *Mrs Rab-i-son* when he dropped by with our meat. My father supplied the rest of our food from his grocery store, greenhouse and kitchen garden.

The throwaway society had not yet been properly invented, nor food-sharing or environmental awareness. Yet my mother was a *de facto* environmentalist. While Petra had made a life choice and followed it consciously and conscientiously, my mother simply lived it without thought. And she was not alone, for everyone was an environmentalist in the sixties, and sustainability was the norm. Petra, on the other hand, swam against the tide of consumerism and empty need with an energy that appeared effortless. It was as if she'd realised she'd been gifted a moment of life and she was determined to fill her lungs with air and dive in – as deep as she could.

3. Looking for Marcella

We left Duisburg in watery sunshine. Whatever lay ahead today I knew that Marcella, who had once lodged with us for a few weeks in the Peak District, would be waiting for us at the end of it. It was our fifth day of cycling and the daily task of turning the wheels now felt comfortable and familiar, the saddle as easy as our living room sofa. Well, almost.

My bike trip had become an unconscious journey in mindfulness. I was living in the moment, focused on the path in front of me, breathing in the cold and damp of earth and leaf. I was tuned into the lap of shore and the honk of geese feeding on Rhine-side meadows. The sky exploded with the increasing urgency of the birds' mating songs, singing loudly, persistently and sweetly. For them, spring was here regardless of the weather.

My father loved the month of May, roaming the fields in search of his beloved birds, hoping to log the first call of the cuckoo. He'd stop his grocery van at the end of his country run to catch a glimpse of the first summer migrants, or one of his favourite residents, and to listen to the first mating songs of the year. *Saw yellowhammer and goldfinch today . . . Great bird activity in the country*, a couple of May entries in his pocket diary exclaimed. And the next day: *Saw a green linnet* (presumedly a green finch). His entries were terse, simple observations rather than self-reflective, and surprisingly positive. They referenced work and worship, interspersed with birds, flowers and his garden. There were lists of places he frequented – Oxford Island, the River Lagan and coastal areas of County Antrim and Down – and his wildlife sightings. In between there were repeated phrases like meditative chants: *Lovely day*; *Good week in shop, thank you Lord*; *Praise the Lord for his goodness*; *Lord, grant us all the will to follow thee and to love each other more until that day*; *Busy all day, praise the Lord*; *May we have sweet fellowship together.* Sunday entries were often identical: *At the remembrance of our Lord Jesus Christ. Amen.*

Of any inner – or outer – conflict there was no sign.

*

It was still early in the day when we reached the medieval village of Kaiserswerth. It was already milling with tourists who'd come to look at the ruins of Emperor Barbarossa's ninth-century castle, stroll through the cobbled streets of the old town and linger in terraced *Biergärten* overlooking the Rhine. We were tempted to join them but we had almost fifty miles to do – and Marcella would be waiting with her father to take us to the Eifel, a rural hinterland west of the river beyond Cologne and Bonn.

Marcella had come to stay with us in England because of Andrea, whom I had met in the hostile environment of 1980s Derry in Northern Ireland. I was a student and Andrea a language assistant at an Omagh school. The German *Stammtisch*, or 'gathering', was an oasis in the troubled atmosphere of the city – away from the armed soldiers and police jeeps patrolling the near-empty streets; away from the threat of bombs, crossfire and mob skirmishes. Later I stayed with Andrea's parents when I went to Germany hoping to earn some money and improve my language skills. I'd planned to spend a few days with the older couple but ended up staying four months, finding a series of jobs in their village. After I returned home to the UK, Andrea and I dipped in and out of each other's lives, losing contact for up to two years at a time then picking up effortlessly. Sometimes, she would contact me to ask if I would take in some unknown German. Marcella was one of them. She needed to spend some time in the UK as part of her education. We were able to offer six weeks. But it was a risk. What if she was difficult? What if she didn't fit in with our household? We waited nervously at the airport for Marcella to arrive, but when she came through the barriers, a German Goldilocks with long blonde hair tied in plaits, her open face breaking into a wide smile, our fears evaporated. She worked hard but always had time to join me for coffee, chatting with ease. When she left us to return to Germany, we missed her presence in our home.

Now, Jamie and I were edging in slow motion towards Marcella, and I felt joy at being on the road. Was this not freedom? Was it not life in its simplest form, uncomplicated and lovely? I felt I was beginning to out-cycle my depression. I realised that I needed to see my depression as something outside of me: it made it easier to objectivise any dark and destructive thoughts. Instead of allowing the black dog of depression to drag me along by its leash, I needed to call it to heel – to be in control.

But I also began to acknowledge I had a pain so securely locked away that I no longer felt I could lift the lid on it – a pain that was making me ill. I saw history repeating itself. The experience of the war years was my father's secret, but I too had a secret I was hiding from my siblings and parents that forced me to live a lie. And there was my fragile relationship with my father, borne of another secret from a single night long ago that no one spoke about in my family. I had convinced myself and my therapists that my illness had been the result of my job, not my childhood – refusing to dig deeper.

*

My joy at being on the road soon turned sour. I'd been warned that the headwinds on the Rhine were a force to be reckoned with. Until now, however, we'd only experienced short, violent gusts that died away in a whimper as quickly as they arrived. This time the wind persisted, pushing against our bodies and bikes. Against speeds of 30mph, it felt as if I was cycling through a wind tunnel. I pressed down hard on the pedals, but my bike barely seemed to move. The spokes sung a mournful tune from the crosswinds as I inched forward.

'Mum, you need to cycle faster. We're never going to reach Düsseldorf today at this rate, never mind Cologne!'

The ever-tolerant Jamie was finally losing patience with me. As we passed by Stockum, the wind gathered force until it felt as if I was at a standstill. It was almost midmorning when we reached the outskirts of Düsseldorf at Golzheim. I sat down on a bench exhausted and reached for our sandwiches. We'd cycled a paltry twenty miles. If I didn't quicken my pace, we'd have to cancel our meet-up with Marcella and find somewhere to spend the night between Düsseldorf and Cologne. If I didn't quicken my pace, we'd be lucky to reach Basel after three months, never mind Istanbul!

Düsseldorf wasn't the ugly industrial city I'd imagined. Sleek skyscrapers of glass reflected the Rhine; buildings twisted and curved like folded origami paper. Steps led up from the river-bank to a large plaza edged with cafés and museums, offices and shops. I wanted to stop but we had to press on. The path climbed up and over a bridge onto a long finger of land. We passed marinas, little cube houses and allotments of vegetables and flowers, then squeezed through housing estates until we were spat out of the city's heart. It had taken us an hour and Cologne still felt a long way off.

At Volmerswerth, still in the outer reaches of Düsseldorf, I messaged Marcella, saying I didn't think we could make it that day. The wind died away at Leverkusen, only a dozen or so miles from our meeting point with Marcella, but instead, hailstones the size of marbles fell and pummelled us. For the first time, I wanted to be back home in the warmth of my own house. I pulled my mobile out to phone Marcella, my fingers so cold I could hardly hit the number on the screen. 'We're going to try and make it,' I said through chattering teeth.

'Good. Head past the city until you hit the fifth bridge at Rodenkirchen. We'll be waiting for you at the car park.'

We counted the bridges down through Cologne. Across the Rhine, we could see the soaring twin spires of the cathedral but there was no time to linger. We pushed on, and the sun was now dropping in the sky – the track alongside the railway line seemed interminable. Finally, we came to the car park by the bridge. There was no sign of Marcella and her father. Were we at the right bridge even? I rang again.

'You're on the other side of the bridge from us,' Marcella finally worked out.

Crossing the bridge, we found Marcella, grinning. While her father loaded the bikes onto the trailer, we climbed into the back of the car and settled with relief into the wide, leather seats with back supports.

4. Monika and the Chilean Seaman

Memories of the wind and hailstones of the Rhine corridor quickly receded in the suburban house below the woods. Monika, Marcella's mother, embraced us in a big German hug.

She was tall with a strong bone structure, yellow hair and eyes that sparkled glacier-blue behind her frameless glasses. Enrique, her Chilean husband, was small and stocky with a thatch of black hair that swept down to bracken eyes. His peppered beard and moustache revealed a perpetual smile suggesting *joie de vivre* – or *alegría de libro*.

No sooner had we arrived than a large plate of food was placed in front of us. It was a big, noisy table with dishes clattering and laughter threading a jumble of words in German and English. We felt at home straight away with Monika, Henri (as his German friends called him) and Marcella's sister.

Henri, I discovered quickly, sang in a local Latino band. The music was wild and pulsing, sensual and loud. He showed us videos of the band and took Jamie down to the basement to show him his guitars and play for him. Henri's zest for life was endearing, and his openness and enthusiasm was infectious.

We were spending a few days here and I enjoyed the stillness of the house after the perpetual motion of bike and the battering of weather. One day, we drove out into the Eifel, an area familiar to me from that summer I'd spent in the home of Andrea's parents – a soft landscape of hills and valleys thick with deciduous and conifer woodland, broken only by occasional meadow. It was odd to revisit Bad Münstereifel with Jamie. The last time I'd walked the cobbled streets by the canal among the *Fachwerkhäuser*, the overhanging timber-framed buildings, Jamie was a toddler just above my knees. I'd held tight onto his tiny hand to stop him stumbling on the uneven streets. And here he was now towering above me, guiding us on our ride and making sure we didn't get lost in the remote Rhine villages when the trail led us away from the riverbank.

On the Friday night, Monika invited Andrea over. It was *Feierabend*. There is no equivalent in English. The word does what the German language does so well: describes in one neat compound adjectival noun what requires a whole sentence in English. *Celebration evening – work's done; I'm letting my hair down.* Monika's coffee table was crammed with sparkling water, German beers and wines with olives, pretzels and other nibbles. It brought back memories of long evenings with Andrea in Blankenheim that summer long ago: out on the balcony; in the mock-Austrian kitchen parlour of one of Andrea's friends; and in living rooms across the village and beyond, when we had laughed and chatted late into the evening by candlelight.

Back then, my summer interlude in the Eifel was far removed from my life in Northern Ireland, distilled to church and countryside. Candles were thought to be papish in the Puritan austerity of my home, wine and beer the drinks of the devil. In this part of Catholic Germany, there was a different culture, a different tongue, a different past and another way of seeing the world. In the Northern Irish Brethren upbringing of my childhood, there was only one possible world view: the indisputable Word of God. There was no sense of irony when the Brothers argued over its interpretation in their weekly Bible studies. As far as they were concerned, Andrea's family and friends were going to hell because of their secular-Catholic West German view of the world. They were not born again.

'I don't hate Catholics,' my father said. 'Just their religion.' But the bitterness that crept into his voice suggested something different.

'They should bring back the B-specials.' The B-specials were a police force entirely made up of Protestant Unionists and were known for revenge killings and reprisals against Catholics. 'They should bring back hangings,' he said when another IRA killing hit the news.

I had begun to see that my father was a strange mix of independent thinker and conditioned Unionist, and I no longer felt I was walking in step with him.

5. Ghosts from the Past

On the morning after the *Feierabend* gathering we called in on Andrea, who still lived in the house where I had spent that summer. Her parents, Lisbeth and Bernie, had found me work, not only in a *Gasthaus* and adjoining restaurant in the heart of the village, but also in the youth hostel up on the Finkenberg and at the *Altersheim*, the old people's home above the main shopping street. I was a source of much local information and they would enjoy gossiping over coffee and cake.

Inevitably, things had changed at the house. Gone was the kitchen garden with its rows of old-fashioned dahlias and lupins, the Canterbury bells and delphiniums, the vegetables and fruit from Bernie and Lisbeth's day. In their place was a long stretch of narrowing lawn, pointing an arrow to the village centre. The garden was strewn with hammocks and chairs and an assortment of natural objects from Andrea's beachcombing trips to the Netherlands, England and Ireland – mainly shells and driftwood.

Behind the hedge, the open-air swimming pool, once ringing with splashes and laughter, was now closed and silent and spreading weeds. It was here that Andrea's niece and nephew had dared me on to ever-higher diving boards to jump and dive. Above the house, the road climbs up to the Finkenberg, a hillside of pines where most of Andrea's friends lived and I'd cleaned the private hostel. To the left of the garden, Blankenheim's castle teeters on the hillside, poking out of ash and oak.

From the base of the hill, Andrea's father, Bernie, had secretly spied on Lisbeth with his friends as she'd exercised in the castle courtyard above him. Lisbeth was a member of the Bund Deutscher Mädchen, or the League of German Girls – the girls' wing of the Hitler Youth movement. Bernie was in the boys' wing.

Bernie, like my father, was conditioned by the culture and politics of his youth and adulthood. Unionism and National Socialism had one thing in common: they were driven by a fierce patriotism stirred up by self-interested politicians, and the perceived threat of a minority group. In my father's case, Catholics; in Bernie's, the Jews. Bernie looked back to this time with nostalgia: the fireside songs; the marches through woodland; the whittling of sticks and food cooked in billy cans over the campfire; the banter and camaraderie. How much of Hitler's insidious xenophobia entered his consciousness back then wasn't clear. Was there a filter?

Later, the British took aim at Bernie's house, Bernie and Lisbeth told me, missing its target and landing on the sewage tank in the yard instead, damaging the goat stall in the basement of the house. The excrement landed on the hall ceiling, and the gables of the house were left at a peculiar angle. Some of the soldiers quartered in the house were injured and had to be taken to the military hospital in nearby Ripsdorf. Fortunately, Bernie's parents were unharmed.

As war ravaged Europe, Bernie joined the *Marine*, the navy. While my father mopped up blood from the victims of German raids in Belfast, Bernie was quietly sailing up and down the Baltic Sea, side-stepping any action.

I have a photo of Bernie at sea, dressed in crisp white flairs and a singlet. He's standing on the steps of his ship, looking dapper, leaning casually on a stairway railing between decks. He looks like a young Elvis Presley with his strong handsome face, muscled arms and floppy hair swept back from his brow. It's only when you look closer at the photograph that you spot the Nazi insignia on his singlet: the spread-winged eagle and the swastika below it.

If Bernie was nostalgic about his time in the Hitler Youth, he was even more enthusiastic about those wartime years in the navy.

'*Komm*, Helen,' he beckoned to me that eighties' summer. 'I want to show you something.'

He led me into his study, a shrine to his time in the *Kriegsmarine*. On the wall, there was a framed knot board, a great macramé anchor and a photograph of Admiral Dönitz, who'd risen to the position of navel Commander-in-Chief in the war. There were also pictures of Bernie's ships: the *Bismarck* and the *Köln*. Luck was on Bernie's side, for he had swapped ships to the *Köln* just before the *Bismarck* was sunk by the British. Below the picture, there was a cabinet containing a model of the *Bismarck* and other paraphernalia. There were also flags: the Marinebund flag and the Reichskrieg flag.

Later, when I recalled Bernie's memorabilia, Andrea had squirmed: 'Oh dear, I'm afraid it makes my dad look like a real Nazi – which he probably was! He kept telling us that he had the time of his life. Anyway, the *Marine* gave him the chance to leave Blankenheim and see the world.'

In truth, Bernie had mixed feelings about the war years. He'd seen the economic depression before Hitler came to power, and he'd witnessed how Hitler had pulled the country together, regulating trains and rolling out motorways. Hitler had made things work and lifted Germany out of an economic mire. He'd given German citizens a sense of pride and a sense of worth in a time of desperation, and above all a feeling of unity. It was a potent mix. When Bernie harked back to the good old times, referring to Hitler as *'der Adolf'*, Andrea was livid. 'You'd think Hitler was your brother, the way you talk about him!' She belonged to a generation who felt ill at ease with their history and their parents' links to the past.

For Bernie it was more complicated. Retrospect is a wonderful thing. He acknowledged Hitler was an evil man, and he claimed he knew nothing of the concentration camps when I asked him. His mind was muddled, for he had to unlearn his earlier conviction that all was great and good under the National Socialists. And there were those warm memories still coursing through his blood. It wasn't easy.

Now in the house, Bernie's memorabilia was gone and in its place were racks of Andrea's clothes, walls of books, an assortment of tongue-in-cheek kitsch and Royal Family china. The Reichsflagge had been replaced with the British Union flag. In a strange twist of irony, Andrea celebrated the enemy who had bombed her house and helped bring down her father's heroes.

Andrea was also a product of the war in a more literal sense. Hidden in the undergrowth below the castle, Lisbeth was unaware of Bernie watching her. He soon found an occasion to introduce himself. Then war separated them – Bernie flung north to Scandinavian waters, Lisbeth to work as a radio operator in Buxtehude.

Finally, in 1944, Bernie and Lisbeth were able to marry in a double wedding with Lisbeth's sister. It was the end of the winter and the war was slowly grinding to a halt – although they didn't know it yet. The guests had no money for wedding gifts and instead the pairs were offered flowers picked from gardens.

At the end of the war, Bernie was captured and detained in a P.O.W. camp near Hamburg. His British captors were kind and lenient, he made a point of telling me, plying the German prisoners with cigarettes and other treats. One day, Bernie, dressed in civvies, just walked out of the camp with a friend. He swam across the River Elbe and made his way to Buxtehude to pick up Lisbeth. Reunited, they started the long journey back to Blankenheim. It would have been a daunting journey at any time, but at the end of the war it was practically impossible. Germany lay in ruins, its public transport in disarray. Bernie and Lisbeth hitched lifts where they could, borrowed bicycles and simply walked large stretches of the journey.

I thought of the journeys that people continue to make because of war. It is as if humankind is unable – or unwilling – to learn the lessons of history. The Syrian refugees were in the news again. The boats that crossed the Mediterranean were landing with increasing frequency. There were pictures of travel-worn men, a baby or small child with a hand slung over their fathers' fluorescent-orange life jackets; older siblings clinging to their mothers' skirts. It was as if they feared the sea could still engulf them as they staggered up the beach.

But the story of migration was not just one of war and separation, but of love and determination – or pure curiosity, like mine: Asher stumbling through the windswept snow of the Dutch polders; Lisbeth and Bernie trying to find their way home through the ruins of post-war Germany; the small dark Chilean Enrique, who'd abandoned his country, oceans away, to set up home in a strange, northern land with his tall, blonde Monika.

Here in the present, as I wandered from house to garden, I could still feel Bernie and Lisbeth's presence – although they were long gone. Here I was, returning to their house decades later and everything had changed. A woman governed the country and Germany was opening its doors to a flood of refugees. The *Willkommenskultur* was still strong. I couldn't know it yet, but as Jamie and I continued on to Istanbul the mood would turn sour and the anti-immigration, anti-Muslim party, Alternative für Deutschland (AfD), would take hold. Europe would swing to the right again and xenophobia would once more rear its scowling head. Later, I would wonder what Bernie and Lisbeth would have thought about the turn their country had taken.

*

6. Hitler's Birdsong

'Would you like to visit Vogelsang?' Monika asked.

'Vogelsang?'

I was curious. During my time with Andrea's parents, Bernie had rolled his Volkswagen out of the garage to take Lisbeth and me out into the Eifel. We'd explored most of the area over that summer, but I could not recall Vogelsang. The name had a seductive ring to it: *Vogelsang* – birdsong. I imagined a tranquil place set in nature.

'It's in the Eifel National Park,' Monika said, confirming my thoughts.

I frowned. I had definitely visited the national park before. I remembered Bernie halting the Volkswagen above the Obersee, Rur and Urft reservoirs. We'd watching sailing dinghies on the sunlit water. Bernie had talked about the national park, the black storks and the wildcats, but he'd never mentioned Vogelsang.

Later it would transpire why: Vogelsang had been out of bounds to the public for decades – the twelve-acre complex of buildings, which included a castle and training centre, was abandoned by the Nazis after their defeat and taken over by the occupying Allied soldiers. It was only in 2006, after the Belgian forces had vacated the area, that Vogelsang was handed back to the German government. They struggled to know what to do with the sprawling monstrosity, a site littered with Nazi symbolism depicted in mural, stone relief and statue – along with a life-sized torchbearer who'd had his balls shot off by the Belgian troops.

The idea for the Vogelsang training college was first given an airing in a rousing Berlin speech by Hitler in 1933, when he called for the creation of education centres fit for the future leaders of his National Socialist German Workers' Party. These centres would train the brightest, toughest and the strongest young men of the Third Reich – a sort of military finishing school for the Nazi elite. The qualification process would be rigorous: entrants would have to prove their Aryan purity, pass a stringent fitness test and have a track record of party activity and military service.

Hitler and his cronies were not afraid to think big. Their puffed-up plans were as ostentatious and crude as they were grandiose. Greek and Roman neoclassical styles were thrown up side-by-side with a more modern utilitarian look at Vogelsang, all sprinkled liberally with symbols of Christianity and German legend. It was an architectural mish-mash that was as pompous and ridiculous as its Nazi pseudo-religious cod philosophy.

The four-lane road leading up to the complex heralded its overblown proportions, as did the wide entrance gate adorned with two great columns (added at Hitler's behest after his 1937 visit). They were decorated with stone reliefs of horsemen: a medieval knight brandishing a sword and the modern torchbearer.

The first building to be erected was Ordensburg – a medieval-style castle with an adjoining forty-eight-metre high water tower. Inside, a large brick swastika was laid out on the floor (the offensive symbol hastily covered up by a sports mat when the Belgians arrived). The castle, requiring the labour of 1,500 workmen, took two years to complete.

But this was just the beginning. The Nazis didn't see any reason to rein in those dreams. Several other projects were planned on the site: a massive library they named the Haus des Wissens, or 'House of Knowledge'; a *Kraft durch Freude* hotel, or 'Strength Through Joy' hotel – a Butlin's-style holiday for the working classes, where Nazi indoctrination was combined with good old-fashioned fun; and the biggest sports facility in Europe.

However, the outbreak of World War Two put paid to some of the more ambitious plans. The sports facility was completed, but the Nazis only got as far as building the foundation walls for the House of Knowledge, while the *Kraft durch Freude* hotel never came to fruition. The *Gemeinschaftshaus*, or Community Hall, and the *Adlerhof*, or Eagle's Yard, were completed along with the tower, and east and west wing. Ten *Kameradschafthäuser*, each housing fifty cadets (or comrades) were also built along with four *Hundertschafthäuser* holding another hundred each. And, of course, a 'House of Female Employees' had to be added for them to look after all the carefully vetted young men.

In 1936, the first 500 cadets arrived. Tall, blond, blue-eyed and muscle-bound – or at least that was the vision. There would be no shirking, and a demanding schedule filled the day:

> *6am, early morning exercise*
>
> *7am, muster*
>
> *8–10am, project groups*
>
> *10am–12pm, lectures in the large auditorium*

all afternoon, sport

7–8.30pm, more project groups

10pm, rest

Lectures focused on 'race science', geopolitics (including the development of *Lebensraum*, creating more space for Germans in the east) and pilot training.

The elitist military school experiment was short-lived, however. By 1939, the young men had been sent home – or to war – and Vogelsang was handed over to the Deutsche Wehrmacht, the German Army.

I sat in the dimness of the auditorium contemplating all this. It felt like I'd been caught in a time warp: the padded walls and ceiling, the torch-flame uplighters and the dark wood – they all had the stamp of Nazi design. Outside, I tried to shake off the feeling of claustrophobia. Standing on the events stage, the apron-shaped *Thingplatz*, we looked out over the wooded hillside to the reservoirs in the valley below, pools of light catching the sun as it broke through the clouds. It was a place of great natural beauty and brutal ugliness: The Beauty and the Beast of the Eifel.

I thought of my father driving to Eire to buy butter, swapping the giveaway labels of his contraband with something less incriminating to sell in his father's grocery store, and his nights in the blacked-out streets of Belfast, searching through rubble. I thought of my mother selling shoes bought with precious ration cards, having to fight off nothing worse than over-eager homesick American GIs on her local train. I thought about Bernie scrubbing his ships' decks on the Baltic Sea, and

Lisbeth with her headphones, busy working as a radio operator in Buxtehude, far from home.

And I thought of another friend whose father had been carted off by the Nazis to be executed.

My parents, and Andrea's, had been let off lightly in comparison – but they were all victims of a runaway nationalism. Churchill had called for a united Europe in the rubble of a post-war Germany, but now a new tide of nationalism was quietly rippling through Europe in the twenty-first century. I suddenly felt cold on the *Thingplatz* as the sun slipped behind the clouds again.

Afterwards, we drove down to the bottom of the hill to look at the Nazi swimming pool. Marcella and I pressed our noses against the glass, and watched a solitary woman swim lengths under the larger-than-life fresco of three muscular and naked blond men frolicking through the waves. It was a surreal moment, and yearning for normality, we found the car again and drove down to the tourist town of Gemund to stuff ourselves with Italian ice cream.

*

Thinking back, there was silence at Vogelsang – or had I misremembered? In my memory, there had been no birdsong, just a stillness and emptiness inside the complex of stone-hewn buildings.

*

7. Romance and Death on the Middle Rhine

We'd spent three days in the Eifel recovering from wind and rain. My skin had softened to indoor living and my bottom had lost its ache from long hours on the saddle. I no longer felt I was bouncing oddly as I walked (as I had done when I'd dismounted from my bike after five days of cycling). Monika had plied Jamie, skinny as he was tall, with jumbo packs of salt-and-vinegar crisps, as if he were a camel that could carry the surplus in the bump of his tummy along the rest of the Rhine.

We'd drunk our fill of German wine and sat for hours around the kitchen table chatting and singing silly songs. Marcella had regaled us with the *Trololo* song, the lyrics nothing more than a series of meaningless sounds that bounced along, and the night descended into raucous scout songs and intoxicating silliness.

Henri had serviced our bikes; making sure the tyres were well pumped up, checking the brakes and oiling the chains. There was nothing left to detain us. In the morning, we packed the panniers and Henri loaded the bikes onto the trailer again.

Henri and Monika offered to take us to Bad Godesberg, south of Bonn, which sliced off around twenty-three miles of our Rhine journey. I was disappointed to be missing out the small section of the Rhine between Cologne and Bonn but didn't want to inconvenience this generous family. On the banks of the Rhine, Henri unloaded the bikes and Monika pushed a packed lunch into my hand. The couple waved us off as we wobbled down the path. Our mood was muddled, but we were happy to be on the road once more.

It was a Sunday morning. The sky was clear and the air still and there was a spring-like warmth in the atmosphere we hadn't experienced since Dordrecht. I felt my body and brain come to life in the open. There was something about the stale, draft-less air of indoor living that was soporific. Like my father, I preferred to be outside.

'Want to go for a walk?' he would often ask after tea.

We'd slip out of the house and pass our neighbour, Manfred Cousins, always there, leaning over his driveway pillar while chewing on a piece of grass. We'd continue on down the lane to the old farmhouse, scrambling over the gate to pass my favourite climbing tree, the one in which I'd learned to test my weight on its branches. We'd reach the stream – my place to build dams and gather frogspawn in jam jars – and the hummock where I'd lit fires and cooked crab apples with my brothers. On the other side of the river, my father and I would pick primroses from the ditch banks in spring – and in autumn, blackberries and rosehips from the surrounding hedges. In the season, we'd drop down to a nearby field to gather mushrooms for supper. Sometimes we'd loop round to Manfred Cousins' field, where I'd played on his abandoned dumper truck with friends, running up and down its dumper to make it rise and fall. My father and I would skirt the border of the field to the place I built secret dens in thickets. On rare winter days, when the ground was covered in snow, we'd crunch over the hardened earth, the Mourne Mountains shining pale in the sunlight. Then spring again and the cuckoo.

Now, as I cycled along, I was listening out for the cuckoo as my father had done, but the only sound was that of families and couples by the river on roller skates, scooters, bikes and on foot. We weaved through the crowds until the way ahead lay clear, then picked up speed, pedalling through sprinkled settlements and out into open countryside. At Bad Breisig we cycled into a tree-lined promenade with chairs spilling out onto the street from half-timbered hotels. I slammed on the brakes beside a terrace café overhanging the Rhine. It was mid-morning after all, and who could resist coffee and cake in such an inviting location? Little piers dotted the waterside and tankers and pleasure boats floated by.

From Bad Breisig, vineyards sloped down to the valley floor, and monasteries and castles appeared on the skyline above the Rhine: Schloss Brohleck, Burgruine Hammerstein, Burg Nahmedy, Schloss Marienburg, Stadtburg Andernach and Schloss Neuwied. It was as if every town and settlement had its own ancient castle or fortress – or at least a romantic ruin. After the harsh industrial towns and cities of the Lower Rhine, with their cranes and concrete docks, it felt as if we had pedalled into a Grimm's tale.

But just as we were lulled by the bucolic scenes of folklore, the path fell into step beside a busy carriageway, pushing us up on to an embankment between road and railway line. An inter-city train thundered past and into a tunnel, almost causing me to fall of my bike. Beside us, signs in bold colours and angry capitals protested the weight of railway traffic. 'BAN GOODS TRAINS AT NIGHT!' one sign shouted. 'TRAIN NOISE DAMAGES HEALTH!' 'THE TRAINS ARE SLEEP ROBBERS!'

I remembered taking the train from Basel to Cologne decades earlier, enjoying the same picture-postcard views of the Rhine from a carriage window, as I did now from my bike. It wasn't hard to understand the locals' resentment as train frequency and speeds increased, and carriers were increasingly using rail rather than the river. Sleep deprivation doesn't bring out the best in anyone.

*

Around midday we found ourselves approaching the Deutsches Eck of Koblenz, the 'German Corner' – where the Mosel river meets the Rhine. On the other side of the bank, we could see an impressive statue of Wilhelm I, resplendent on his horse. The path forced us along the banks of the Mosel to the west for a few minutes until we came to a bridge that took us into the old town and returned us to the Rhine. We went to have a closer look at the German king and found an inscription beneath the statue: *Never will the Empire be destroyed as long as you are faithful and true.*

In a truly ironic strike, an American artillery shell had badly damaged the statue in 1945 and it was not until German reunification in 1990 that the statue was reconstructed and reinstated in all its glory, now a symbol of the newly reunified Germany. Next to it, three sections of Berlin Wall sat side by side, commemorating the victims of the divided post-war Germany.

When I travelled on a train from Switzerland along the Rhine in 1990, just after the fall of the Wall, an East German student, sitting opposite me, had described her life under Communist rule. She'd explained how limited her freedom had been under the Socialist Unity Party: everything decided on her behalf, from holiday destinations to university – even the subjects she took. And now she was travelling through West Germany, a place that had been once part of her country and was close in every sense, yet had been out of bounds just a few months previously.

The student sat at the window with the wide eyes of a child. When we reached the Lorelei, she'd jumped up with excitement, and I had peered with her from the carriage window at the cliff on the opposite bank of the river, wondering why a lump of rock would cause such delirium – not understanding the student's bumbling explanation, nor appreciating how dizzying her freedom felt; not grasping that she could now see a part of her past that had, not so long ago, been reduced to story and fairy-tale.

Jamie and I reached the Lorelei after a night in Boppard. We locked up our bikes outside the guesthouse opposite the rock and ordered our morning coffee from a disgruntled waitress. Across the river, the pinnacle of slate rose up from the bend of the Rhine. On the train, it had gone by in a grey-brown blur; now I could take in its scale and magnitude.

Written on the gable of the guesthouse were the words of Heinrich Heine's poem, *Die Lorelei*:

Ich weiss nicht was soll es bedeuten,
dass ich so traurig bin.
Ein Märchen aus uralten Zeiten;
Das kommt mir nicht aus dem Sinn:

('I don't know why I am so sad about this ancient tale; but I just can't get it out of my mind.')

I knew the words well, for a German friend and I had sung them in Derbyshire pubs accompanied by guitar and accordion. Greta and I were hopeless, often missing our opening and descending into immature giggles. Our guitarist would start again, nodding more emphatically to indicate when we should join in and off we'd go, singing the sad ballad in German with doleful voices. The song suited Greta well with her sad eyes and voice that held a hint of pain.

As with Andrea, the Allies had dropped a bomb on Greta's family home. The four-year-old had crawled under the basement table with her mother, terrified, and while they'd survived, the house didn't. The community rebuilt their home brick by brick, but no one could breathe life back into her father's dead body – not a victim of the Allies' bombs, but of the Nazis. As a Jehovah's Witness and conscientious objector, he'd refused to go to war, stating with firmness it was against his religious beliefs. Sentenced to death, tiny Greta watched her father depart by train for prison, not knowing she'd never see him again.

Now, sitting on the terrace of the Lorelei restaurant, I sang the words quietly to myself:

Die Luft ist kühl und es dunkelt,
und ruhig fließt der Rhein;
Der Gipfel des Berges funkelt,
im Abendsonnenschein.

('The air is cool and it's growing dark, and the Rhine flows quietly by; the mountain peak gleams in the evening sunshine.')

Decades went by and Greta still didn't know what the Nazis had done with her father's body. She assumed they had buried him in an unmarked grave – until some seventy years later a letter arrived in the post, informing her of her father's resting place, a picture of his headstone enclosed.

Greta was a beautiful woman, a Brigitte Bardot who perilously drew the wrong kind of men – until she met her third husband. It was as if she was intent on punishing herself with a survivor's guilt. She was Lorelei in reverse; Lorelei, who'd sat aloft the rock combing her golden hair and luring unsuspecting boatmen to their deaths with her beauty and mesmerising melody. Eyes fixed on the cliff, the boatman had paid no attention to the current and underlying rocks, until he realised his boat had struck them and the waves were taking him under.

The Lorelei could also have been a premonition of 1930s Germany – the beautiful woman now a preposterous man who could magically weave poisonous words into a seductive song; leading his people astray and taking them under with him. It was a fairy-tale gone wrong, a Grimm tale that haunted the minds of its victims more than half a century later. Greta and my father, struggling with the darkness of their minds, were just two of them.

8. Cycling through Vineyards

When English friends, Richard and Chris, heard we were cycling the Rhine, they offered their holiday house in Ungstein.

'Is it far from the river?' I asked Chris.

'Not much more than a dozen miles from Ludwigshafen,' she reassured me.

'And what about hills?'

'Flat. No problem.'

It was an offer I couldn't resist, and we looked forward to a couple of days on our own, where we could spread out across an entire house and relax.

When we studied the map in Bingen, however, it seemed easier to cut due south to Ungstein rather than follow the Rhine through the ugly industrial development around Mainz before turning west again. Wouldn't it be quicker and more picturesque to cut over the vineyards to join the *Weinstrasse*, the picturesque 'Wine Road'? The German word for vineyard is *Weinberg*, literally 'wine mountain'. The clue was in the word: it should have been a warning.

It was still early when we headed out of Bingen, alongside the Nahe river, looking not much more than a stream after the mighty Rhine. The road hugged the riverbank initially, the cycling pleasant on the flat floodplains. As I looked down this slow-flowing subsidiary of the Rhine, I caught a flash of blue, low on the water. A kingfisher! I stopped my bike, but it had gone, now hidden somewhere deep within the riverside vegetation.

Back in the 1970s, at the beginning of the Troubles, my father bought the first edition of the *Reader's Digest AA Book of British Birds*. Had his interest in birds arisen during World War Two? Perhaps they had been an escape from the horrors he'd witnessed in Belfast – a healing even, along with his devotional meditations. And then the birds and their songs may have continued to soothe him through a new civil war, a return to the death and injury he must have imagined we'd left behind on our island.

When the narrow hardback arrived, I leafed through it with excitement, nosing the fresh-print smell of its glossy pages and delighting in the romantically named sections:

'Seacliff and Rocky Islands', 'Broadleaf Woodlands' and 'Parks and Gardens'. Each page had a large illustration of the bird at the top and sidebars with maps showing the distribution of the birds and their migratory patterns, with notes at the bottom describing their appearance, nesting and feeding habits. The picture of the evil-eyed sparrowhawk, pupils and razor-sharp claws the colour of mustard gas, appealed to my inner world and fuelled my imagination. But it was the page with the absurdly bright-coloured kingfisher that I returned to again and again. How I longed to see one of those beautiful river-birds with its orange-red breast and shimmering steel-blue head and back. I read that the kingfisher had transparent eyelids, enabling it to see its prey when diving under water. A magical bird!

My father was also taken with the kingfisher. In a diary he'd written a few years before he became ill, he recorded his sightings of the bird: *Saw the blue flash of a kingfisher*, and, two days later, on my birthday, he got lucky again and wrote, *Praise thee. Saw a kingfisher*, delighting in his glimpses of this shy and elusive bird.

As I cycled alongside the Nahe, I wondered about the German word for the kingfisher: *Eisvogel*, or 'icebird'. 'King-fisher' seemed a much more apt description, but on learning that *Eis* comes from the old German *eisan* – and therefore related to 'iron' – I realised the name more likely referred to the bird's gleaming metallic and iridescent steel-blue feathers. Which is equally apt for this mesmerising creature.

*

We left the river behind and cycled through villages of cobbled courtyards draped in vines and dotted with tables and chairs, half-hidden behind the heavy oak gateways of the *Weingüter* – the wineries. I longed to stop for a glass of wine, or two, but knew we had to push on: there were close to fifty miles ahead, and I needed to stay upright on my bicycle.

After Sprendlingen, Jamie abandoned the roads that linked village with village, seeking out the vineyard lanes that ran through a patchwork of green corduroy. Still early in the growing season, there was no one to be seen except a winegrower, putt-putting through fields of vines on a miniature tractor. Soon we came to a crossroads. Above us, the Via Vinea climbed through the vineyards to a powder sky. Jamie studied the map on his phone, then, to my relief, took the route that skirted the base of the 'wine mountain'. We plunged down into Gau-Blickelheim. It was our first proper freewheel since we'd reached the Rhine.

His Rhine cycle book no longer of use to him in this hinterland of vineyards, Jamie was dependent on the Google maps on his phone. The warp and weft of country lane was more difficult to navigate than the linear riverside route with its well-signed pathways, but Jamie seemed to translate the three-dimensional topography of land and road, reduced to the wriggle of white threads on the tiny screen of his mobile, with relative ease.

At Flonheim we had no choice but to take the road that rose out of the village, forcing us to push our bikes on tip-toes. At the top, Jamie mounted his bike and pushed off, only to feel the back tyre give. There was a short, quiet hiss. He looked down to see a telltale trail of green below his wheel – the slime we'd filled our inners with before leaving England. He'd had his first puncture. Fortuitously, we found ourselves outside a wildlife centre with outside tables. I ate my *Butterbrot* of salami and cheese, and watched Jamie take off the back wheel, and then the inner, feeling for the source of the puncture. It was a pointless exercise, but at least he was getting to grips with the mechanics of his bike. Wheel on again, he pumped up the tyre, the slime inside the inner solidifying to seal the hole like glue, and we set off once more.

The way climbed again. My calf muscles began to throb and my lungs wheezed like clapped-out bagpipes, and with each rise we conquered, another rose beyond it. Having, at last, approached the highest point above Alzey, I looked forward to the long freewheel into the town, only to find the track had disintegrated to rough stone. I sighed, dismounted from my bike, and began to walk towards the settlement far below us in the valley.

In a town-centre café, the waitress refilled our water bottles, assuring us the road to Ungstein was not hilly. But inclines, invisible to car drivers, are painfully obvious to cyclists. The road unfurled like a whipped-out ribbon, taking the bikes ever higher across the land until I thought my legs would crumble. We refuelled with apple strudel slices at the supermarket on the edge of Flomborn, where Jamie, determined to find every farm track that criss-crossed the Rheinpfalz, careered off-piste again.

Around Wachenheim, the sky darkened, tipping a bucket of rain on us; then the track ran out, forcing us out onto the busy 271. At Grünstadt, we found ourselves caught up in a motorway approach, the passing cars gathering speed in anticipation of the motorway. Their wheels flung up rainwater, and the rush of air from the too-close vehicles turned my already jelly-legs to fluid. I was miserable. With each new settlement, my heart lifted, but the signs never read Ungstein, and the Wine Road teasingly dipped in a brief respite before climbing again until my inner child screamed: *Are we nearly there yet?*

Then, just as I was beginning to feel the road had no end, we dropped hard and fast into Ungstein. In retrospect, we sift the joy from the misery, holding on to the gold and discarding the rubble. It was only in the soft dimness of the cottage living room afterwards that I came to appreciate the cycle through the vineyards. I quickly forgot the slog of each rise, only remembering the pleasure of reaching the top with views extending across the Palatinate to red-roofed villages folded into blankets of green. I no longer remembered the aching calves and the tightness in my chest, just the exhilaration of tumbling off hillsides and the blast of cold air catching my face. I remembered the arches of vines that bridged the narrow streets of stone-built dwellings, not the noise and fumes of traffic. And I remembered the human contact of old men loitering in a sleepy village, their toothy smiles emerging from leathery faces as they shouted '*Wohin?*' – 'Where do you want to go?'

*

Before leaving England, Richard had emailed me a long list of useful instructions for the house. The last instruction, however, had puzzled me: *Don't forget to feed the hens!* I was curious. It seemed odd to keep hens when Richard and Chris spent no more than a couple of months out of the whole year in Ungstein. Did they encourage an endless stream of visitors just to feed the hens and prevent them from starvation?

Jamie soon found the street where Richard and Chris had

their cottage. Our instructions told us to collect the key from some neighbours, Karlheinz and Ingrid. I rang the bell and a man with snow-white hair answered the door. His lips spread a welcoming smile under a thick handlebar moustache, curled up in Regency splendour to match his goatee beard.

'*Willkommen; willkommen in Ungstein!*'

Karlheinz led us down the street to a bright, whitewashed house that protruded onto the road at a right angle. He gave us a tour of the garden that Chris had so lovingly described before: the long strip of lawn with its tended flowerbeds that funnelled down to a wildflower meadow and orchard flanking the fields beyond. To one side of the garden, Chris' vineyard striped the plot with vines of fresh green leaves.

As we returned to the house, Karlheinz paused by the barn, with its yard piled high with rubble, old buckets and packing cases. Behind the broken mesh of the old hen house, my eye caught sight of the hens among the stones and buckets, sitting in a pile of hay with their brood of chicks.

I burst out laughing: the hens were made of porcelain. It was then I remembered that Richard had once told us the story of the old woman they'd bought the house from – how she'd loved her hens and how Richard and Chris had installed the porcelain hens in her honour.

While the house outside had a pristine German appearance, Richard and Chris had created on the inside a distinctively recognisable English interior of ornaments, sofas and armchairs. In the softness of that little house in Ungstein, I opened all the shutters and dropped into the sofa to watch the day dim to night. I breathed out, enjoying the stillness – happy in the knowledge that the next couple of days would bring the simple pleasure of sleeping in, wandering around the corner to the bakery for freshly baked croissants and rolls for a leisurely breakfast and lunch. We would read and sleep and explore nearby on foot, leaving our bicycles chained up by the barn.

We finally forced ourselves out of the house late in the afternoon, walking out of the village and on through vineyards to a reconstructed Roman villa. The Romans had cleverly sussed out the potential for winemaking in this northern part of Europe, protected from the wind and rain in the shadow of the Haardt Mountains, and it was to the Romans that the Germans owed the pleasurable taste of white blossom, almond and grapefruit in the local Rieslings.

As Jamie and I gazed out between the great Roman pillars, we followed the line of blood-red poppies through the vines to the ribbed waves of rolling vineyards below. Caught between the vineyards and forested hillside of the Palatinate, the valley stretched out level from the nearby town of Bad Dürkheim, held in a gentle glow of light-filled haze. I noted the flatness of the topography with satisfaction: we'd be heading out there in a couple of days, back to the Rhine.

By evening, we'd unchained our bikes again – the need for food driving us to cycle into Bad Dürkheim, where a festival was being held. We wheeled our bikes through the narrow streets and squares of the old town, which were filled with colourful stalls, fairground rides and long trestle tables. Adults sipped on wine or beer while children with candyfloss ducked through the crowds. The smell of sausage, burger and fried onion permeated the air.

The next morning, friends of Chris and Richard took us out sightseeing in their car, but I felt disorientated by the speed of our travel, with no time to gather the passing blur of landmarks into a coherent impression. As we returned to Ungstein, I realised the pace of modern life felt strange and unnatural now, and to my surprise, I found I was yearning for the slow and gentle rotation of my bicycle wheels on quiet Rhine-side paths.

With our short sojourn in the vineyards of the Rhineland-Palatinate at an end, we handed the keys back to Karlheinz and Ingrid. They shook our hands and wrung theirs as they said goodbye.

'Watch out,' Ingrid said, gripping my hand again. 'You are just a girl.'

I laughed at Ingrid's words – it had been a long time since someone had called me a girl.

'No, seriously. Eastern Europe . . . it's not like here. Please, be careful,' she said, echoing the words of the Alsatian e-bikers.

9. Cuckoos and Storks on the Upper Rhine

The sudden storms of the Upper Rhine seemed far away and the day was filled with birds and mellow sunshine as we cycled away from Ungstein. Just north of Leopoldshafen, we caught sight of our first storks, a pale glow of white on the dark earth of the field that curved with the road. One lifted off, black-tipped wings pushing down in a powerful beat before surfing on a current of air. Jamie and I dismounted from our bikes and watched the bird in silent flight, mesmerised by our first experience of the Rhineland storks.

From Karlsruhe, we had a short reunion with the Rhine, but soon the wetlands and backwaters of the Altrhein, the Old Rhine, pushed us back from the main body of water again. I realised the call of the cuckoos I'd first heard back in the Netherlands had followed us all the way along the river and was still with us here on the Upper Rhine. It was as if my father was persisting on staying by my side on the cycle. I heard his voice in the two-note flute of the cuckoo, even though he was trapped in a urine-stained armchair in his care home far away. It was the birds that glued us together. Even now.

Birds had been the backdrop and soundtrack to our bound lives, roaming the damp earth of fields to tune into the sky, I, knee-high, thigh-high, then waist-high to my father. And I had followed him everywhere, rising early sometimes to walk with him into a dawn of milky light and sweet staccato notes.

Listen, my father said year on year, *the first call of the cuckoo!* And the long days of childhood and birdsong unfurled through the seasons like the pages of a picture book. The birds and their voices, he presented to me like gifts: the blackbirds' early morning chitter-chatter; the lark high above the dunes; swallow-tails tipping pond-water; pale geese arrowed southward; the robin's melancholy winter tune.

Near the village of Elchesheim-Illingen, Jamie caught sight of a nest of storks from the corner of his eye as he cycled past. We stopped and craned our necks to watch a pair of scrawny adults with their gawky young high above us in an out-sized nest. It was precariously balanced on the stumpy fingers of sheered-off branches at the top of a poplar, the stripped trunk like the long arm of a waiter holding high a twiggy plate of wriggling fledglings. One of the adult pair fed its young, a grey-beaded eye fixed sternly on the chicks.

An information board revealed the story of the Illingen storks: in 1999, as the Lothar cyclone swept across Europe, it had sliced off the crown of this poplar where the storks had nested year on year. Undeterred, the pair rebuilt their nest the following spring in the remaining branches, raising their young there until 2007. But then disaster struck: the trunk snapped and the nest was flung to the ground, the young crashing to the hard earth. The nest was destroyed, but the storks survived, and the villagers of Illingen, with the support of a local ornithologist, sprang into action. The stunned and injured storks were taken to a rescue centre and nursed back to health – but there was still the issue of the damaged trunk and the destroyed nest. Once again, the community rallied to create a manmade nest of steel lined with willow. Luckily, it was accepted by the storks.

I gazed back up at the storks, the adult concentrated on feeding her five young. Long ago, my father would have appreciated this family of storks in their twiggy castle, lording it over us from their sawn-off treetop in the sky. Now, I wasn't so sure.

We cycled on, aware that the geography of the Rhine had changed in a fundamental way. Ever since Emmerich, on the border with the Netherlands, Germany enclosed the river on either side. We'd swapped from side to side, sometimes cycling on the left bank, sometimes on the right. We'd criss-crossed bridges, back and forth, but always in Germany. Now France lay on the far bank. We could have crossed to experience another country, another culture – but I didn't speak the language.

Here in Germany it was easier. Jamie and I made a concession: we cycled onto an artificial island, a strip of land that lay in the middle of the dammed Rhine. The German–French border sliced through the man-made river island, where a *casse-croûte* on the French side served up coffee and snacks. The Alsace owner responded to my order with a fat, slurred accent. "*Voilà,*" he said, pushing the cups of coffee at me in a quick impatient movement.

Back on the German side, the Rhine path hugged the river, mile upon mile of gravel that snaked with the broad sweep of the waterway. As the sun slid down the sky, Kehl, our destination, seemed beyond our reach, and the day disappeared into the ribbon of path. We dreamed of food as afternoon slipped into evening, Jamie yearning for deep-fried chicken. At last, we cycled into the corridor of warehouses and cranes that eked out from all Rhine cities. We veered off into a jumble of high-rise buildings, car parks and warehouses where we found our accommodation for the night – a tower block that sprang up from the urban mess. And there, planted in front of the hotel, in the gravel of a wasteland car park – as if flung down by God in answer to Jamie's prayer – was a mobile snack bar selling deep-fried chicken.

That night we bedded down in our own lofty concrete nest, lording it over the city of Kehl and the river like the Rhineland storks.

*

10. Ingrid's Redstart

On the Upper Rhine the character of the river changed again: the romance of the Middle Rhine, with its castles and monasteries, disappeared; and the rocky cuts that forced the river through narrow chasms and steep-sided valleys ribbed with vines, gave way to dirt tracks edging a flatter, tamer landscape. Here, the path followed the wide brushstroke of river, except when it was pushed back from the banks where the Rhine's veins branched off into a watery world of marsh and woodland, interrupted only by sleepy villages. While it didn't have the drama of the Middle Rhine, this stretch of the water had its own gentle charm.

After Kehl, I sensed the transition from north to south. A chorus of softly throbbing crickets joined in with the coo of wood pigeon. Accents grew thicker, seamlessly shifting to southern dialects. We were greeted with *Grüss Gott*, rather than the lofty *Guten Tag* of High German; a true sign that we were in the south. For the first time, we saw the mountains, distant and faint to begin with, then sharpening in definition and magnifying in size as we pedalled southward.

There was something else too: we were cycling from spring into summer. My feeling of well-being deepened as I felt the heat of the sun on my hands and face. The wind that had hounded us in northern Germany had limped away and the air was warm, and the wheels of our bikes seemed to spin of their own accord. We skirted peaceful villages and dropped into ash woodlands where cool air eked from the undergrowth like a fridge door left open.

The cuckoo was still following us, its soft soporific double note floating through the air from some faraway location. It was such a gentle sound, heralding kinder days: the soothing balm of warmer air; the stretching out of light-filled hours and the sudden burst of spring-flower colour. As a child, I had thought the cuckoo a benevolent bird with its innocent, hide-away 'peek-a-boo' call. But my father revealed a story of cunning ruthlessness: the parasitic cuckoos laying their camouflaged eggs in the nests of other breeding birds; the young, when still bald and blind, kicking out the eggs of their unwitting host while mimicking the cries of the ejected chicks, ensuring their foster parents continued to feed them. The truth of the cuckoo was a far cry from the gentle two-note carried through the air – echoing the innocence of my childhood that protected me from the harsh realities of the world in my edge-of-town fields. Knowledge and self-awareness would come later.

Through Germany, we continued to follow the birdsong, the aroma of coffee and pastries and the fresh sharpness of ozone along the riverbanks. I loved the simplicity of our lives here on the Rhine: sleep, eat, pedal and repeat. But it was much more than that – for we glided effortlessly through a world alive with sound and sight, smell and taste – and around each new corner, there was a new onslaught on the senses. I felt a rediscovered equilibrium that gave me a fuzzy happiness as I cycled along.

*

I slammed on the brakes and looked on in dismay. The Rhine had burst its banks and the path in front of me was submerged somewhere beneath a lake of water that held a pair of mute swans. A family stood staring at the flood, too, the sullen teenage boy in a bad temper – furious that his parents had marched him along the Rhine only to be halted in their tracks. The parents shrugged and turned around, dragging their unhappy son with them.

I was not pleased either. We'd travelled a good number of miles along a dirt track from the last village, and now we'd have to add an additional dozen to our day by retracing our route back to the road in a long detour. Still I stood there, frowning at the water, as if my disapproval would make it recede. On the other side of the flood, I could see a cyclist approaching us. He stopped and dismounted from his bike and gave us a cheerful wave.

'Just wade through,' the man cried out.

I looked at him doubtfully then back at the flood. This was no puddle – more of a pond. I stepped closer to the water. While the edges looked shallow enough, I thought the dip in the middle looked unmanageably deep.

The man stood hesitantly on the other side, too, despite his confident call. Then he sprang into action. He pulled off his trousers, socks and shoes, lifted the bike above his shoulder and waded through the flood in his underpants. I watched the water come to his ankles, his knees and then his lower thighs at the deepest point, but soon he was through, triumphant and pleased.

'Go for it,' he laughed as he slapped out of the water.

Jamie looked doubtful.

'Let's do it,' I said, not caring for the extra miles.

Before Jamie could say anything, I'd pulled off my socks

and shoes. I wasn't going to strip down to my underpants, however: I was British. *Please!* I rolled up my trousers as far as I could, pulled the panniers off my bike and hoisted them onto my shoulder. Jamie watched, still unsure, as I pushed through the water, then he followed before returning across the flood to fetch the bicycles. A group of other German cyclists had now caught up with us and there was much laughing as the cyclists stripped off and negotiated the flood. The ice broken – or the water parted – we all lingered to share cycling tales.

At the youth hostel in Breisach, I emailed Karlheinz and Ingrid to reassure them that everything was going swimmingly – and that we'd nearly had to swim through the Rhine floods in southern Germany. Karlheinz sent me an excited email back:

You've brought luck at Richard's house. Just after you left, we discovered a redstart had nested in the roof of the front door porch – and the nest is now full of its young! In Germany, if a redstart builds her nest in a house, it brings good fortune – and we are sure it's a good omen for your trip.

11. Manuela

Somewhere back on the Rhine, my Swiss friend, Manuela, had messaged me: *You need to cycle more quickly and get to us for the weekend. We're waiting patiently.* I smiled as I read the text: it was typical of Manuela's humour.

Years ago, Manuela and I had met in a rural youth hostel somewhere between Bern and Luzern. Manuela, sixteen or seventeen, was on a cycling trip with school friends, and I, a couple of years older, was inter-railing on my own around Europe. Manuela was round-faced with a layer of puppy fat, living off cake as her mother didn't cook much. Later, she told me she'd thought I was sophisticated and worldly-wise, whereas I, with my sheltered Brethren upbringing in provincial Northern Ireland, thought Manuela sophisticated with her chic continental clothes and her cultivated European outlook.

I remember Manuela lowering herself onto the floor of the hostel to look up at me with focused intensity from ice-grey eyes. She had a way of positioning herself lower to whoever was with her, so that they had the feeling no one else existed. Men found her irresistible, and Manuela went from one intense love affair to the next over the years.

Back home, we started writing letters to each other on tissue-thin airmail paper, Manuela's writing long and sloping and exotically foreign in appearance. After a year or so of correspondence, I returned to Switzerland to stay with Manuela in her village. She introduced me to her friends in a trendy bar laid out with deckchairs and a sand floor – there was nothing like that in Northern Ireland in the 1980s. I had found another world. Manuela had a boyfriend whose father watered his balcony marijuana plants when they went on holidays. I didn't know anyone with a balcony, much less a marijuana plant.

Manuela approached everything in life with the same intensity and passion – it was hard not to be seduced by her enthusiasm. She had a weakness for hyperbole, hamming up her drama-queen acts with a well-developed sense of the absurd and dark humour. It would stand her in good stead for medical school and her training as a neurologist. Not everyone 'got' her, but for those who befriended her, she was fiercely loyal – and despite the distances that divided us, our friendship had endured for thirty-five years. In truth, our backgrounds and lives were so different, we'd never have been friends ordinarily, and we valued our friendship all the more for it.

A couple of years after that first meeting in the hostel, Manuela came to Ireland to work with disabled people at a Camphill community, ahead of her medical degree. One day during that time, I confessed to her that I wanted out of Northern Ireland, away from the small-town conservatism of my birthplace and its entrenched sectarianism. I also wanted away from the shackles of my Brethren upbringing and the weight of my parents' fragile peace agreement.

'I'd love to have the courage to leave my job and go and live in Switzerland.'

'Well, what's stopping you?'

I started to make excuses, then stopped. She was right. There was nothing. A little while later I bought a copy of *The Lady* magazine with its pages of nanny advertisements, hoping to find a Swiss family who'd employ me as an *au pair*.

When I told my father I had found a job in Switzerland, his face dropped.

'But there's nothing for me here,' I told him. 'I need to experience something different, explore the world. I want to be happy and have fun'.

'But we are not here to have fun. You shouldn't be pursuing happiness. You should be content with what you have.'

I looked at him oddly; somehow this puritanical aspect of my Brethren upbringing had passed me by. Later, I realised this was a desperate argument from my father, who simply didn't want to let go: his children, his *raison d'être*, were slipping away, one by one. It was when my youngest sister left a few years later that his depression set in.

*

Manuela had good reason to jokingly ask me to cycle quicker: she had a busy week ahead with practice consultancy hours and a medical conference. It was a shame. Nonetheless, as Jamie and I drew closer to Basel, too late for the desired weekend, I was looking forward to seeing Manuela. In one sense, I would miss Germany for the few days I would be in Switzerland. Its pure High German was much more accessible, for even after three years living in Switzerland on and off, I still barely understood the dialect.

For all of that, Switzerland felt more like home and despite its 'too-perfect' image I loved its mountains, the clean air and the easy organisation of it all. I felt embarrassed to admit my love affair with the country – no one ordinarily confessed to liking this law-abiding, conservative country. Even Manuela dismissed her own land 'with its stupid cows and boring mountains'. Basel, at least, was industrial, even rough in places and more laid-back – and lay right on the German border. It was here Manuela set up home with a skeleton suspended from a hook in her book-filled study, deep within the immigrant quarter of the inner city. It was as far away from chocolate-box perfection as she could get.

There was another reason why I felt a rising sense of excitement as we neared Basel. We had almost reached our first major goalpost – the end of the southbound stretch of the Rhine.

From here on in, we'd head east before turning north again for the Danube.

Just north of the city centre, Jamie and I cut away from the Rhine and unceremoniously crossed the border into Switzerland. If it hadn't been for the painted white cross on the pedestrian footpath and a small sign half-hidden in bushes, we wouldn't have realised we had entered another country: German suburbia merged with Switzerland's seamlessly, and there was a sense we'd sneaked in through a back door.

Manuela kissed us Swiss-style, right, left, right, and marvelled at Jamie's height. Long gone was her soft round face, the puppy fat and the waist-length hair, sometimes swept up in a loose roll. Her face was gaunter now, her body taut and skinny, her hair cut in fashionable shoulder-length layers.

Manuela dipped in and out of the house over our three-day visit, still finding time to bake *Zopf*, (plaited bread) and cake, and to cycle with me into town to rummage in second-hand shops. We spent evenings chatting and eating *raclette*, made with strong Swiss cheese, and *Spätzli* with smooth red wine – as we'd done down the years, first alone, then with our men and finally our sons. Those years had gone by fast and furious: one minute, Manuela and I were young women on the cusp of life, the scores to our future still unwritten; the next, mature women with teenage sons. It was hard to believe Jamie was around the age Manuela and I had been when we'd first met.

I had told Manuela we would stay five days, but in the empty house I felt the black dog of my depression scratching at the door. Just as I felt it had gone forever, it came creeping back in. I had the urge to find the Rhine again. I missed the fresh air and the constant movement. And so we packed our bags, wheeled the bikes down the little garden path, pushed the gate closed behind us and free-wheeled down the hill. Back to the river.

12. Back and Forth

From Basel, we stayed on the German side of the Rhine, but I knew that the next stage of the ride would see us cycling backwards and forwards between Germany and Switzerland, and between past and present.

Soon we were out of the suburbs – the refineries, power stations and sluice gates replaced by open fields. By early afternoon we were cycling into Bad Säckingen, where our CouchSurfing host, Hans, had offered us a couple of sofas for the night. As the retired teacher wasn't expecting us until late afternoon, we explored the town, peering into its Gothic church and wandering through cobbled streets around the main square. We found an ancient wood-covered pedestrian bridge, the longest in Europe, and crossed into Switzerland at Stein, lingering there until it was time to find our host.

*

'I'd like to cycle part of the route with you, if that's okay?' Hans said in the morning.

'You're welcome to join us, but I have to warn you that I cycle very slowly,' I laughed.

It didn't seem to put Hans off, and after our host had cooked us a boiled egg to accompany the usual German breakfast of rolls, meats and cheeses, he wheeled his bike out to join us on our way east. As we cycled towards Laufenburg, the air nipped and a low fog hung over the Rhine, softening birch and willow to an Impressionist painting in the early morning mist. For the first time, I put on my cycling gloves – to keep my hands warm, rather than for protection. Had the summer weather north of Basel been a fleeting tease? It felt as if we'd returned to winter.

Hans was good company. His easy chatter was a refreshing change from Jamie's withdrawal into a world behind his ear-plugs. Jamie was happy, too, pleased to drop behind and listen to downloaded podcasts on his mobile. At Laufenburg, we paused to look at the handsome half-timbered terraced houses mushrooming from the river on the Swiss side, the town still sugared in misty light. I'd also come here with Manuela when our boys were small. We'd sharpened sticks to spear *Bratwurst* and barbecued them over a fire on the river beach.

As Hans, Jamie and I headed out of Laufenburg, the mist dissolved and the sun broke through: it was another fine May day. And at mid-morning, Hans waved his goodbyes before turning back for Bad Säckingen. At Rheinheim we lost the signs for the Rhine path and found ourselves on the bridge crossing to Bad Zurzach in Switzerland. We were cycling blind and beginning to feel frustrated, but an elderly couple stopped to help us, then accompanied us up a steep hill on their bikes to show us a shortcut – causing me to feel great shame at my incline phobia.

From here on in, the climbs became more persistent. Deep down, I knew the hills were as much a psychological problem as a physical hindrance for me. Ahead lay Hohentengen am

Hochrhein: *hohen* and *hoch* indicating height – and twice over. Sometimes, linguistic ignorance is bliss, but the way ahead turned out to be a gradual schlepp, rather than an insurmountable climb. Jamie, for his part, was in a rare bad mood and I was struggling to cheer him up. In the end, I gave up and left him to guide us in and out of German and Swiss villages, back and forth over borders until at last we came to the long freewheel down to the Rhine Falls.

I'd come to the Rhine Falls with Tom long ago. Later that year, we returned to Bodensee, getting engaged at Konstanz. It seemed appropriate. A quarter of a century later I was still with this man who stood consistently by my side, giving me space to grow, encouraging me in that growth. He was indeed the constant in my life.

That day back in 1990, we'd walked the river to the Rhine Falls as the light faded out. There was no one there but us, as we kicked through wizened leaves in the chill of dusk. Now, here with Jamie, the place was heaving with tourists. Japanese, French and Spanish mingled with tens of other languages. I squirmed at the crude tourism of the place – a far cry from that muted winter's evening when I'd come with Tom. Jamie and I didn't linger, climbing out of Neuhausen am Rheinfall and on through the tangle of suburban streets that led to the old centre of Schaffhausen.

When I'd visited with Tom, we'd wandered through the same streets and squares of Renaissance buildings decorated with frescos and surrounded by statues. We'd enjoyed the autumn-winter taste of charred chestnuts – our senses heightened with fresh love. Here in the present, the place was bright with spring sunshine. Jamie and I found a place for the night with a couple of artists, where I made pasta on a hot-ring among the tubes of oils and paintbrushes and great canvasses of abstract paintings.

After our makeshift meal, Jamie and I looked at the map to work out our route over to the Danube. This would be my first major challenge, and the thought of the hills that lay between the two rivers made me nervous.

'We could put the bikes on a bus,' I suggested.

'No, we can't do that.' Jamie's voice was firm. 'We're cycling. You can do it.'

I nodded contritely. Jamie was increasingly taking over the role of his father and I was pleased that he was growing in confidence daily.

*

Just after 8am, we cycled out of Schaffhausen. The road eased us up its incline and on through a narrow valley, squeezing between thick woodland, before opening out into meadows dotted with sloping farmhouses and solid wooden barns. The way took us past bales of hay and ruler-straight woodpiles. Glossy Swiss tractors lay in farmyards, looking like they'd never seen a muddy field. These were the rural scenes of Switzerland I knew so well from the past.

I struggled on, the incline now sharper. My legs felt like lead and the pedals fought against me as I pushed down on them. My head, still sluggish in the early morning, held onto a stubborn resentment against the rise.

Around Bargen, we cycled into Germany, then promptly back into Switzerland, the two border signs just yards from each other. On the edge of the village we turned right onto

Steigstrasse. The name told me everything I needed to know: 'Climb Street' was like a wall in front of us. We dismounted and wheeled the bikes up the narrow country lane, joking we needed to rest our numb bottoms. It was a bike-hike, as Jamie christened our new mode of travel. But it didn't matter; I was pleased to slow down to a walking pace and take in the views around us. We headed on through forest and onto the plateau, weaving through wildflower meadows. Overhead, a bird dipped and rose with the hills that unfolded in waves of yellows and greens before us.

The skylark!

One early summer, just before my father left Wood Lane forever to enter the sterile world of the care home, I had taken him and my mother to Eire. I wanted to show him the parts of Ireland he couldn't reach on his day trips. Tom and I had rented a cottage overlooking Dingle Bay. I'd planned to take a boat out into the bay to show my father Fungie, the resident dolphin, but he'd looked at the boat and shaken his head before shuffling back to the car. We'd climbed the pass over to Brandon and drove the Ring of Kerry, his head drooping into his lap. We'd taken him to the Burren in County Clare, where Tom and I had scrambled over the table-flat slabs of limestone to find early orchids, mountain avens, even spring gentians, but my father had hung back, disinterested. Then in County Mayo, on the dunes above a littering of islands, he'd lifted his head and craned his neck skyward.

'The skylark!'

We'd stood there together, my father and I, watching the dizzy skylarks bombing and flittering and shooting vertically up into the sky before dropping down again like a plumb line.

We tilted our heads backwards to spot the birds so high above us – small dots in the heavens, a darting of energy. And from these tiny birds, ping-ponging high above the Earth, came their song sharp on the air, yet also gentle, sweet, bubbling, intricate. I looked at my father and saw the old light in his eyes, an excitement that I thought had gone forever. But it was to be short-lived, as fleeting as the skylark's movements across the clouds.

'The skylark!' I said to Jamie.

We stood amid the beauty of Switzerland's uplands and observed the bird's acrobatic twittering and flight, just as I had done with my father in Country Mayo. A moment captured, a moment repeated: father and daughter; mother and son. And I silently promised myself that I would never allow my depression to cause me to lose sight of Jamie, or the skylark.

From Blumberg, Jamie and I freewheeled to Donaueschingen, zig-zagging through German country lanes and on past farms reeking of cow manure and fields of pungent rapeseed that tickled the nose. The air was a cold compress slapped on my face and the iciness of wind caught my throat.

We followed the ditch canal into Donaueschingen with satisfaction: we'd completed the Rhine from Rotterdam as far as Schaffhausen and had reached the source of the Danube. I'd conquered my fear of those first hills and made it across. It didn't matter that I'd wheeled the bike up the steepest sections. I'd done it, and, more importantly, I was emotionally alive.

GERMANY AND AUSTRIA

1. Starting Out on the Danube

From its source at Donaueschingen, to its mouth at the Black Sea, the Danube is 1,768 long miles – it is Europe's second longest river (after the Volga). The Rhine we'd left behind was less than half the length of the Danube, and the journey ahead, following the twists and turns of the river, would take us through eight countries: Germany, Austria, Slovakia, Hungary, Croatia, Serbia, Bulgaria and Romania.

The scale of our journey was now sinking in. Apart from a short section before Schaffhausen, the Rhine route had been largely flat, and while large sections of the Danube offered easy cycling through floodplains, there were challenges to be met in the vineyards of Croatia, and in Romania where the Carpathians drop down to the river.

Finding the karst spring at Donaueschingen's castle, I was disappointed to see it surrounded by rubble, planks and scaffolding: the Danube's source was under restoration and a mess. It was an anti-climax after the pictures I had seen of the spring surrounded by a grand ornamental wall and wrought-iron railing, with an imposing marble statue of a woman and child representing the hills and the Danube – Mother Baar pointing the way east to the child, the Danube.

While Donaueschingen has grandly claimed the river's source, the Danube actually has two sources on higher ground: the Brig river that begins deep in the Black Forest just northwest of Furtwangen, and the Brigach that flows from the north.

The two rivers conjoin at Donaueschingen and it's at this point on the outskirts of the town (not in the castle park) that the river becomes the Danube, keeping its name in all its different forms to the Black Sea.

As Jamie and I needed to find overnight accommodation, we headed for tourist information. The helpful assistant pointed us in the direction of the Jägerhaus, the Hunter's House, lying deep in woodland north of the town. When we arrived at the guesthouse, there was no one there but the owners. We parked our bikes in a dim hall with a bowling alley and blinked through the darkness to the reception area. The woman took us upstairs to a roomy suite with a kitchenette.

'Great. We can we cook for ourselves.'

'Not for one night,' the woman said sourly. 'It's too much work.'

'Ah, we'll eat in the restaurant then.'

'No, it's not possible. We closed the restaurant last year.'

Arriving for breakfast in the morning, I found, to my surprise, the dining room filled with guests. The husband courteously served breakfast in breeches, checked shirt, a western bow-tie and cowboy boots, but without making eye contact. The guests whispered among themselves, and we ate our breakfast in muted discomfort, the room having all the atmosphere of a school examination hall. I looked at the hunting paraphernalia strung around the room and then to the woodland outside, almost expecting Little Red Riding Hood to burst through the door followed by the wolf and the hunter. I suppressed a desire to giggle. It really wouldn't do.

*

There was a sense of anticipation as we cycled out of the town to a new river and a new stage of the journey. The valley lay wide and flat in front of us, the path parting wildflower meadows edged with blood-red poppies. A series of sharp lefts and rights led us through open countryside, and we lost the Danube for a while until we crossed the bridge at Pfohren. With a short, sharp rise out of the village, we were on our way again, loving the speed of the wheels on the tarmac.

At Tuttlingen, the riverside park tempted us with its sculptures and hammocks, but we pedalled on. Less able to resist Mühlheim, perched on a skyline ridge with an imposing reconstructed medieval castle at one end, Jamie and I pushed our bikes up the steep-sided hill and under a gateway of cobbled stones. We paused to quench our thirst at the fountain under a statue of a mother carrying a basket on her head, her children clutching her apron. The main street of pastel timber-frames stretched the length of the ridge, the ancient houses bulging and sagging with age.

The landscape changed again from wide meadow to narrow wooded gorge. After Fridingen, pinnacles and walls of white chalk protruded from thick deciduous woodland. The fast tarmac paths soon deteriorated to a rough gravel track that rose and fell on the hillside. This quiet backwater of the Upper Danube was possibly even more enchanting than the Middle Rhine. Palaces, castles, churches, monasteries, ruins and grottos called to us on the skyline. I yearned to stop and explore, but we still had sixty miles to go before reaching our destination with its hilltop youth hostel at Sigmaringen.

*

We were both speaking German, but weren't communicating.

'Where? Is-tan-bul? Unbelievable.'

The cyclist sitting at the next table next to ours on the terrace café was on a ten-day cycling trip along the Danube. He'd complained about the 'freshness' of the weather and the winds. For me the weather was perfect, with its partial sunshine and light cooling breezes.

'Yes, Istanbul. But we've almost three months and we can take it slowly.'

'I just can't imagine that,' he said, frowning. 'To have to unpack and repack every day – and live like Gypsies for months. That can't be easy.'

'It's okay, actually. We don't have much with us, so it doesn't take long to gather our stuff. And I love the adventure. Around every bend, there's a new view and a new experience.'

The cyclist shook his head in puzzlement. I turned around again to talk to Jamie. From behind me I heard him muttering, 'Istanbul. Madness.'

As we cycled away from the terrace garden in Bertoldsheim, I thought about the German cyclist's words. Everything I'd said to him was true. When we'd set out at the beginning of May, I hadn't known how I would feel after weeks on the road. Would it get to the stage where I wouldn't want to sit on a saddle again? Would I yearn for home? But the further south and east I travelled, the more joyful I felt. There was something wonderfully liberating about turning the pedals and waiting for the world to unfold. On the German Danube, we spun through buttercup and wildflower meadows of ox-eye, viper's bugloss and yellow rattle and on through poppy-splashed barley fields. We bumped along cobbled streets of rainbow-painted towns and villages. Just outside Donauwörth, we slipped into a beer tent to listen to the locals singing Bavarian folk songs in *Lederhosen* and *Tracht* (traditional costume for women) with a belly full of *Weissbier*. It was only mid-afternoon.

Once a grass snake slithered across our path – and a fawn ran out in front of our bikes. We saw an enormous carp rise from the water as we ate our *Butterbrot* on the edge of the river, sending rings across the broad width of its surface. On the Danube's backwaters, we passed ponds of screeching frogs, sounding something between a chorus of demented Donald Ducks and a battery of gunfire. Storks adorned riverside meadows and herons stood frozen on the Danube's banks. I dismounted from my bike to watch one of the slender herons on the Danube's edge, I, too, frozen on the river's edge, as I waited to see if the bird would move from its spot.

If I were asked to choose a bird that best matched my father, it would have to be the heron: solitary, still, watching, sharp-eyed. My father was drawn to this elegant creature, too, recording multiple sightings in his diary in his usual shorthand: *Saw a heron in country . . . Saw a heron in flight . . . Saw a heron at the Lagan Bridge. Praise the Lord . . . Watched a heron for a long time.* I saw from his diary entries that the birds and his God were an outlet for the emotions he was unable to express. When he abandoned his expressions of faith, the birds and his countryside, he had abandoned himself. It was a truly dark place.

*

As Jamie and I continued on our journey, the smell of wild garlic in the Danube woodlands filled our nostrils. The gentle two-note of the cuckoo still accompanied us, dipping in and out of our soundscape each day. Continuing through Bavaria, the accents grew even thicker, the landscape more rural.

Bavaria, along with Baden Württemberg, is Germany's most affluent state. Everything was solid here, from the sturdy houses to the bulky farmers in their dungarees and brace-held trousers and the housewives in their nylon housecoats plucking fruit in their gardens or preparing vegetables under shady trees.

They reminded me of my mother, who also wore a nylon housecoat throughout the day, although she preferred to chop vegetables in the kitchen, venturing only into our small garden to pull stalks of rhubarb for pies, and scallions and lettuces for salad. She hated the sunlight.

My father, in contrast, revelled in the outdoors: the songs of the sky, the slap of wet grass against his leg and the pungent smell of damp earth and vegetation. At this time of year, we tramped our fields edged with the white blossom of hawthorn, the air filled with its scent, just as it was here in Germany.

What was it that had drawn my parents to each other? Perhaps the fact that my mother was a farmer's daughter. She lived in County Down, the adjacent county from my father's home county of Armagh. He'd met my mother at a Brethren conference, seduced by her eyes, dark as wells, across the pews. My father had cycled out to her family farmhouse near the small town of Dromore, intent on wooing my mother. He liked to tell us the story of that first visit: how he'd cycled along the drive to the large panelled door and rang the bell. When one of my mother's sisters opened the door, it almost fell off its hinges. No one used the front drive or door, preferring to slip through the back door in the farmyard.

My mother's many brothers teased my father for years after about his grand entrance. My uncles were pranksters – and loved to play practical jokes on their three sisters' wooers, whether it was letting down tyres or hiding their bicycles up trees. Sometimes I wondered if my father was drawn as much to the countryside where my mother lived as to her large brown eyes, while my mother was equally drawn to the boy from the town. During their courtship, my father thought nothing of the fourteen-mile round trip on his bicycle, along the twisting roads of the Down drumlins – in sunshine, wind and snow. Later, he abandoned his bicycle for the car that became something of a love affair despite his affiliation with the outdoors. But he would roll the window down, whatever the weather.

In spite of the fragile relationship I now had with my father, I knew I was very like him. When we went outside, it was as if something reconnected in our brains. We both felt alive. The countryside was our natural home. As I cycled on along the Danube, I knew he too would have once revelled in its nature on two wheels: the rising carp, the racket of frogs, the bolting fawn and the light playing off blossom trees.

I'd turned my back on him all those years ago – after that terrible night in in our kitchen – but still he was here at my side, occupying a stubborn place somewhere inside my skull that simply wouldn't leave.

*

2. In the Wars with Klaus

We arrived in Ingolstadt under heavy skies that were befitting this medieval city of castles, towers, walls and gates and grand gothic buildings. It had sprung up around a fortress – its horseshoe ends meeting at the Danube to create a loosely circular enclosure – and the locals refer to themselves as *Schanzer*, the 'people of the fortification'. It's here that scientist Victor Frankenstein built his monster.

Klaus, our CouchSurfing host for the night, lived outside the fortified old town, across the railway track and down a quiet suburban street. I'd written to him further up the Danube to ask if he could put us up for the night. He'd replied: *You're very welcome. Just one condition: my team 1860 is playing against Kiel in a relegation match and I have to watch the match the night you are here.*

No problem, I'd reassured Klaus, wondering how a football team had ended up as a number (it transpired 1860 was Munich's lesser known team, and its number referred to its founding date). While I'd promised Klaus I wouldn't hinder him from watching his match, I inadvertently managed to cause a distracting commotion in the middle of the game. Perhaps it was the wine our hospitable host had plied us with, or perhaps it was just a case of my scattiness, but on returning from the toilet, I'd forgotten the clear glass doors that separated the hall from the living room. As I looked at the TV screen ahead, I went slap – straight into the doors – nose first.

There was blood everywhere: on the tiled floor and all down my clothes. Klaus was torn between my plight and the football match. 1860 won and I slunk off, embarrassed, to wipe up the mess and change my clothes. It was a pure slapstick comedy moment – and despite the hefty nosebleed, it was mainly my pride that had taken a dent, not my nose. The irony of me losing so much blood when 'safely indoors' was not lost on me, as Jamie and I hadn't had any accidents on the bikes, bar a cut finger on that third day when I'd fallen into the ditch.

The football match out of the way, Klaus busied himself in the kitchen preparing pasta, while I chopped up salad. He filled up a jug of his homemade lemonade, with mint picked from his garden, and poured me a glass: it was deliciously refreshing. As he put on the pan of water to boil, Klaus told me about his childhood: he'd grown up in a small village just five miles or so from 'the Wall', born a decade after its erection. His parents never spoke about the time before the country had been split down the middle – it was as if East Germany didn't exist. Klaus knew the names of some of the villages across the border, just a handful of miles from where he lived, but that was it.

'We all knew there was something on the other side, but we didn't know what it looked like. It was like the dark side of the moon.'

I thought of the East German student I'd met on the Rhine train and her excitement at discovering the West. How the East Germans were kept in the dark about the FRG is well documented, but now Klaus was telling me he had been just as ignorant on the western side. There was something fundamentally tragic about a people who had shared a nationality, language, history and heritage to have been so arbitrarily separated.

'The thing is, no one expected the Wall to come down. We all just assumed it would always be like that, and when it fell, we couldn't believe it. There was massive excitement. In no time at all, we built up links with our neighbouring villages on the East German side, and before long, I was playing football matches against those East German villages that had just been names all my life.'

'How much do you remember about the days after the Wall came down?'

'I remember there was a mad flow of traffic in both directions. Everyone wanted to know what it was like on the other side. A whole new world had just been opened up to us – and it was right on our doorstep. It was bizarre. All of a sudden, our little village was inundated with people from East Germany.'

I wondered how Klaus had felt in the Cold War. Had he been afraid? Had he felt threatened living under the shadow of the Wall, so close to the border?

'No, not at all. You know, I had a good life. It was really quiet where I lived, but I had good friends living in the surrounding villages and we'd all meet up in town and have a ball. We never talked about the Wall. It just wasn't a topic. At the same time, it was kind of cool for me as a kid living so close to the Wall – we had a sort of 'sponsorship' with the *Bundeswehr*, the federal armed forces. They came at least once a year to carry out manoeuvres, the US army too. I remember German and US soldiers sleeping in our house. They made a point of building up good relationships with our village – showing us their weapons and so on. I even got to sit on a tank once. You can imagine how that felt for a young boy! I remember the US army had a band too. I loved it when the army came. Our quiet little village would come to life – there was so much to see and do. But no, I never felt unsafe.'

I thought of my parallel upbringing in Northern Ireland. There was no physical wall in the place where I grew up, but the divisions were real enough for all of that. The Catholic and Protestant populations lived at opposite ends of my town like bookends, separated by the town centre. By the time the Troubles had begun, there were no Catholic families left on our street. A mutual sectarian purge was taking place in council housing estates: Catholics were threatened and evicted from Protestant strongholds, Protestants from Catholic. It wasn't long before self-imposed segregation had taken place across most of our town. Like in Germany, our (albeit invisible) wall divided us from unknown places – places unsafe for us to enter for fear the other side would ask you for your religion. It was the dark side of the moon, as Klaus had said.

But I was curious about these alien Catholics. What were they really like? Were they as bad as people said? Would they really stab you in the back with a knife if you turned around, as some Loyalists I knew claimed? At secondary school, I met my first Catholics (bar the next-door family from early childhood). They were normal human beings, I discovered, not these fearsome monsters portrayed by some people in my community. It was a revelation. I started to argue with my father over politics. Discrimination against Catholics wasn't the answer, but rather integration and equal opportunity. Catholics weren't the enemy. When my father ran out of counter-arguments, he dismissed me with a *You'll understand one day when you're older*. I was already in my twenties. But bit by bit, the Troubles rumbled to an end. Years of negotiations had brought us a peace deal. It was a painful birth into a new era, an uneasy peace.

Reunification in Germany was another matter: the events unfolded almost overnight. I watched the crowds chisel away the Berlin Wall on the TV screen of my flat in Switzerland. Could this really be happening? As a friend of a friend was writing a dissertation arguing that the Wall would never fall, it collapsed. Overnight, my East German unit at university became obsolete. Reunited, friends and families in Germany hugged and cried after decades of separation. The joy was palpable, even through the glass of my TV screen.

'I remember the moment so clearly,' said Klaus. 'And the Year-12 trip to eastern Germany on the day of reunification in October 1990. We went to Weimar and Dresden and stayed overnight at the Elbterrassen – you know, on the Elbe. Everyone was celebrating. It's an experience I'll never forget.'

3. Blah-blah with Kat

I had messaged Kat from a room in the eaves of a rickety hotel in Ulm. Kat wrote back quickly: *You're in luck this weekend – I'm at home. If you come after 5pm, I will be here and you can surely surf my couch.* The last sentence made me smile – I had visions of standing on Kat's couch with arms outstretched as if balancing the waves on a surfboard.

Like Klaus, Kat lived on the other side of the railway line in a quiet suburban street on the outskirts of Straubing. She opened the door, grabbed my bike and hauled it down to the basement, and then we climbed the steps to her attic flat. Kat opened the door to a rooftop jungle: plants hung from the ceiling, crowded shelves and crept along the wooden floor. Between the sloping eaves, an enormous L-shaped sofa took up most of the floorspace.

Kat and Jamie discovered they shared the same taste in music. 'You're in charge of the CDs, Jamie. Pick out something good.'

While Jamie sorted the music, I helped Kat in the studio kitchen as she prepared a Bavarian *Kartoffelsalad* and fried *Leberkäse* and eggs. *LeberKäse* is neither liver nor cheese, despite its name. It's pure comfort food: a mix of corned beef, pork, bacon and onions, all chopped up finely and compressed in a loaf-tin, then baked in the oven. It's a meal beloved of southern Germans, Austrians and the German-speaking Swiss. The loaf-shaped *Leberkäse* is sliced and fried along with eggs that are placed on top and accompanied by potato salad. It's a rich and tasty meal, and while it may not be the finest dining, it was a calorie-packed treat for hungry cyclists.

We settled down to chat. Kat was full of stories – but she was also interested in our lives and our cycle trip. She explained that she used the company BlaBlaCar to car-share. It was a more sociable and environmentally friendly way to travel, and cheaper too. 'BlaBla refers to the test you take when you join, to let your driver know how sociable you are – and how sociable they want you to be,' Kat explained. 'Blah-blah-blahs are the people who never shut up, while the blahs are the silent types.' Kat had clearly mastered the art of 'blah-blah' herself. She was good at conversation and she was good at listening.

While our previous host, Klaus, had grown up in the shadows of the Wall on the western side, Kat was on the other side as a small child, living in the heart of the 'dark side of the moon', as Klaus had called it, near Dresden.

Kat was lucky to exist at all. When the British and Americans carpet-bombed Dresden in February 1945, around 25,000 Dresden inhabitants were killed. Kat's grandparents were eighteen and nineteen years old at the time, and were fortunate enough to escape the bombing as they lived on the edge of the city. Having survived the war, her grandparents lived in poverty, as German rations were even more meagre than their British counterparts'. Germany had to rise from the ashes and rebuild in every sense of the word.

Kat's parents were born just a couple of years before the erection of the Wall in 1961, too young to remember the life 'before'. But for her grandparents, it must have been a shock: the Wall had gone up virtually overnight, with kilometres of barbed wire rolled out as people slept.

1961 was also the year my parents gave birth to me, far away in Northern Ireland. Two weeks after my arrival, Germany was torn down the middle and Berlin was split up by the Allies, with the British, American and French sectors of the city becoming an isolated island in the middle of the new East German Republic. As German tensions rose with the Cold War, Northern Ireland was still at peace, my parents quietly living in Wood Lane on their edge-of-town development flanked by sleepy countryside. When East Germans were being shot at, as they tried to cross no man's land into West Germany, someone planted a rose field opposite my house. Colour filled our front windows and sweet perfume permeated the air for a couple of summers until the business venture was found to be unprofitable.

There's a picture of me in one of my mother's homemade dresses, with its flounced border trimmed with lace and little white buttons down the centre. My sister, Audrey, is holding my chin up, forcing me to look at the camera. I'm grabbing her hands, or maybe pushing them away, and I have a sly smile on my face. My mother is wearing a dress of lilac flowers and my father is wearing his suit, a hanky in his pocket. We are standing between the rose bushes in our Sunday best, in among the lemon, bluish-red and dusty pink rose-heads with emerald-green fields stretching behind to low-lying cottages. It's a picture of childhood perfection, if you don't look too closely.

I asked Kat what she remembered about the Republic before the Wall toppled in 1989.

'Well, I wasn't born until 1983, so I wasn't really aware of the politics. All I have are my memories and the warm feelings I had from that time that I've carried with me into adulthood.'

As Kat talked about her early childhood in Dresden, it reminded me of the opening scenes of *Good Bye Lenin!*, set in East Germany during the Cold War – with its soft camera shots and warm light and the soundtrack of children's laughter in the garden of a cosy *dacha*. The similar expression of nostalgia in Kat's childhood reflections was striking.

'There was a strong community, for sure. I remember lots of barbecues and parties. We kids were always running in and out of each other's apartments in our block.' Kat smiled at the memory. 'I remember all the bathrooms were on the ground floor and that it was really scary for us kids when we had to go to the toilet in the middle of the night.'

She laughed. 'You know I'm one of the GDR baby boomers. In East Germany at that time, you were stuck with your parents until you got married, so people tended to marry young. They had their kids young, too, because childcare was excellent and there were lots of benefits.'

Kat's parents both worked, as was usual in the GDR: her father for the local transport company; her mother in the sweet factory filling *Schultüten* – the little cones of bonbons every child received on starting school. Kat went to nursery at the factory from the age of six months, surrounded by other babies and small children until one of her parents picked her up at lunchtime.

'I remember the small grocery store at the bottom of our apartment block too. When they got a stock of exotic fruits, we kids got first dibs and were sent straight to the front of the queue, ahead of all the grown-ups. The child was king – or queen – in the GDR! Children were seen as the future and to be nurtured.'

Kat's shared memories helped me understand why so many East Germans look back to the GDR era with longing, as a time when every citizen was looked after from 'cradle to grave'. The harsh reality of fierce competition in the newly reunited capitalist Germany hit the *Ossies* hard: you had to find your own job and head off any competitors. No one was guaranteed a job anymore and you had to secure your own childcare – and pay for it. If your business couldn't compete, there was no one to bail you out. And so, the euphoria that Klaus had experienced on the Elbe river was short-lived: East Germans felt disadvantaged compared to their West German cousins, while *Wessies* thought the *Ossies* were whingers and needed to learn to compete like everyone else in the real world. Kat was one of the survivors: young enough to adapt, smart enough to get ahead. But she still looked back on her early years in East Germany with gratitude.

'Did your parents miss the German Democratic Republic after reunification?' I asked.

'Well, they were happy enough in the system. They were given a flat when they got married, they received lots of benefits when they had a family, and their places of work provided them with cheap holidays. But everything was decided for them.'

Kat absentmindedly pushed a piece of potato around her plate, then said quietly, 'They didn't really know what true freedom meant until the Wall came down.'

'And you, do you remember the fall of the Wall at all?' I asked Kat.

'Not much. I asked my dad about it recently and he told me we had missed out on being in the centre of Berlin when it all happened. Instead we spent the evening huddled around the radio. My parents were really excited when the news came through – but they were also scared because they didn't know what the future was going to hold: and sure enough, my mum lost her job. But then she took the opportunity to go back to school.'

'How did things change for you?'

'I was only six, too young to really understand. I remember Saturday school stopped all of a sudden. And I remember my parents receiving their Trabant in 1991 after we'd been told we wouldn't receive it until 2002! We all drove down to Bavaria. I think we were the slowest car on the motorway. And I remember thinking Bavarians had really strange accents – and that their lives were very different from mine. Little did I know that I would end up living here.'

'Do you think your experience of East Germany influenced you politically?'

'Good question . . . I think my grandparents were more open-minded from their experiences of the War, but the generation who grew up in the GDR had had little experience of the outside world. So now they fear they'll lose their jobs and they worry about the future. They worry about how women are treated differently in Islamic cultures. That generation didn't travel, so they fear what they don't know and what's different, whereas I've had the chance to explore other places and different cultures. But then again, my mum didn't have that either, and in spite of everything, my parents raised me to be open-minded. They don't support AfD – you know, the extreme right-wing party, Alternative für Deutschland – but many other East Germans do, especially those who are not so well-educated. It breaks my heart that Dresden, my hometown, is the heartland of the anti-Islamic party, Pegida (Patriotic Europeans Against the Islamisation of the Occident).'

'And did the lack of freedom in the GDR feed your desire for travel?'

'For sure. My grandmother has never seen the sea to this day. Isn't that incredible? My mum knew what it was like not to be able to travel wherever she wanted. Before I finished school, she said to me, "You go, girl. Be smart and travel the world. Do what we were never able to do." So, I took her advice. I remember having this intense feeling, this urge to travel beyond the horizon of the country I was born in – to go beyond those boundaries that locked my parents in.'

Kat stopped speaking. There was just the drone of frogs outside the window. I thought about the descriptions of her childhood: so different from mine in Northern Ireland – and yet not so different. We both shared a romanticised view of our young lives, where love was unconditional and the light soft and warm: Kat roaming the Dresden streets with friends and screaming through the flats in her apartment block; me playing British bulldog, red lights, kerby and German jumps on our road just down from the rose field. We shared a soundscape of high-pitched screams and bubbling laughter and the too-loud voices that children use.

In my father's photograph album there are pictures I keep returning to: me in a cumbersome pram, my father's arms proudly enfolding its hood; me as a smiling toddler on my father's knee, little hands resting on his legs; and another one, of my father carrying me, as I clutch the lapel of his shop coat with a chubby fist. There's me as a young teenager leaning into my father as he rests his hands on my little sister's head. We are smiling in the blurry picture, confirming the rose-field view of my childhood. Everything we needed was there in our childhood places. It was only later I yearned to explore the world beyond our streets and fields.

The light was fading and I could just make out Kat's eyes shining in the gathering dusk. Then Kat laughed again. 'You know, when my grandfather remarried, he started travelling and I'm convinced he's going to keep going until his feet won't let him anymore. He and his wife have been a huge inspiration to me, ever since I was a child. They're almost eighty now but they know what it means to be free – and that they can make friends wherever they go in the world.'

4. *Auf Wiedersehen Deutschland*

On 31 May, Jamie and I cycled into Passau. We'd been on the road for a whole month.

That first chilly day in May, when we'd emerged from the belly of the ferry in Rotterdam, blinking like newborns in the daylight, seemed such a long time ago. Now cycling was as natural as breathing. And Germany, along with the pocketful of days in the Netherlands and Switzerland, had been an easy home the length of the Rhine and Danube to this point. Meanwhile, Britain was receding in my memory – a half-forgotten island from the past.

We found a little guesthouse sandwiched between tall thin terraces in a side street on a narrow spit of land between the Danube and the Inn rivers. That evening, Jamie and I wandered along the banks of the Danube, which was lined with cruise ships, and on past towers and churches, castles and grandiose baroque residences. When we ran out of land at the Dreiflüsseck, or 'Three rivers corner', where the Inn, Danube and Ilz converge, we followed the promenade back along the banks of the Inn.

Wandering through the narrow streets of Passau, I thought back on our journey along the German Danube – of the poppy-splashed pathways, the wildflower meadows and the pastel-coloured townhouses teetering on hilltops. The Danube had been glassy and still in the mild spring weather, wispy cloud and powder-blue caught in the mirror of water. On that last stretch of the river, we had been covering enough ground to allow us to make detours. Between Munderkingen and Ulm, we'd followed the Blau tributary to the Blautopf at Blaubeuren – a pond of such intense blue, it stung the eyes. In Ulm, Jamie and I had had a rest day, wandering the cobbles of the fisherman's quarter, its ancient houses leaning drunkenly over canals, their midriffs bulging like beer bellies. At night, a light show played off the tower of the Gothic Munster, the tallest church in the world, and bright neon lights gleamed shocking-pink and electric-blue from modern blocks, spelling out *Weltblick*, meaning 'vision' (but literally 'world view'), and *Sehnsucht*, meaning longing, a word that can't be translated very precisely into English, but is roughly 'a yearning to the point of obsession or addiction'.

Those words could have been a personal message especially lit up for me. Like Kat, I had longed to escape the confines of my life. There had been no physical walls – just mental ones. The bike ride had originally been intended as my lifeline, something that would see me through the next years at my stifling school, until I could afford to leave. But my breakdown had brought it all to an abrupt end. Recovering at home, the *Sehnsucht* was an itch that wouldn't go away. I had a *Weltblick*, a vision – a long-distance view of the world – that extended all the way to Istanbul. I believed it would save me.

And, sure enough, the journey was healing me slowly and gently, more effectively than the pills my doctor had prescribed to me. Somehow, the waters of the Rhine and Danube were washing me clean; and the birdsong that I imagined had been sent by my father was a balm for my tortured soul. The meadows thick with wildflowers were a much better gift than any get-well bunch of flowers. And the human connection with old friends, and the simple trust of strangers along Europe's rivers were more soul-restoring than the rounds of therapy that had been arranged for me.

There were other experiences that were less positive. When we'd reached Regensburg, we found ourselves caught up in a student demonstration against racism. We felt the atmosphere thick with ugliness, emitting from the skin-headed neo-Nazis, who goaded the demonstrators from street-side cafés, arms folded across thick chests in alpha-male threat, beer and testosterone spilling from metal tables. I'd experienced the same ugliness in my own country: the mob mentality, the troublemakers hurling insults and bottles, even petrol bombs. The air curdled with hatred.

But as we walked back to our Passau Gasthaus, it wasn't the neo-Nazis I was thinking about, but rather Klaus and Kat, who had lived under the shadow of the Wall; who'd taken in Jamie and me – two foreigners of unknown character – and fed and sheltered us in the Middle-Eastern, Islamic tradition of hosting strangers. This cycle was more than a physical journey – it was also a spiritual journey that nourished and fed my soul. And I realised that when people live in hope, not fear, and when we see our place in the world as a force for good, not one of threat, then we are naturally inclined towards reaching out to our fellow human beings in kindness.

*

5. A Detour along the Inn and Salzach Rivers

When you are cycling thousands of miles along Europe's great rivers, what's another hundred? And why not add another couple of rivers? So, we took a right turn at Passau, abandoning the Danube, and headed south towards the Austrian Alps along the Inn and Salzach rivers to visit friends who lived in Oberndorf, the town near Salzburg where the Christmas carol *Silent Night* was written.

Mental preparation and practical planning are everything when cycling. If you know there are hills ahead and the paths are going to be rough in places, you brace yourself. If you realise the temperature is going to soar, you get up at first light. But we'd been lulled by easy cycling from Ulm, with tarmac paths and flat terrain. Cycling sixty miles in a day had been easy, even on the Tank.

Just beyond the bridge that crossed the Inn at Passau, the climbs began. Jamie missed our turn-off and we found ourselves pushing the bikes up a near-vertical hill. We backtracked and discovered our path sandwiched between river and railway track, where we crossed into Austria. It was already hot, although it was early in the morning. The sudden heatwave was unexpected.

At Wernstein am Inn we wheeled our bikes onto the pedestrian bridge to catch the breeze off the river. The waterway was Air Force blue, blotched green by the reflections of the dense woodland that flanked the river's banks. Above the woodland, inky-green gave way to lime meadow, and on the skyline, the towers of Schloss Neuburg castle stabbed the unbroken blue with pointed roofs of red. Below us, Wernstein's castle stood more modestly at the water's edge, its little wooden balcony wrapping stone beneath its roof. I breathed in the ozone of water and felt the early morning sun like a lamp-glow on my skin.

Every day brought new surprises on this journey – in the beauty of its natural landscapes and in man's own poetic shaping of Europe's rivers. We stopped just outside Wernstein to look at the monastery of Vornbach spread out along the shore on the German side. Two mute swans, book-ending a line of cygnets, glided towards us in search of food. I felt a sudden sadness that my father had turned his back on the outdoors, preferring to sit in his armchair with the TV on silent, flicking with disinterest from channel to channel. What if he had been prescribed country walks instead of electric shock treatment and pills? Would it have made a difference? While still at home, we'd tried to encourage him to take his evening walks to the fields again, but he'd barely made it to the end of our road before heading back again. Perhaps, my father had yearned for us to reach out to him, in the darkness of his mind, but I, for one, had never asked. We had merely followed the doctors' orders.

After passing through Schärding, with its colourful baroque architecture, we temporarily left the banks of the river and climbed up through woodland to hilltop villages. A freewheel flung us down to the water again, where a farmer, surreally, was ploughing his field under a large parasol attached to his tractor. Our bikes continued to shoot across the floodplains from the momentum of the downhill, a welcome cooling breeze in my face and a respite from the heat. As the afternoon drew to a close, we cycled into Braunau am Inn, a pretty riverside town – and the birthplace of Hitler.

Braunau's wide main street of narrow, terraced houses and pencil-sharp roofs, and café terraces sitting under shady trees, combines Gothic grandeur and Mediterranean cool. With its onion-domes, cupolas, turrets, arched doorways, frescos and brightly coloured buildings, the settlement exudes an odd mix of sugary sweetness and solid respectability, as well as centuries-old wealth.

But for the local residents, a dark shadow smears a stain across their colourful town. If you google Braunau am Inn, it mainly references the town as Hitler's birthplace, reflecting the outside world's morbid fascination with the dictator. But the people of Braunau would prefer it if Hitler had never been born here. On one of the town's websites, it's only the obscure Hans Steiniger that's listed as a notable resident, documenting his two-metre-long beard (the 450-year-old beard still on display at the local museum). The website even pays homage to a visit from Emperor Franz Joseph. Of Hitler there's no mention. It's as if he had been erased from the town's history.

The history books, however, record that Hitler's father, Alois Hitler, having progressed from humble cobbler to senior custom's officer, was relocated to Braunau am Inn in 1875 – with Germany just across the bridge on the other side of the river. In 1889, Alois, now on his third marriage, held his newest child in the apartment block on Salzburger Vorstadt 15, a child he and his wife named Adolf. A sickly, weedy infant, the young Adolf only lived in the apartment block for three short years before he and his family moved on to Passau. This didn't stop

Braunau from basking in the reflected glory of the Führer in the years preceding the war, renaming Salzburger Vorstadt as Adolf-Hitler-Straße, and the town plaza as Adolf-Hitler-Platz.

Hitler's private secretary, Bormann bought the house on Salzburger Vorstadt and opened a Nazi-style art gallery and library (which was seized by US troops at the end of the war). After the war, the town's association with Hitler soon turned from pride to shame as the extent of his crimes sank in. Now, the only indication that Hitler ever lived in the house is a piece of granite, from a quarry near Mauthausen Concentration Camp, inscribed with the words *Für Frieden, Freiheit und Demokratie. Nie wieder Faschismus. Millionen Tote mahnen*: 'For peace, freedom and democracy. Never again fascism. Remember the millions dead.'

Despite the plaque, the building has become a place of pilgrimage for neo-Nazis, a blot on the old town's hosed-down, scrubbed-up and freshly painted streetscape. Never has a building caused so much fierce discussion: its defenders asserting that we should confront history, not bury it; its opponents arguing the house had become a shrine for white supremacists and should thus be dismantled. I, too, was torn between the rationale for confronting history and the feeling of distaste at the idea of seeking out Hitler's birthplace. In the end, we turned our back on Hitler and went for a pizza.

*

It was another cloudless day as we left Braunau, although the air was still deliciously cool in the early morning. A few miles outside of town, we came to a junction on the river, with the Inn continuing towards Innsbruck and Switzerland in one direction, and the Salzach twisting west then south towards Salzburg and the Tirol in the other. We took our leave of the Inn to follow the Salzach to visit our friends, Chris and Maria, in Oberndorf.

Maria had already sent a text, wanting to know our ETA and urging us to arrive by Thursday. Something stirred somewhere in my brain, but it didn't quite reach my consciousness at the time: it was out of character for Maria to push – even gently. But as we headed along the forest road behind the Salzach, I felt a thrill of anticipation: Manuela, in Basel, seemed a long time ago and I longed for familiar faces.

At Duttendorf we emerged from the forest and cycled on through field and suburb to Ach, where, at last, we caught a glimpse of the Salzach again. *Ach* – or 'Oh!' – is a wonderful name for any village, and is particularly appropriate for this one: views across the river reveal the German fortification of Burghausen spread out along the ridge above the town for more than half a mile (it's the longest castle in the world). Like an illustration from Chaucer's *The Canterbury Tales*, towers, courtyards, chapels, residences, serving quarters, gates and draw-bridges fill the skyline here, while below the battlements, the town's terraced houses line the Salzach in a colourful concertina.

From Ach, the river twisted this way and that before settling down to a long straight slash through woodland. Here the trees closed in on the river on either side as we cycled, and the sense of claustrophobia was palpable in the heat of the day. I drooped over the handlebars as the track stretched out interminably in front of us.

Then familiarity: the curve of houses on the bank of the Salzach at the town's edge; the promenade that loops with the bend of the river; the gravel beach where Tom and Chris had once tried to throw stones across to Germany on the other side of the river, and failed miserably; the pedestrian bridge that connects the two countries; the diminutive Silent Night Chapel; and, finally, the hub of roads that congregate at the corner of Chris and Maria's apartment complex.

The cycle along the town's riverbank felt unreal. Were we really arriving at Maria's doorstep on a *bicycle*? I remembered taking the train from Winterthur to Salzburg, decades earlier, to visit Chris and Maria in their old flat – a journey of several hours through Switzerland, Liechtenstein and Austria. It had seemed such an adventure at the time. Then, years later, driving from England to Oberndorf when the boys were small. I remember distinctly thinking with wonder that we'd driven all that way. And now we'd arrived by bicycle from Rotterdam – across half a continent.

*

Maria was a friendly, approachable language assistant at Southampton University, where I studied German. I liked her straight away. She was gentle and tough at the same time; she embraced her femininity but was an unashamed feminist. We met up once or twice but other than that my contact with her was limited to brief encounters around the small German department. Maria had already made good friends with her colleagues. Plus, she was increasingly spending her time with another student – a final year student called Chris. It was only after Maria had left Southampton that I really got to know her, through my visits to Austria over the years as a student, then with Tom and finally with our children.

Maria and Chris were queen and king of *Gastfreundlichkeit*, translated literally as guest friendliness. While they worked hard during the week, the weekends and holidays were given up to pure indulgence. Breakfast would start late – an Austrian mountain of breads, cold meats, cheeses and eggs – and we'd spent hot afternoons dozing in the hammock, followed by long, balmy evenings on their terrace with good food and wine. When we came with our young children, the boys had drawn pictures of African animals, which Maria added to a collage of paintings from children in the commune.

'Come in, come in,' Maria called.

The door flung open and we were caught up in Maria's hugs. We went into the living room and spotted the boys' pictures still hanging there. Jamie and I collapsed into chairs: we'd been cycling for seven consecutive days and felt hot and tired. Cups rattled from the kitchen area and the coffee machine began to gurgle.

'I need to go to the doctor in the morning,' Maria chattered as she prepared the coffee. 'Then we'll head to a local outdoors shop in town, where we can buy the camping mattresses and sleeping bags you need.'

This was good news. As we'd headed down the Inn and Salzach, I realised we couldn't hold off camping any longer: the temperature was soaring into the thirties, and we were discovering Austrian guesthouses were not cheap. Meanwhile, Tom had promised to post out some lightweight tents to Oberndorf.

'Have the tents from Tom arrived?' I asked.

'Not yet, so maybe you'd better stay in the house in the morning in case the postman comes with them. You'll need to sign for them.'

'No problem. There's nothing I'd rather do than sit on the terrace with a cold drink!' I laughed.

I was worried about the tents though. I sent a message to Tom: *Are they going to get to us before we leave Oberndorf?*

I'll track their progress, the reply came.

Then a second ping the next morning: *They're in Austria. They should arrive any time.*

*

'Helen, your tents have arrived,' Maria called out. 'The postman's at the gate. Can you go and sign for them?'

I wandered down the grassy path and opened the gate onto the street to see . . . not a postman, but Tom standing there with two suitcases.

'Your tents,' he said, holding up one of the cases. 'Mattresses and sleeping bags too.'

I stood with my hand over my mouth and laughed, unable to speak. Tom and Maria, as it turned out, had been scheming for weeks and I had suspected nothing: Maria had not gone to her local GP, as I'd assumed, but had picked up my very own Doctor of Philosophy.

All along the Rhine and Danube, Tom had been my champion, but he missed Jamie and me terribly. The house felt incomplete. He also worried about the next stage of our journey – the unfamiliarity of Eastern Europe. Now the reality of what he'd agreed to was sinking in. He fretted over the stories of aggressive pack dogs out in the countryside, the opportunistic thieves, the thundering lorries on the narrow Eastern European roads, and the isolated villages miles apart, just as I did. But while I would be there to deal with it and take the decisions with Jamie, he'd be hundreds of miles away – and everything that would happen to us would be beyond his control.

Our weekend together went by in a blur of activity and inactivity. We visited the local food market for our breakfast ingredients with Chris and Maria, and walked along the river and over the pedestrian bridge into Germany for ice cream, as we'd done in the past. We drove to a nearby lake and drank local beer on a hilltop above the Salzach. Chris and Maria treated us to a fine meal in a monastery garden, and Tom and I dozed together in the hammock after long brunches that stretched into the afternoon.

At the end of the weekend, it was hard to say goodbye to Tom.

'I'm going to come out again in three weeks, when you are in Budapest,' he whispered. 'I'll bring Patrick with me next time. We'll celebrate my birthday on the Danube. What do you think?'

6. Cycling with Coffins

It had taken us two days to cycle from Passau to Oberndorf, but just a morning to return to the city. We'd decided to put our bicycles on the train to save time. By the time we reached Passau, the heatwave had broken and dark clouds hung from the sky like funeral drapes. Still, we had our new tents and I was keen to try them out. We stopped in Lindau for our campsite ingredients and cycled on a handful of miles to Camping Kohl-bachmühle. The glum manager, body bent like a broken spring, reassured us that no storm was forecast even though the sky was smeared an angry black.

Jamie and I shook out our tents and quickly erected them. We had chosen lightweight ones, but now that they were up, I could see that each one was not much bigger than a coffin. Getting into the tent needed the skills of a contortionist. Jamie tried his out and found that he could not fully stretch out. There was definitely no room for his panniers, which he had to chain to his bicycle. I could fit mine in, as long as I lay straight and stiff as a corpse.

We observed the sky, swollen with water now, and headed for the campsite restaurant to slowly sip coffee and take shelter in the warmth of the room. As we stared out of the window, the rainwater broke from the pregnant sky and any sense of eager-ness I'd felt about sleeping out in the open evaporated with the earlier sunshine. When the rain finally stopped, we ventured outside, to find a man shivering at the entrance with his bike, a wet shirt clinging to his back.

'You wouldn't have a spare jumper or coat?' he asked hope-fully. It was a desperate request. I shook my head a regretful no and the man slunk away. Despite the fact that we only had one waterproof and one jumper each, I felt guilty.

Down by the water's edge, the Danube was softened by mists. Beyond, the hills of Austria were sponged an impression-istic watery green. Just as we contemplated setting up the stove, the rains came down again and we scurried into our coffins, where all we could do was listen to the hammer of water on canvas and try to sleep. When the rainstorm finally stopped, we took refuge again in the campsite restaurant, comforting ourselves with *Spätzli und Wurst*, our plans for pasta cooked on the stove forgotten.

That night was the longest of our trip. I cursed our sheet bags (bought with the summer temperatures of Eastern Europe in mind) and sliver-thin self-inflating mattresses that didn't properly self-inflate. I lay in my coffin and listened to the thunder, dreaming of the guest rooms above the restaurant. Emerging from my tent in the morning, the campervanners opposite us shouted a cheerful hello.

'We felt so sorry for you last night in the storm.'

But you didn't invite us into your warm, dry campervan, I thought sourly while smiling cheerfully.

*

From the Austrian border, the Danube stretches out with barely a kink until it hits the Schlögen – the Loop. The Danube here, encountering impregnable granite, is forced to double back on itself, taking a 180° turn to create a watery noose around the forest of Sauwald, before looping round once more to head east, then south. It's a particularly haunting stretch of the Danube, narrow and thickly wooded. Man has barely left a mark here. As we approached Au on the curve of the loop, the heavy rain from the previous night had left the deep-cut valley washed in mist.

From Passau we had kept to the left bank, but at Au, where the river slices through a deep incision of land, cyclists have no option but to switch to the right bank. Our bike book offered us two options: a short ferry-hop directly across the river to the other side, or a boat ride along the second loop that stopped just short of the hamlet of Grafenau, dropping its passengers off on the same side of the river. Jamie had decided on the second option, but when we arrived at the departure point, we found it unmanned. We returned to the first ferry.

On the other side, the track undulated through woodland, with no sign of human habitation until we came to a guesthouse with a little kiosk attached to it. We slammed on the brakes and ordered *Gulasch mit Brot* – the goulash dish somewhere between soup and stew and served with crusty bread. It was delicious and filling and good value at six euros and would serve as our main meal that day. *Radeln macht hungrig*, as the Germans say – cycling makes you hungry.

Twenty-three miles later, we were pushing up the steep uphill into Ottensheim. We had chosen the village for its campsite, but now the sky was a threatening black again. We could see the campsite below us by the water's edge. We hesitated then took a turn into the town. Our camping days seemed to be over before they had properly begun.

*

Tourist Information sent us to Frau Hemmelmayr, a widow who lived in a wood-clad house down a quiet side street on the outer edges of town. She took a look at our soggy tents sitting on our bike-racks and suggested we spread them out in the garage among the garden tools and household equipment.

'Come in, come in,' she said, leading us up steep steps to the house entrance. We climbed yet more steps to the first floor. Frau Hemmelmayr pushed open the door to a room filled with heavy oak-carved furniture and gold-gilded framed pictures, depicting religious figures and romantic Austrian landscapes in thick oils. We'd been delivered into the nineteenth century.

In the morning, our host pulled freshly made rolls from the oven and sat down with us on the corner bench of the breakfast table to chat. We talked about her business, her failing eyesight and her garden with its cherry tree, visible from the kitchen window. I told her how the wood pigeons had discovered my own cherry tree and came every year now without fail to strip off every last cherry, not leaving us a single one. I asked Frau Hemmelmayr for advice.

'Shoot the buggers,' she said, screwing up her shrewd eyes and throwing her head back with a roar of laughter. And with her giggles still ringing in our ears, Jamie and I retrieved the tents from the garage, packed the panniers and freewheeled back down to the Danube.

As with Asher, my father would have enjoyed Frau Hemmelmayr's mischievous character, her no-nonsense manner and glint of eye. And like me, my father had had to contend with wildlife raiding his food – only his thieves were foxes, not wood pigeons; and his victims were chickens, not cherries. Near our house was a farmstead with a little pocket of land that no one seemed to want, so my father rented it. Behind the house, he installed hens to provide us with eggs, but despite his best efforts to keep the chickens safe, a fox returned night after night to pick them off – leaving a trail of bloodied feathers across the garden until every last hen had been taken.

My father kept a pair of heifers, too, in the fields that straddled the farm track. It was a chance for him to have a go at being the hobby farmer he'd always dreamed of. But this project was equally doomed as the cattle escaped the fields on a regular basis. He called my brothers to help him round them up and herd them back to their own field. Giving chase again and again, the cattle didn't put on much beef and made little or no money at market.

Then there was the goat my father brought home. We called her Betsy and my sister and I paraded her on a long rope around the streets of our town (to the astonishment of my cookery teacher). But when it turned out that Betsy was Benjamin, my brother sold it on, unimpressed we had a useless goat and no chance of goat's milk for our kitchen.

Finally, a local builder purchased the farmhouse and land for a steal. The fields were left fallow for a while and it became a playground for local children. My friends and I scrubbed out one of the henhouses as best we could and set up our gang HQ in the wooden shack, spying on the enemy – a pretty, if haughty, girl from down the road who had probably snubbed one of the boys in the gang. The builder put up fencing to keep us out, but to no avail. We ran wild on the farm, gorging on bitter gooseberries and blackcurrants in the garden and climbing a tree to break into the boarded-up house through the skylight. Once he came around to check the premises when we were in the coal bunker. He stood outside, his feet visible just inches from us, as we crouched in the tiny space, holding our breath and hoping that none of us would sneeze in the dusty bunker.

Despite the builder, I was grateful to my parents for giving me the opportunity to be a wild child in nature. And I felt saddened for my father and his failed farming venture.

*

On the river path opposite Linz, we negotiated skaters, skateboarders, cyclists and walkers. The edge of the city was heavily industrialised with the kind of riverside wharfs, factories, chimney stacks and cooling towers we'd not seen since the Lower Rhine. With relief, we left the city behind, ducking in and out of dark woods and sleepy villages until we reached a bend in the road.

'So,' said Jamie, who'd by now taken on the additional role of tour operator and cultural organiser as well as map reader, 'you make the choice: we can either visit Mauthausen Concentration Camp or the open-air museum at Mitterkirchen, but we don't have time for both.'

How do you choose between a Nazi death camp and a folk museum celebrating Celtic life? It seemed too crass a decision. The previous winter, Tom and I had visited Krakow on a week-end break. Part of the package was a trip to Auschwitz. I had had my reservations about the tour. Wasn't there something ghoulish, even perverse, about visiting a concentration camp? But we had gone, and I had tried to take in the sheer scale of the inhumanity: the mounds of hair, the heaps of shoes, the mountain of suitcases. I tried to latch onto something that would personalise the objects and humanise the individuals behind the vast numbers – a name on a suitcase, or a glimpse of life in the photographs of the stony-faced and shaven women lining the walls in the corridor of one hut. And I found that humanity in a picture of Helena Bargiel: her smile and direct, fearless gaze transcended the death camp.

I left Auschwitz, despite all my reservations, with a sense of gratitude that I'd had the opportunity to pay my respects to all those who had died – that I could bow my head and say 'sorry', whatever that meant. It was hopelessly inadequate and yet it felt important and necessary. But most of all, I'd left the camp with a picture of a defiant Helena in my head.

Some of the Auschwitz inmates had made the journey from Poland to Mauthausen. Not Helena, who'd entered Auschwitz in January of 1943 and was dead by October. But for those who had made it to Mauthausen, there was no comfort in knowing there wasn't the ruthless and efficient organisation of killing found at the Auschwitz gas chambers. At the Austrian camp, there was no quick release – no trains that delivered passengers directly to the gas chambers. This was death by torture, slow starvation and work-exhaustion. It was long and drawn-out, cynical and callous.

The Nazis were endlessly inventive, cruelly creative. At Mauthausen, the quarry that had supplied the stone outside Hitler's birthplace in Braunau was reached by a long stairway of hewn steps known as the Stairway to Death. The prisoners were forced to race up the 186 steps carrying granite boulders, one behind the other. When a prisoner fell, often backwards, on top of another, it created a domino effect all the way down the stairs, crushing the prisoners below. For those who survived, they often had to face the next challenge at the 'Parachute Wall'. On the edge of the quarry face, inmates were given a choice: take a bullet in the head, or push a fellow prisoner to their death below. It was a macabre game show of moral choices and survival.

As we stood on the elbow of the road, I peered up the little lane towards Mauthausen, hidden in the folds of meadow and woodland, just out of sight. The road ahead looked so innocent, the scene absurdly bucolic. I turned around to Jamie and quietly said, 'Let's cycle on to the museum at Mitterkirchen.' I'd seen the rows of functional huts at Mauthausen on the internet, just like Auschwitz, but I didn't know if there was a Helena.

I turned my back on Mauthausen, a feeling of guilt weighing me down. But as I freewheeled down the hill to the town, I was carrying the picture of Helena Bargiel in my head, her eyes staring fearlessly into the camera, a smile curling on the edges of her lips. I would carry her confidence and optimism with me across Europe, her courage and defiance, not the scenes of brutal cat-and-mouse games at Mauthausen.

We cycled into Grein campsite late afternoon and unpacked our coffin tents. The sun slipped out for a few moments from behind the clouds, and suddenly I was grateful for my life.

7. Mary Poppins and the Lock Keeper

Iris and Brian cycled into the campsite as Jamie was setting up the camping stove. Iris, small and sturdy, was bent over her child-sized bike with an expression that was both bullish and cheerful. Brian was a few pedal rotations behind his wife – a cycling Prince Philip.

The campsite was filling up with touring cyclists: a Frenchman cycling to India; a Berlin couple, whose eyes lit up when they recalled the fall of the Wall; and now the retired English couple. Brian and Iris unpacked their bags and erected the tent in a series of quick confident steps, in an artful *pas de deux*. I watched Iris unpack the panniers like Mary Poppins emptying her carpet bag. The couple had the best camping equipment: a large two-section tent; top-of-the-range mattresses; four-seasons sleeping bags and silk liners; pots and pans; kettles, cups and plates; even a tiny foldable camping chair with a back. And much more besides, as Jamie and I would find out later. It was hard not to succumb to equipment-envy.

While the campsite had looked idyllic as we'd ridden into Grein, with its green park of shady trees edging the Danube, the reality was quite different. Caught in the curve of a busy road, the sound of traffic echoing around the Danube valley kept me awake that night. The plummeting temperatures didn't help – even though I was wearing as many layers of clothes possible. I tried not to think about Brian and Iris in their luxury sleeping bags.

I woke to the early morning song of thrush and blackbird and waited for the day to take on full light, glad when the sun finally heated my coffin tent and brought some warmth back into my tomb-cold body. While Jamie still slept, I made some tea. Not having any breakfast ingredients, we packed up and headed up through cobbled streets to the market square, finding a little café-bakery that sold steaming coffees and warm croissants. Outside, I closed my eyes and cradled my coffee cup, the soothing sound of running water from the fountain in the square almost lulling me to sleep again after my restless night in the cold.

As we left the café, bellies full, that sleepy sense of warmth and well-being was rudely shattered by Jamie's panicked voice: 'Mum, I can't find my mobile – I must have left it charging in the hook-up at the tree.' We raced back to the campsite to find Brian scrolling through the phone, trying to find some way of contacting us. I could have given him a hug. Instead, we cycled with Brian and Iris over the next three days.

Having retrieved the mobile, we headed down to the ferry on the Grein quayside, now crowded with cyclists – including Brian and Iris. Disembarking on the other side, we found our-selves falling into step – or rather into pedal stroke – with the gregarious couple. Iris, in particular, chatted and joked with everyone she passed. We made an odd-looking pair: Iris, short and wiry, bent low over her small bike that had been especially made to fit her compact frame; me, not much bigger in height, but feeling like a giant, towering above her with my high saddle and handlebars.

Iris frowned in disapproval at my bike. 'Did you have the bike before the trip?'

It was obvious she was baffled by my choice of heavy town bike, clearly unsuitable for a long-distance cycle. Her indirect question, it turned out, was unusually discreet for Iris. Not put off by Jamie's shyness, she chattered away to him as we cycled through woodland along the banks of the river in the ever-nar-rowing valley. With him, she was more direct: 'Jamie, you need to pump up your tyres.' Despite Tom's best exhortations, Jamie and I neglected our bicycles, never bothering to check our tyres (after all, they were filled with slime) or oiling the brakes or chain.

'Jamie, you need to raise your saddle. You will have a much stronger downward push and it will make cycling easier.'

While Iris persuaded Jamie to pump up his tyres and oil his chain at the next campsite, she simply couldn't persuade him to raise his saddle. I shrugged and held out my hands. Jamie could match Iris's motherly bossiness with a good dose of his own stubbornness, and although Iris returned to the subject again and again, Jamie refused to raise his saddle.

As for me, I let Jamie make his own decisions, recognising his mule-like obstinacy in myself. No amount of cajoling
would make him change his mind: he would have to come to
the decision by himself. I was pleased how our relationship
was developing on the cycle. Jamie was not only in charge of
the route-finding, as he had been from the beginning, but was
continuing to make decisions about budgets and sight-seeing
side-trips. In truth, I was happy that Jamie was taking over more
and more of the decision-making. Our relationship was shifting
on the cycle – less mother and son and more cycling partners.
I tried to give him space to be the adult he was and step back
from my role as mother – otherwise it was going to be a long
three and a half months for him.

As we cycled towards Melk, Brian, as the older man, took
over the map-reading. Jamie was not impressed, fuming when
Brian had taken us off on an unnecessary detour.

'But you didn't explain to Brian why you thought he was
going wrong,' I said to Jamie.

Communication was not his strong point. It was one of the
few times I criticised him on the journey. More often, Jamie
would chastise me – he was both young for his age and a wise
old man.

Brian also chatted freely with Jamie. While Iris was wiry
and square of shape – a little work pony on her bicycle, Brian
was string-long and somewhere between weedy and sinewy.
He had a strange method of cycling, making several quick
rotations of the pedals before freewheeling into a long glide,
as if on ice-skates. Before retirement, Brian and Iris had lived
in a little Water Board house on an island in the middle of the
Thames, where he operated the locks. His adventures on the

water matched any tale in *Wind in the Willows*: he'd rescued escapee barges, uncovered a pair of dead bodies from the river and pulled a non-swimmer from the water. He'd acted as a flood and storm-warner for boaters and farmers alike.

On the other side of Melk, we baulked at the price of the local campsite, not helped by the boorish attitude of the owner, and cycled on to find a *Pension*. I was a bad influence on Iris and Brian, who'd religiously camped along the Rhine and Danube before our meeting. We climbed the valley above the Danube to Aggstein and a hotel that stood on the hillside opposite the ruins of a crumbling castle, once darkly known as Dunkelsteinerwald, or 'dark stone forest'. It was a fitting name for this Grimm story setting, where its medieval owners, known as the robber barons, had held their rivals to ransom, tying their victims to the rocky ledge below the castle, while threatening to throw them to the gorge below if they didn't pay up. As I sat on the balcony overlooking the castle ruins on the skyline with a glass of wine, I was glad to be living in the twenty-first century rather than medieval Wachau. When Iris and Brian arrived on the balcony, I bought them an evening meal in thanks for rescuing Jamie's mobile. Twenty-first-century problems I could handle.

After Aggstein, we emerged from the shadowy riverside into the bright light of the apricot orchard plains. The sun broke through the clouds and the sweet scent of the ripening fruit hung in the air, the dew of the trees dripping on my knees – until I realised it was my leaky water bottle. Our wheels nosed forward effortlessly and I felt joy at being in this fruit-scented landscape of orchards.

There was a sense of contentment at being in the outdoors. It was something I shared with my father from the days when

he'd been well. The oft-repeated two-word entry in his diary –
In country – held so much meaning and contained so much of
what my father was. Once, he wrote more eloquently, *Lovely day
in country with my Lord*. I felt my father's deep sense of peace
and serenity as I cycled along, if not his religious devotion. But
perhaps it was the one and the same: I just didn't give it a name.

When we'd reached the campsite at Tulln the sky had darkened again and I was reluctant to camp. 'Okay,' said Jamie, our
business-headed budget manager. 'But if there's nothing under
fifty euros, we camp.'

Even the youth hostel cost more than that, and I reluctantly
followed Jamie to the campsite, where we found Iris and Brian
again. On erecting the tents, Jamie found one of his pole attach-
ments had splintered at the end. Iris dipped into one of her
'Mary Poppins' Ortlieb panniers and triumphantly pulled out
some duct tape and toothpicks to help Jamie with his DIY job.

After a campsite dinner, she was determined I should go
swimming with her.

'I need to clear up,' I protested, not wanting to swim.

Iris took the dirty saucepan from me: 'I'll do the job for you
while you get ready.'

There was no arguing.

But Iris was right: the water in the lake beside the Danube
was warm and soothing, a balm on my cycle-tired muscles. We
swam in the soupy weed, then floated on our backs, our voices
drifting in the gathering darkness.

*

On Friday 13 June, we cycled into Vienna, white blossom drifting across our path like snow. We had reached the outer edges

of Western Europe. Here the Ottomans had been driven back. It was another landmark on our journey.

8. Sabine and Sisi in Vienna

Sabine met us at the Messe exhibition centre. Dressed in black, she crushed us in a tall, strong-boned embrace before stepping back to peer owl-like at me through thick black-rimmed glasses. Sabine was a Tigger, bouncing everyone along in her passion for music, photography, art, architecture and theatre, all punctuated with exuberant cartoon sound effects. She was the perfect guide for Vienna. More than that, she'd set aside the whole weekend to show Jamie and I around her adopted city.

It was our love of music that had brought us together from our respective homes in Vienna and the English Midlands to Northern Ireland. Our paths had crossed in Belfast, where we'd travelled to see Duke Special, a quirky indie musician who combined soulful songwriting with old gramophones, theatrical props and song-sheets for sing-alongs. The musician personified all that Sabine and I loved: theatrical music, storytelling, vaudeville, cabaret, the absurd, the darkly humorous and emotional songwriting.

Not surprisingly, Sabine had turned her back on her rural birthplace, a deeply conservative hinterland of Austria close to the Slovakian border, to come and live in the theatricality of the *fin-de-siècle* Habsburg city. Now in Vienna, I saw that all the

Austrian towns of onion domes, twinned-towered churches, ornate statues, carved masonry and colourful frescos Jamie and I had cycled through were just the overture to Vienna. Everything in the historical quarter declared unchecked grandeur: a penchant for pomp and circumstance, unfettered wealth and a self-indulgent formality of architecture spread out across this part of the city.

From the newer, shinier, stripped-back Messe – a trade fair centre of concrete and high-rise glass that doubled the cityscape in shimmering reflections – Sabine led us into Prater amusement park. We dodged children with candyfloss and parents with prams. We carried on past stalls reeking of *Bratwurst* fat and fried onions and through garish amusement arcades to the *Riesenrad* – the Viennese big wheel built for Emperor Franz Josef's Golden Jubilee in 1897. The surviving gondolas looked strangely like Victorian garden sheds. We entered one, and slowly the wheel swung us to the sky. High above the city, black clouds parted and shafts of sunlight bathed the city's rooftops in pools of golden light. It seemed a fitting baptism for this city of decadent opulence.

We finished the evening in the Café Central, sitting below chandeliers and decorative arched domes. Penguin waiters in black waistcoats and white knee-length aprons delicately danced around marble columns and customers while holding silver platters of pastries high above their heads. Adolf Hitler, Franz Kafka, Sigmund Freud, Arthur Schnitzler and Hugo von Hofmannsthal, all familiar names from my university degree, had come here to philosophise, politicise and to write essays and poetry. Had they sat in this very corner where Sabine, Jamie and I now sipped on our drinks? In all probability. I felt the hand of history in this café. But it was the portrait of Empress Elisabeth of Austria on the wall beside her husband Franz Joseph I that caught my attention: 'Sisi', as she was often called, in her porcelain-white silk dress to match her porcelain-white face; Sisi with her delicate beauty and needle-thin waist; Sisi with her clear gaze and determined chin. It would be Sisi's story that stayed with me as Sabine showed us round the inner city the next day.

'And this is where Sisi had her apartments,' Sabine said, pointing up to the building that curved with the circular Michaelerplatz. 'She was only fifteen when she married Franz Joseph I and came to Vienna.' Sabine took us to the rose garden in the Volksgarten behind Hofburg, the empress's summer palace. I sat by the shade of the fountain, listening to the tinkle of water and the hum of traffic in the background. In front of me, Sisi stood frozen in Laaser marble, chalk-white hands folded demurely in her lap in front of her snap-thin waist.

'Sisi was derided and dismissed by Viennese society,' Sabine explained. 'At best, she was admired for her beauty, only becoming a much-loved figure in Vienna after her death.' The empress was deeply unhappy in Vienna, I learned. Her all-consuming vanity was at odds with her desire to be taken seriously. In all likelihood, Sisi suffered from an eating disorder: she was known for her binge-eating and punishing exercise regime, and rumoured to have a secret stairway accessing the kitchen. She was obsessed with her health, her ankle-long hair and her weight – sewing her tiny waist into the tightest of corsets. At the same time, she seemed to loathe the excesses of Viennese society, preferring to escape to a simpler life in Hungary, where she felt more of an affinity with the Magyars – causing deep resentment in Austria. She became more and more of a free spirit, turning her back on Viennese society and spending time in Madeira or Malta, or alone on board her steamer on the Mediterranean, writing poetry in the style of the poet Heinrich Heine. Each time she returned to Vienna she became ill. It was clear she had a psychosomatic aversion to the city.

'Her life was tragic,' Sabine told us by the statue. 'She'd married into the Habsburg dynasty at a very young age. Then her son committed suicide – and she was murdered by Lake Geneva. An Italian anarchist rammed a file into her heart. She still managed to walk the distance to the steamship. It was only when they removed her corset – that had been stopping the flow of blood – she died. After her death, Sisi's rejection of Viennese life was quickly forgotten by the Austrians. Instead, they remembered how she connected with ordinary people, her philanthropy and beauty. Now she's a sort of saint.'

I could understand Sisi's dislike of Viennese extravagance. I also felt an aversion to the overwrought baroque buildings with their shop windows piled high with designer goods and luxury chocolates. I preferred the shabbier, narrow side streets beyond the inner ring road: the quirkiness and fun of the multi-coloured Hundertwasserhaus, the graffitied walls by the River Danube and the bohemian boathouses with their deckchairs and bars and artificial beaches.

On our last day in Vienna, Sabine took us on the bus to Kahlenberg above the vineyards with their courtyard wineries. Below us, the Danube sliced southward through the city before disappearing into the green of the Danube National Park, where it would emerge at the border. Tomorrow, we would be heading that way. I felt a thrill as I saw our route stretched out in front of us, yearning to be on the open road again, and at the same time feeling a nervousness at cycling into the unknown – over the other side of the hill – into Slovakia and Eastern Europe.

PART TWO

EASTERN EUROPE

SLOVAKIA, HUNGARY
AND THE WESTERN BALKANS

1. Slovakia

Jamie and I cycled out of the city, leaving the early morning stirrings of Viennese streets to plunge into the empty tree-lined avenues of the Prater parkland. I breathed in morning dew and damp earth, enjoying the splinter-sharpness of chilled air after the stuffiness of the hotel room. We overtook a road-cleaning lorry and splashed through soaked tarmac before climbing the spiral cycle path onto the bridge that led to the Donauinsel, or the Danube Island, which is a dagger of green stretching between the old and new Danube. The artificial island was created from the spoils of the channel that had been dug out to create a flood defence. I wanted to stay and explore the leisure island with its beaches and cafés, but we had forty miles to cycle between Vienna and Bratislava, the Slovakian capital. We crossed another bridge and continued along the left bank.

'I love Bratislava,' Sabine had told me. 'It's a beautiful city. Sometimes, I take the boat there and the train back, but do be careful – especially around the ATMs. Best to change your money inside the bank, and keep your belongings close to you. It's not like here.'

Again, those words: it's not like here – whispering all the way along the Rhine and now here on the Danube.

'Your adventure will begin in Eastern Europe,' Klaus had commented back in Ingolstadt. And now I felt a tightness in my stomach at the idea of adventure. Everything about the Germanic countries we'd passed through had an easy familiarity of language and culture, whereas the Slavic countries were still, primarily, a half-formed place in my mind – created by words on a page or images on my computer screen.

Or founded on rumour.

But that fear of the new and unknown, as always, was pushed aside by my curiosity, driving me on. I fought against any preconceptions, deciding instead to cycle into Eastern Europe with openness. But it was difficult to bat off all the warnings we'd received. I felt a tugging at the bike's spokes, a dragging of the wheel – at least in my head.

In reality, we were covering ground quickly. The cycle path shot straight as an arrow through the Donau-Auen National Park between poplars, elms and willow, the river lost in marsh and bog. There was little to distract me and I thought of Sabine and Sisi again. I too had felt out of sync with the world I grew up in. At first, you just are; at first, it just is. You stand in the centre of your world and it reflects back at you in harmony. Everything radiated out from my town: the surrounding villages and the seaside settlements beyond, always returning me to the place that rooted me. Somewhere beyond that, there was an English world of strange accents, too far away to contemplate, and beyond that again, the unknown – a world of incomprehensible languages, customs and belief systems.

But when I was about twelve, I learned in geography that my small town in provincial Northern Ireland was just a village in comparison to mainland cities such as Birmingham and Glasgow, and it was even far down the list of Northern Irish towns by population. I was shocked and I had to rethink the significance of my epicentre. Up until that point my world comprised of my home, my school and my meeting hall. The

Brethren were at the centre of it and the unbelievers they spoke of were a tiny, stubborn, led-astray-by-Satan smattering of individuals who would, hopefully, one day see their wrong. Everyone eventually got saved. Didn't they? And if they didn't, they were too entwined in their own selfish wayward-ness. They were beyond redemption.

Our path continued through the trees of the Donau-Auen. There was a heavy stillness in the forest, apart from the sleepy hum of insect and the rustle of small mammals in the under-growth – a wood mouse or weasel, perhaps. And once, from somewhere deep within the trees, I heard something thrash-ing through the vegetation, the snapping of branches echoing through poplars. I wondered if it was a wild boar or a red deer, but we saw nothing bar the funnel of green that stretched out endlessly in front of us, and the dance of midges in front of the bikes.

I returned to my inner world. The first person to challenge my childhood reality was a supply teacher in my final year at primary school. She was an exotic creature smelling of perfume and always carrying an outsized bag over her arm as she swag-gered along the school corridor in tight trousers smoothing out her closely cropped hair. She was the vicar's wife from an outlying village, who was now teaching me hell was a metaphor, not a real place.

Hell was central to our gospel meetings, a place that preach-ers spoke about with low, hushed voice or with raging thunder. It was the weapon the Brethren used to persuade sinners to seek salvation. In our next art lesson, the supply teacher asked us to draw our own idea of purgatory. I defiantly painted flames in blood-red and left comic-strip religious tracts on her desk,

warning of the perils of rejecting salvation and portraying hell
as a fiery reality. She held up the miniature booklets, flashing
scarlet-painted fingernails while raising a finely plucked eye-
brow, quiet bemusement curling her lips. When my father came
to pick me up from school at lunchtime, as he often did when
it rained, I expressed my outrage about the supply teacher. But
my father sat there quietly, head slightly bowed over the wheel,
and I felt confused and abandoned by his silence.

For a few more years, I pushed away the possibility of other
realities, but a larger, alternative world was revealing itself to me
through books. With no TV in my home, I read ferociously,
hungry for knowledge of the world that lay beyond my provincial home: Hardy and Lawrence, Atwood and Drabble, and a
host of other novelists. I read the philosophers, Sartre, Camus
and Russell. I *read The White Hotel*, by D.M. Thomas, and
mourned the loss of my innocence.

But it was too late. I didn't have the arrogance to simply
reject other opinions, another *Weltanschauung*. Wasn't our
perception of the world deeply rooted in our culture and in
our experiences? If salvation was only to be found in Christ,
then it was heavily tilted in favour of the Christian-centric
West – and specifically to the tiny number of evangelicals that
mushroomed in small pockets of the world. If you were born
into a Northern Irish Protestant household, you had hit the
jackpot, but if you grew up in Communist Cuba or Islamic
Iran, the odds were stacked against you. The Brethren argued
over predestination, and whether a person could be sent to
hell if they had not been exposed to the Gospel, but it was a
simplistic argument that didn't consider culture and upbringing, and the thoughts and beliefs that live inside our heads.

This narrow view of 'truth' over perception didn't sit comfortably with me.

The problem was, I could see the world from other perspectives. Slowly, I was shifting away psychologically from the narrow boundaries of my home, my town – its religion and politics. My father shook his head. My mother tutted at my rebelliousness as I entered adulthood. Like Sisi, I felt hemmed in. I didn't quite belong.

Here, in the darkness of the Danube-Auen forest, I also felt hemmed in. There was an eerie quiet but for the rumble of our bike wheels. Once, somewhere above an oak, the silence was broken by the sweet machine-gun rattle of a blue tit.

Just before Hainburg, we emerged from the forest, blinking in the light after the gloom. Across the other side of the Danube, black clouds leaned into the river and the sky grew shadowy. We contemplated waiting out the coming rain in a riverside restaurant but Bratislava was calling on the other side of the hill. We cycled past low-slung terraced cottages, the kind depicted in Russian folk tales or in a Chagall painting, more typical of Slovakia than Austria, although we'd not yet crossed the border. On the top of the hill, the clouds sagged, then burst like an overfilled paper bag, tipping cold, hard water on Jamie and me. I tried to shelter under a tree but was soon soaked through, regardless. Then the rain stopped as suddenly as it had begun and we freewheeled past fields, shivering in damp clothes, down towards the city.

*

Heading into Slovakia, the changes were immediate. At the border, the customs buildings lay empty, weeds squeezing through broken concrete, render cracked and windows smeared with grime. Communist-era high-rises filled the skyline and the cycle path was cracked and uneven.

We left the main road and followed the cycle path as it swept north again to the Danube, then east along its banks. Still following the line of the border, we passed a pair of bunkers, one converted to a museum. Now, the concrete, humpbacked bunkers lay like beached whales in fields of weeds and yellowed grasses. The Czechoslovakians had built these fortifications in the 1930s as a defence against the Germans. Later, a border was created to keep its citizens in – the Iron Curtain. During the Cold War, this area had been heavily manned, barbed wire strung along the border in hostility. How quickly the barbed wire had unravelled in the dying days of Communist rule, when Eastern Europeans had flooded into Austria from Hungary and Czechoslovakia. Now the border soldiers were gone, the lookout posts and the barbed wire too. I marvelled at the open land between the two countries. I could have dismounted from my bike and wandered between Austria and Slovakia at will.

At New Bridge, leading into the heart of the city, we passed a curious observation tower, part retro with its brutalist Communist architecture, part futuristic with its UFO-shaped viewing platform. Across the river, Bratislava's castle gleamed white on the hillside in the watery sunshine. We cycled into the old town, the cobbled bricks in the pedestrianised streets shifting below the wheels of my bike with the rainwater that had oozed through the cracks, and on past a bronze figure pulling himself from a manhole. It felt like Bratislava was at sea.

In keeping with the watery Bratislava, we booked ourselves into the Botel – an old cruising ship anchored on the Danube that looked like it hadn't been renovated since the seventies. It was filled with swirly carpets and moth-eaten curtains, and stank of stale cigarettes and cheap coffee, but we liked the feel of the water beneath our cabin beds and the open decks overlooking the river. More than that, it was cheap – a fraction of the price of our modern hotel in Vienna.

*

We were lost. On the other side of the city's railway bridge that spanned the dual carriageway, the diversion signs for the Danube cycle route had run out. For once, Jamie was disorientated. We backtracked over the bridge and started again, but still we couldn't find our way out of the city to the Danube. Eventually, I saw a middle-aged man at the side of the road having a pee. I held back and waited until he was finished, then approached him for help.

'English?'

'No. No English.'

'*Deutsch?*'

'*Ja, Deutsch.*'

This was the first time, but by no means the last, that I would find German useful in Eastern Europe. I asked the stranger for directions to the river. After a series of complicated instructions, the man noted the look of confusion on my face and said he would show us the way, swinging his bike around to lead us through the city. After ten minutes or so, we came to a spaghetti junction of overpasses with still no sign of the river. Our rescuer got off his bike and pushed it under the knot of overpasses, along a worn grassy track and up onto a bank. I started to feel uneasy, but followed behind, pushing my bike up an incline and out onto a path. And there it was, our old friend the Danube, stretched out in front of us.

The man gestured to the river, climbed back on his bicycle and disappeared off into the city from where we'd found him. I thought of the warnings from the Alsatian e-bikers, Ingrid and Sabine, and how this stranger had taken half an hour out of his day to cycle in the wrong direction in order to help two foreigners. I wondered, too, about the perceived need of human beings to define themselves, even justify their superiority, through the 'othering' of those outside their own culture, race, ideology, language and home. The physical borders of Europe may have been long gone, but the psychological frontiers remained.

Back on the Danube our bikes sped along the riverbank almost of their own accord. Our bodies had become sails, pushed along by the wind. It was exhilarating.

Just west of the little settlement of Čunovo, the borders of Austria, Hungary and Slovakia meet in a group hug. Following a straight-line northeast, an artificial arm stretches into the Danube: part of the Gabčíkovo hydroelectric power plant and dam engineering. It had started out as a joint project between Hungary and Slovakia but had ended in acrimony when Hungary backed away from the project – the two countries fighting it out in the International Court of Law. While the Slovaks continued the project on their side, the Hungarians refused to follow though the agreement.

We pushed against the wind out onto the dam. The ghostly clang of metal on yachts rang around a marina. Ahead, a low-slung contemporary building of glass and concrete sat on a peninsula, dotted with colourful sculptures. We dropped our bikes to explore this unexpected museum of modern art in the middle of nowhere, and spent a couple of delightful hours viewing the contemporary paintings and a quirky exhibition of comical creatures created from shells, bones, feathers and other bits and pieces from nature.

From the museum, we cycled along the sliver of land that separates the Danube and Hungary from Slovakia and the dam until we came to the village of Gabčíkovo. Google had earlier revealed cheap rooms with bathrooms here, for less than ten euros per person in an ugly Communist-era building – much better value than the cost of a pitch in the Austrian campsites. It fitted our dwindling budget. I could live with the brutalist high-rise at that price. And we'd be looking out, not in.

We cycled past a crumbling building on the edge of the settlement that looked like a half-abandoned factory, but couldn't see our 'hotel'. In the village, a woman tried to rent us a room for fifty euros, but with a room for less than twenty somewhere down the road, I was determined to find our bargain. As I walked away, the furious B&B owner snatched back the piece of paper on which she had written her offer and ripped it in two. With the help from the seller at the kiosk across the road, we cycled out of the village again and found the elusive bargain . . . back at the 'crumbling factory'.

Inside, the receptionist behind the glass stared down her sharpened nose at us, shaking a hatchet head at all language offers. She wrote the cost down on a piece of paper with an angry flourish, along with the room number, and sent us off to grope our way down dark corridors. We wheeled our bikes into a minimalist room with an en-suite that included something that was half-bath, half-shower, the ceramic chipped under a copper showerhead. Outside on the balcony I leaned over the rusty iron-railings to a car park of Ladas and cracked cement pushing up weeds. But the room was clean and cheap, and that was all that mattered. It was only later, when I read the information board in the foyer, I realised we'd booked into university accommodation available for the summer recess.

*

It was our second day in Slovakia and we were learning to negotiate the sudden bumps and cracked pavements of the cycle paths, obstacles that hadn't existed in Western Europe. Just as I felt we had left the solid prosperity of Bavaria and Austria behind, we entered a small village to find a coffee house advertising German and Austrian beers. A coffee house! So far from Vienna! I gazed at it longingly then turned to look for a grassy slope on the dyke for our picnic lunch. As we ate our sandwiches, sand martins flittered on the banks of the river.

I couldn't remember watching sand martins with my father, but I remember a long hot July and August in my childhood when a corncrake had taken up residence in the ditch across the road from our house on Wood Lane. My father was full of excitement – to my bemusement, not realising that these once fairly common birds were beginning to disappear from our fields and ditches. At night, I lay in bed and listened to the corncrake's rasping sound, like someone running a fingernail over a metal comb – *crex*, *crex*, which also happened to be its scientific name. In retrospect, it was a thing of beauty, a dying call from a disappearing world. I could still hear the *crex*, *crex* here on the banks of the Danube, mingling with the real-time chirrup of the sand martins. But when I tried to remember my father's face or voice, they were as indistinct as the darting martins.

How easily we disregard the worlds we live in until they disappear. I'd walked away from Wood Lane, never to return. I removed myself so thoroughly from my father on an emotional level that any interaction with him had become cold and functional on my part. Why had he behaved so coldly, so indifferently, indeed so cruelly that night in our kitchen? The anger and resentment I felt towards him had become a metal-cold wedge between us. Now when I tried to remember my childhood conversations with him, they remained elusive. I wracked my brain for even the smallest shared dialogues, but there was nothing. How come they evaded me when the map of our evening walks was sharp with detail? And I felt a sorrow for the lost soundscape of our shared lives.

When we'd finished our sandwiches, we headed into the coffee house for a caffeine shot. Inside, I settled into one of the benches that wrapped around the dining table, covered in a red gingham tablecloth so typical of Austrian houses. A heavy chandelier lit the shadowy room of wood and stone. The sense of displacement was heightened by the Austrian paraphernalia cluttering every wall and surface. Crests, medals, crosses and flags hung from the ceilings and packed glass cabinets, along with wartime photographs, tankards and heavy oil paintings romantically depicting the Austrian Alps. At first, I thought I'd entered a Nazi shrine; then I realised the crosses and medals were from the Austrian Red Cross, not from Hitler's National Socialist Party. I breathed a sigh of relief and wallowed in this little piece of Austria – a two-day cycle from Vienna.

In the middle of the afternoon, exhausted from battling the loose gravel of a dyke that had been like cycling though quicksand, we reached the town of Komárno with its sister Komárom across the bridge in Hungary. We hesitated, wondering whether we should stay in Slovakia a little longer or cross over the Danube into our sixth country, then decided on the latter and headed over the bridge into Hungary.

2. Into Hungary

At our spa hotel in Komárom, we ran into Geoffrey and Leone, an older Australian couple we'd first encountered back in Hainburg on the Austrian border. Geoffrey had white feathery hair, surprised-round eyes and a pencil moustache that made him look like something between a retired colonel and a snowy owl. Leone had the kind of sharp features that could have been chiselled from rock, and her hair was cropped close to her head. Her leathery, weather-beaten face was as tough and grooved as an elephant's bottom, and she wore cheap jewellery – dangly earrings, heavy chains and thick bracelets the colour of Cheetos that seemed at odds with her skin-tight lycra.

'I wear all the jewellery because I look quite masculine otherwise,' she admitted.

'I can tell you, when we're in bed together, there's no question she's a girl,' Geoffrey said, his eyes coming to life.

Geoffrey and Leone were also touring cyclists and recommended returning to the north bank and Slovakia: 'There's a new path with a good surface.'

But Jamie, remembering the quicksand gravel of the

previous day, opted for the Hungarian south bank with its tarmac roads. They came with their own challenges, however – namely the Hungarian lorries that rolled and tipped past us like drunken killer whales just inches from our bicycles. With relief, we turned off Route 1 and onto the quieter 10. We were pleased to see a sign forbidding lorries, but our sense of well-being was soon destroyed as the heavy artics followed us with no regard for rules and regulations, crashing along the narrow pot-holed road while driving perilously close to our bicycles. When yet another lorry threatened to throw me into the ditch, I shook my fist at the driver, shouting angrily at him.

'Move out! Do you want to kill us?'

I took to holding my arm out to force the drivers out.

'Not sure that's a good idea,' Jamie said drily. 'They could take your arm off.'

Still we cycled on, my knuckles white on the handlebars, lips tight and body tensing when the rumble of lorry approached from behind. The road tipped and rolled above the Danube flood plains, leading us from one settlement to the next. They had strange, unpronounceable names: Dunaalmás, Neszmély, Süttő, Lábatlan and Nyergesújfalu. And every village was shaped by the same low-lying buildings of crumbling render and rough rooftiles, mixed in with the smoothly plastered and custard paint of newer buildings. The streets reeked of diesel and dust, and of frying pork. I began to think of the engulfing gravel paths from the previous day with nostalgia. So it was a relief when we turned off onto the flat, rod-straight road that would lead us, no-nonsense-like, into the heart of Esztergom.

Once again I relaxed and retreated into my inner world. Through my secondary school education, I had clung to my faith. It was what defined my life, my home, even my 'social life' of morning meetings, Sunday school, gospel and youth meetings – sometimes four in one day. If I abandoned my faith to rewrite the narrative of my belief systems, I would lose my identity. But my life was already stripped of certainties because I had seen there were alternative worlds out there.

At the after-school Scripture Union of my secondary school, a pupil returned to the subject of hell: 'So, what is it?'

Our religious education teacher hesitated, then said, 'It's not so much about physical punishment or hell fire; it's more about being separated from those you love forever.'

By the time I reached adulthood I had a guilty secret: I was no longer a believer. And with that came the knowledge there was a gulf between me and my family that couldn't be bridged. I didn't need to die to feel the pain of separation; I had chosen it in life. I longed to be open and honest with my parents and siblings, but I could only imagine the disappointment in my father's face and the sad shake of his head. I couldn't bear the idea of being judged and condemned, being called the black sheep of the family. Neither could I bear the idea of hurting my family or causing them pain. So I held on to my secret through the long decades, knowing I was fooling no one.

Being in the closet was damaging to my mental health. I wished that my family could accept my own beliefs but that wasn't possible because their faith wasn't pragmatic, it was absolute. There was no diverging from a faith they held so deeply and was the very fabric of their lives. There was no way out of that separation since I couldn't lie to myself or compromise on intellectual rationality. It was a problem without a solution. And at times it felt like it was killing me.

The city of Esztergom pulled me out of the past and back to the present. We found ourselves in another baroque town – a Hungarian version of the immaculate Austrian towns, but with crumbling and chipped buildings like old china.

Before the Habsburgs and the Ottomans, the Romans had come to this city, and before that the Celts. It's a place oozing history from every crack. For hundreds and thousands of years it attracted the great and the good and everyone else in between. Hungary's first king, St Stephen, was born in Esztergom and it remained the royal seat for over two centuries in the Middle Ages. It was also the seat of the Hungarian Catholic church for more than a thousand years.

As we climbed the hill in search of a place to stay for the night, the basilica filled the skyline on Castle Hill, flanked by the city walls, while the stately buildings of the bishops gathered at the cathedral's feet on the river's banks. It was a stunning location. We found a room beneath the cupola of the great church. I flung open the little window and leaned out to gaze across the red roofs of the city's Víziváros neighbourhood as the church bells rang out their single solemn note.

As we headed down the stairs, we found Geoffrey and Leone in the courtyard – yet another accidental meeting with the pair. They were revelling in their day's cycle and the excellent stretch of new cycle path on the Slovakian side of the river. Jamie had made the wrong decision. Still, his choice had been good practice for the road sections ahead of us.

I asked Leone for advice on dealing with the murderous lorry drivers.

'When you hear them approaching, move right out. Once you've forced their line onto the middle of the road, they can't easily alter it, then you can move back in, creating a comfortable gap between yourself and the lorry.'

It was sound advice from an experienced cyclist – and would work well for the busy road sections ahead.

As the sun dropped, Jamie and I wandered the streets of Esztergom and observed the ordinary life taking place among the historic buildings. Children screamed through playparks, while parents huddled together in gossip. Youths smoked and horse-played by the canal and on the slipway below the wrought-iron bridge spanning the Danube, their laughter reverberating in the evening air.

Just two more nights and my own fractured family would come together again in Budapest. I missed my red-haired Patrick and his fiery passion. I missed Tom. And as I watched families with prams saunter through the tree-lined boulevard, my stomach flipped like a teenager in anticipation of our reunion.

*

The cycle from Esztergom to Szentendre is a skip and a hop – from left bank to right and back again, with another hop across a sideways arm of the Danube just north of the picturesque town.

In Slovakia and Hungary, we'd not seen a single touring cyclist apart from Leone and Geoffrey. But that changed when we reached the ferry crossing to Szob on the north bank. The floating platform, pulled along by a little tugboat, was swarming with tourers and their bicycles. Leone and Geoffrey were there, and another Australian couple riding a tandem recumbent, a softer Australian version of the brash Leone and Geoffrey.

We crossed the river again at Vác. Geoffrey had shown Jamie

an alternative route to the busy main road leading into Szentendre that meant taking a little ferry crossing the Szentendre Danube, an arm of the Danube that diverged for twenty miles from the main river. When we reached the ferry slipway, we could see the boat sitting on the far side of the river. We waited. After an hour, it made its way across the water to us. At last, we would be on our way. But the boatman climbed out of the ferry, holding up four fingers to indicate we'd have to wait another hour – until 4pm – before he'd be crossing to the far side again. It was infuriating.

'Right,' said Jamie. 'Let's go. It's faster to cycle round.'

We raced along the top of the dyke, back up to the bridge at Káposztásmegyer and down the road to Szentendre. When we reached the ferry crossing point, the boat was still moored on the opposite bank. We laughed. Two wrong decisions in two consecutive days – based on information from the Australians. But what did it matter? We were in no hurry.

We reached Szentendre campsite in the late afternoon, ignoring the hardened surface of the campground in favour of a rickety room with dodgy mattresses, worn bedclothes and its mass grave of dead flies. We spent the evening eating in the campsite restaurant with a demented keyboard player who caused Jamie and me to giggle into our stew.

That night, I couldn't sleep: my family, which I had rent in two, was to be reunited in the morning in the handsome city of Budapest.

Next morning, I slept in and was annoyed with myself for keeping Tom and Patrick waiting. The short cycle into Budapest seemed interminable – the twists and turns, the rough surfaces, the underpasses and road crossings, the traffic and people always in the way. We lost the route, but somehow found our way into the centre of the city. We were now late. Tom and Patrick would be waiting at our hotel, and I was wasting our precious long weekend together. We found our way back to the water's edge – the parliament strung out along the shore, the castle complex mushrooming along the ridge of Buda.

We pushed on, weaving through the crowds. *Tom would be wondering where we were.* We passed bridge after bridge. One of them was ours; one of them had Tom and Patrick waiting on the other side. I counted: one, two, three, four, five bridges. At last, we crossed into Pest and turned into a quiet side street. And there they were – my two redheads, one peppered grey – waiting on a bench outside the hotel in the morning sunshine, father and son with arms intertwined across the back of the seat.

My Christmas Day at Summer Solstice had arrived.

3. Budapest Reunion

Tom and I had met for the first time outside a post office depot in Southampton on a soggy December morning, his head peering out from under his hood as the rain fell, pale as a Celtic ghost, his red-brown hair plastered to his face. He was tall and thin as a string of spaghetti, and looked about sixteen, but his winter-grey eyes, paradoxically, held warmth.

We were both starting a Christmas job sorting parcels that would fling their way across the UK, Europe and the world beyond – one that required good geographical knowledge to sort the parcels into their appropriate cages. The irony wasn't lost on me as I failed to find the entrance of the depot. 'Are you lost too?' Tom had asked. And in that moment, we found each other – unceremoniously in the cold drizzle outside the P.O. headquarters, dripping and half-concealed from each other beneath the hoods of our waterproofs. I hadn't realised at that point that I had met the man who would double my life and then quadruple it with our children.

Tom was in the background over the next couple of days: kind, attentive and friendly. He was the man to go to when I didn't know where a place was; when I didn't know which cage a parcel belonged in. Tom's knowledge of his country's geography was impeccable. I liked his intelligence and soon discovered that he was no sixteen-year-old – he was a PhD geology student heading towards thirty.

As quickly as we'd met, I was gone – a mercy deed to look after my sister's children as she had come down with flu, followed by the Christmas holidays in Northern Ireland. I returned to Southampton and my damp student flat, the kitchen carpet covered with silver snail trails, to find Tom had called. And called again. And I understood his attention to me had been more than casual interest.

The rain fell hard that winter, and the rain brought us together. Twice. I visited Tom, my clothes plastered to my body, caught in a flash-storm. He removed my coat, towelled dry my hair and kissed me.

A relationship is built on moments: Tom cooking a meal for me in his student flat, the kitchen window steaming up; freezing in unison as we stumbled on a deer crossing a New

Forest path one summer's dusk; Tom bent over my floor with a jigsaw as I studied; Tom's arm on my shoulder after lectures as I wheeled my bicycle back to my flat in Portswood.

And in those moments, I realised I'd come home.

*

Budapest is a city made up of two parts: Buda tucked into the hills of the west bank, and Pest spreading out across the sand plains on the east side. The two settlements united in 1873 to form one city: Budapest. It seemed a fitting place for our split-in-two family to come together.

The next three days had a surreal quality to them. Our journey across Europe had metamorphosed into a city break. The bikes were stowed in the underground garage of our hotel and forgotten as we took to the streets on foot as weekend tourists. We breakfasted in quiet cafés in tucked-away side streets and drank wine and beer in hipster bars on the riverbank.

Patrick and Jamie soon slipped back into brotherly needling and camaraderie. Long gone were the boys who had raced on that Northumberland beach – they were young men now, as tall and pencil-thin as their father had been. Like Jamie, we'd measured Patrick at the age of two and doubled our findings to find out his adult height: he had come in at a more believable six foot two. Now, here they were: Jamie's head was in the clouds; Patrick's a few inches below him – the same height as his father. My neck was always straining, my head tilted upwards. We took a series of silly selfies at Buda Castle, my chin cut off at the bottom – Jamie's head sliced off at the top – our mouths wide open with laughter as he failed to fit us all into the picture frame.

That weekend, we walked until our feet stung: by the banks of the Danube and along the ridge from the castle to the Fisherman's Bastion. The days passed in a blur of baroque and neoclassical grandeur; Hungarian cottages of orange, rose, creams, russets and fifties greens; and elegant art nouveau buildings. We climbed to the citadel and saw the city spread out beneath us, a living, three-dimensional map at our feet. I traced the sweep of the river back to Margaret Island, with Szentendre and the hills beyond. The eye took in, with a single glance, what had taken Jamie and me long hours to travel, following the curves of the Hungarian Danube with our bikes, inching forward. It already seemed a distant existence. I tried not to think of our onward journey south and east away from Tom and Patrick. I was determined to live in the moment – but those moments were slipping like sand through my fingers.

We tried to cram in as much of the city as we could – as if we could expand time with a bulging bag of Budapest sights. But it was only when we stopped, breathed in the city and listened to its music that we captured the moment, metaphorically cupping our hands with fingers squeezed tight to hold onto something ephemeral: a violinist scratching Gypsy music across the higher notes on the steps below the Fisherman's Bastion; a wind quartet playing baroque music from the balcony of the National Archives of Hungary; a swarm of buzzing Vespas at Heroes' Square, horns blasting; the whisper of foliage in the park below the citadel; echoing spa halls; and the boys' voices weaving through each other. And Tom's voice, with his softened Glasgow lilt, telling me that he and Patrick would be waiting for Jamie and me by the boat terminals just before the Galata bridge in Istanbul, two months' hence.

This was the soundtrack I would carry with me along the Danube as we pedalled towards the Black Sea and on into Turkey. That, and the fading voice of my father as the cuckoo slipped away and the birds began to hush.

4. A Tale of Two Teachers

I found Eszter, our next CouchSurfing host, among the kayaks and bicycles of her long Danube garden on the edge of Ráckeve. A crumpled car sat at the entrance to the property and Eszter stood in front of the door, arms outstretched in a welcome, her son standing back in the shadows of the hallway.

Eszter, slight and light on her feet, danced around the kitchenette, making tea and chatting in careful, precise English. 'I have a student coming at four for an English lesson. Just relax and make yourself at home until I'm finished.'

She left us with a pot of tea and a couple of fridge-cold snacks called Túró Rudi, which were covered in red polka-dot wrappers. I bit into the chocolate-covered bar and was surprised by the burst of sourness – like buttermilk or cottage cheese – in contrast to the sweetness of the chocolate. The curious taste was surprisingly agreeable to my palette.

'Túró Rudi is our national snack, you could say,' Eszter explained later. '*Túró* means "curd" and *rudi* means "rod".'

That evening, when Eszter's husband came home, we sat round the table drinking some of the best rosé wine in Hungary, followed by a rich paprika stew.

'You know our government is building a wall,' Eszter told us over the stew.

'A wall?'

'A wall because of the black ones.'

'The black ones?' I cringed at my echolalia, but I was struggling to follow Eszter.

'You know, the refugees. It's a big problem in our country.'

Her tone was one of satisfaction, which was a surprise as Eszter had opened her home to so many strangers from around the world – mostly bicycle tourers like ourselves – and she seemed curious and open to other cultures.

'What do you think about the black ones?' she continued. 'Is it a problem in your country?'

'Well, no. I don't think so,' I answered cautiously, not wanting to argue, all too aware that I was a guest in this stranger's home. 'I mean, the United Kingdom once had a large empire and as a result we've taken many immigrants from around the world – and since we invaded their countries and helped ourselves to their resources, it seems only fair to me. So, I personally don't see it as a problem.'

She looked doubtfully at me over the top of her glasses. An awkwardness hung in the air and I changed the subject, asking about work and jobs. Eszter's husband didn't speak much English but communicated with smiles and nods from behind drooping eyes after a long shift at the local Coca-Cola factory.

'Our friends are jealous of his job,' Eszter commented. 'But even though the money is good, there's a price to pay in the long shifts and the extended working week before a leave day.'

This was a family making the best of their lives on the Danube, in an area of high unemployment. They had built around their one-room holiday house to make a family home, the building swelling with the years. In summer they moved into the garden, playing outdoor ball games, or heading down to the Danube with the kayaks or out into the countryside with their bikes.

As we set off in the morning, Eszter sighed at the cloud-covered sky. 'Summer is so late this year.' But as Jamie and I took off down the riverside road, we were pleased to be shaded from the heat of the sun – and grateful to Eszter for offering us a small slice of her Hungarian family life behind the Danube.

*

This was our first day of cycling since Budapest. The Danube bike book had warned against the road out of the city, and we had sheepishly packed the bikes onto the train for the journey to the little town of Ráckeve and Eszter's home. It had taken the train an hour and a half to travel the twenty-five miles. 'You could have cycled faster,' Eszter had laughed. 'The train is so slow.'

Now, as we took a sharp turn right and dropped down to the water's edge, the wheels slapped through puddles and growled on stone and asphalt, as if protesting the friction of earth and wind. The road deteriorated further to rough gravel. Holiday homes lined one side of the lane, some Swiss-chalet smart, others little more than sagging garden sheds. Across the road, families cupped mugs of coffee on landing stages and fishermen cast lines into the water. Once, a scrappy rope half-hidden in the mud on the riverbank sprang to life: a water snake! On the far side of the river, children's voices bounced off the water.

Cycling was now our life. Every day, I took up my existence

on the saddle and pushed out into the Danube blue – green or grey or creamy-white. Was this an escape? A restlessness? A soul unwilling or unable to find a home? Unable to find an inner peace? Was it curiosity that drove me on? Or a yearning? If I didn't stand still, I wouldn't have to think. If I didn't stop, I wouldn't have to acknowledge the world was spinning uncontrollably away from me.

Was this what had driven my father on during all those hours behind the wheel? Just driving, driving, driving. Those long days on my mother's knee in the front seat had seemed endless. But arriving at the end of the road, in front of the Irish Sea or the Atlantic, had made it worth it: the roar of the ocean, the thud of the waves on sand, the wind whipping my hair in my face. Maybe, that was all it was – a joy in the unfamiliar and the thrill of the open road that drove us both on. A freedom.

*

'Call your dogs off. Call off your bloody dogs!'

From Szentgyörgypuszta, we climbed onto the grassy dyke to cycle alongside the Danube. In the dip, a shepherd was crouched on the ground with a smattering of sheep. He and his German Shepherds eyeballed us before the dogs leapt up, bounding along the dyke towards us. The shepherd watched his dogs snap at Jamie's ankles, a glint of amusement in his eyes. This was the best piece of entertainment he'd had all week, I imagined.

I turned around and shouted with fury. The shepherd smirked and the dogs made a deep, low-throated growl. They circled the bikes, and the older bitch sank her teeth into Jamie's pedal.

'Call your dogs off,' I shouted again. Only then did the shepherd stand up and gave a low, lazy wolf whistle, and the dogs slunk back to him.

So these were the Eastern European dogs we'd been warned about. Over the next weeks, street dogs would often run at our wheels, barking furiously – but I soon discovered they were all bark and no bite. They were lousy actors. I found if I stopped my bike, pointed back in the direction from which the hounds had come, and spoke in my sternest voice, they'd slink back into the shadows.

It was mid-afternoon when we reached a green criss-cross bridge of iron and pedalled over the Danube to Dunaföldvár. We pushed the bikes up the hill to the castle tower and Tourist Information, in search of a place to spend the night among the castle ruins and the narrow streets, before pushing on to Kalocsa.

'Welcome. Welcome,' Zita called with a hoarse thick-tongued Hungarian accent, pushing open the door in the garden wall that led into the courtyard. The sun was washing the low-lying building with a caramel light that faded out the grass to a yellow-beige. Summer had come to Zita's garden. Bobo, her golden retriever, bounded around the cherry tree before circling us, tail flicking lightning-fast.

'Please, do you need cloths washed?' Zita asked, her dark eyes peering anxious-to-please from her soft round face as she led us past a series of doors to the kitchen entrance. She held it open for us: 'Please, come in.'

Zita's home lay in a quiet side street, a short distance from the centre of Kalocsa, the paprika capital of Hungary. Like many of the single-story buildings that lined Hungarian towns and villages, Zita's house lay sideways to the road, with only an unassuming gable announcing its existence.

Our Hungarian host led us from kitchen to living room to bedroom, a string of inter-connected rooms (each with a door leading to the outside) filled with dusty ornaments, worn furniture and a lumpy sofa buried in throws – my bed for the night.

Back in the kitchen, Zita indicated the small Formica table. 'Please. I call my son. I have little English. I learn Russian in school.'

In the box-room of a kitchen, Zita and her chef son made us a Hungarian feast. While Zita stood over the deep fat fryer cooking potato wedges, Benedek served ragout with sour cream – thick with chicken, celery, parsnip, swede, mushrooms and peas, all flavoured with lemon juice and fresh tarragon and accompanied by a cucumber salad with Kalocsa paprika the colour of fire.

'Eat, eat,' Zita implored us.

I held my hand over my tummy and puffed out my cheeks. 'It's so good, but I am full.'

'No, please. Eat. You are hungry bicyclists. Eat, eat!' And with that Zita spooned more soup into our bowls.

I licked my lips with a cyclist's satisfaction, but Zita and Benedek were not finished yet. They placed in front of us large bowls of *brassói*, a filling stew of pork, potato, garlic and marjoram, along with the fried wedges.

That evening, Bobo took Zita and me for a walk around Kalocsa, pulling us past the paprika museum and the mustard twin-towered cathedral. Earlier, while Zita was still working at her school, Jamie and I had cycled around the town, and I had felt acutely aware that I was far from home. No one spoke to us. No one acknowledged our presence. We might as well have been ghosts. But with Zita, all that changed – and the town became mine too.

'*Helló!*'

'*Jó estét.*'

'*Hogy állnak a dolgok?*'

I listened carefully for something recognisable in the concoction of greetings, but the language was incomprehensible – with no roots in Latin, or Saxon. Even the word for 'restaurant' – which barely changed all the way to the Turkish border – was an unfamiliar *étterem*. But the faces were friendly and the smiles wide: the language of body and face is universal.

*

In the early morning sunlight, as we prepared to leave, Zita plucked a handful of cherries from her garden tree and poured them into my hand, then presented us with a small hessian sack of Kalocsa paprika tied in a pink gingham ribbon.

We pushed our bikes through the garden door and headed out along the last of the Hungarian Danube, past settlements of hovels splashed with blood-red geraniums and bored children doing wheelies on village greens. Once a café dog adopted us and followed us through an entire town before turning for home. We spent one last night in Hungary – on the banks of the Danube, beside the ferry landing stage at Mohács. In the morning, the long, straight road out of town would lead us to Udvar and the Croatian border.

*

5. Croatia – Bullets, Landmines and Deadly Mosquitoes

On the border at Udvar, a large sign splashed blobs of primary red, blue, green and yellow, with the word Croatia painted in child-like capitals. It suggested a sunny, carefree Croatia – the Croatia I knew from the Dalmatian coast, with its chic baroque quarters, waterside cafés, coastal pine forests and sun-speckled oceans. A terrible irony, I was soon to discover.

I pulled our passports out of my money-belt. It was the first time we'd had been asked for them since leaving the ferry terminal at Europoort.

'Where have you come from?' the border guard asked.

'The Netherlands.'

'And where are you going?'

'Istanbul.'

The guard looked bemused and waved us through. We mounted our bikes and cycled into our seventh European country.

Hungary now lay at our backs, with the future stretching out in front of us in Croatia. As we cycled on, more signs echoed the sun-splashed greeting at the border crossing: *Dobrodošli! Welcome! Willkommen! Üdvözöljük!* I felt a burst of happiness, heightened by the fields of sunflowers lining the roadside, the rows of large yellow faces turned towards us as if in bright adoration. Then, in among the flowers, I caught a glimpse of metal and barbed wire, and a watchtower came into view, reminding me that this country had been at war less than twenty-five years earlier; its scars still visible under the sun.

The watchtower and barbed wire brought back memories of the protected police stations in Northern Ireland during the Troubles. I hadn't questioned my life back then. It was simply how it was. Most of the time I remained unaffected, roaming through fields and climbing into abandoned, tumbledown farmhouses full of broken furniture and spiders – where once we'd found an ancient grocery invoice made out by my grandfather. But the fortified police stations manned by grim-faced officers wearing heavy bulletproof jackets and loaded guns did make me nervous.

As I braced myself for the hills in front of us, Jamie swung left onto a minor road that led through flat fields of dusty crops and into the village of Duboševica. At a crossroads with a sun-coloured church, Jamie missed our right turn and continued straight on.

We passed a trio of capped men sitting over their game of backgammon at an old garden table on the grass verge, their arms shooting up in a friendly wave as we passed. The friendliness of the villagers here reminded me of my old homeland, too, and I wondered how the warmth and friendliness of a nation's people could so quickly descend into violence, murder and war.

In the Brethren, it was generally agreed that believers shouldn't get involved with politics, and some of them didn't vote on principle. But for the Free Presbyterians (founded by Ian Paisley, the leader of the Democratic Unionist Party), church and politics were fundamentally connected. My mother's brother and family were deeply involved in DUP politics, and my aunt's bitter recriminations against Catholics, that would spill out from her kitchen and drift down the hallway to where we cousins played, puzzled the child in me, accepting of everyone.

Now, lost in the village of Duboševica, Jamie took a road that led us through a corridor of conifers and grass dotted with neatly stacked logs. At the end of the avenue, he swung right again to find the road we'd missed. As we came around a blind corner, I was surprised to see a row of abandoned single-storey houses, their roofs collapsing, gables disintegrating and windows pane-less. Inside, I could see smashed furniture scattering rooms. These were the first of many war-ravaged homes we'd see on our journey through Croatia.

Riding on through the villages of Topolje, Gajić and Draž, it was the same narrative – abandoned house upon abandoned house. Then I saw that some of the dilapidated houses were actually occupied despite their cracked and broken windows, with plastic sheeting sometimes covering the roofs.

There was a terrible beauty in these half-ruined villages that was both sobering and uplifting. On the one hand, there was a sense of hopelessness in the damaged homes. I saw one house where the bullet holes had been partially filled in. It was as if the owner had tried to patch up the wounds of the past but had given up: there were simply too many. On the other hand, there was also a visible resilience, for despite the pock-marked shutters, the bullet-riddled brickwork and damaged roofs, many of these homes were splashed with the colours of flowers and surrounded by neatly tended kitchen gardens of fruit and vegetables. Although it was clear that the region of Slavonia had still not recovered from one of the most devastating European wars since World War Two, people smiled cheerfully and waved and shouted greetings as we cycled by.

From Draž, we headed up through orchards and vineyards, climbing steadily until we reached the crest of the hills and Batina. The climb was a shock after long days cycling through the 'bread basket' plains of Hungary, and I looked forward to the long freewheel down to the Danube again. But the road, dropping steeply down, was covered in rough cobble, and I had to apply the brakes hard, rattling over stone with every bone in my body jolting.

Heading towards Osijek, there was still no sign of the Danube, but I knew it lay somewhere beyond the marshlands on our left, just out of sight. Along the straight road that lead from town to town and village to village, I could hear the sound of laughter wafting from gardens behind crumbling walls and rusty, wrought-iron rails, the smell of grilling meat filling our nostrils. Life went on among the bullet holes and half-destroyed houses.

As with Hungary, the older cottages sat gable-ended to the road, with tiny windows in the slant of the roof and decorative detail in the masonry despite their modest structure. Often, there was a little walled courtyard to one side. They had a pleasing simplicity, and I wondered why so many of these lovely old buildings were shuttered and left to crumble beside the newer houses of smooth, freshly painted render and more generous proportions.

As we approached Osijek, we passed by woodland dotted with signs depicting skulls and crossbones in danger red – a warning that the landmines from the civil war had still not been cleared. I needed the toilet, but going in the woods was not an option. We stopped on the cycle path to take a drink from our water bottles.

'There's something irritating my eyes,' Jamie said.

'Me too,' I said, rubbing them ferociously.

Within minutes my eyes had swollen to an angry red. Crossing the bridge into the city, the citadel of Tvrđa, with its cluster of baroque buildings laid around a large courtyard, was just a blur.

'I can't see. I can't cycle on,' I said to Jamie in panic.

'Right,' Jamie said, taking charge. 'Let's find somewhere with internet and I'll look for a place to stay.'

Having found a room that met our budget, Jamie led us deeper into the city. My eyes were so swollen now that they were almost completely closed. I was riding half-blind. Every few seconds, I prised them open to check I was not about to hit something – and it was terrifying. Finally, we came to an office-like building. Jamie rang the doorbell and an older man answered it, leading us down a long corridor with our bikes to a functional bedroom, where I took painkillers and crashed out. When I awoke several hours later, my eyes were back to normal and my brain fuzzy.

The owner's son told me that my mishap was down to the mosquitoes in the woods. 'They're vicious!' he said.

'Perhaps, they should have signs warning against the mosquitoes then, as well as the landmines!' I laughed.

But I was grateful I could function again, and that we could continue on our journey. It was our first – though not last – serious challenge of our two-day cycle through Croatia.

*

6. A Place Broken

In 1969, my youngest sister was born, a bundle of baby sweetness and a late gift to our family. My father slipped us into the hospital where the fierce matron had banned children, and I pressed my nose to the soft skin of my new sister with delight. I was eight years old. That same year, the Troubles in Northern Ireland began – a *Gift* only in the German sense – a poison that created fear and anger, violence and murder.

While I lived my life on the periphery of the Troubles, other children lived in among the stone-throwing, petrol-bombing and raiding of mafia-style ghettos and terrorist strong-holds. I continued to roam the fields at the end of my road, damming streams, picking crab apples and climbing trees, or dreamily peeling reeds to reveal the sponge pith beneath. Now and again, an explosion from the other end of town reached our street with a boom and a vibration. It was usually the railway station – the most bombed station in Northern Ireland – or one of the businesses in the centre of town. In the main street, I would be patted down and frisked at every shop entrance – but that was all I'd ever known, or at least remembered. Some of the shops I visited would be there one day and gone the next, reduced to rubble and char. Other than that, our main brush with the Troubles was at flash road-checks.

Transferring to secondary school, the Troubles became more visible, as I had to walk through the town centre to reach my college. Soldiers manned the streets in pairs. The first soldier guarded the other with cocked gun as the second walked a section of pavement before they swapped over again. As I passed the crouched soldier, the barrel of the gun inches from my leg, I felt uneasy: What if the gun accidently went off?

By 1991, my baby sister and I were both engaged to be married and the guerrilla war in Northern Ireland was rumbling to an end. The political parties and terrorist organisations were in secret talks with the British government. The endless rounds of bombings and violence with no forward movement had been exhausting and the stagnant waters of a crippled economy disheartening. The Peace Process was under way.

As Northern Ireland was yearning for peace in 1991, the Croatian region of Slavonia was about to erupt into bloody conflict. While Northern Irish Republicans were fighting for Irish independence from the United Kingdom, with resistance from Protestant Unionists, Croats were demanding independence from the Socialist Federal Republic of Yugoslavia and the Serb-controlled Yugoslav People's Army – and an independent Croatian state. The Serbs, in turn, wanted their own Serbian state under the banner of the Yugoslav Federation, taking in parts of Croatia, Bosnia and Herzegovina with sizeable Serb minorities.

Vukovar, the town we were cycling towards, had been a handsome baroque city before the war, with a mixed Serbian and Croat population living peacefully side by side. All that changed in the winter of 1991 with the Battle of Vukovar.

I'd watched the television footage back then at home, barely comprehending the events that were unfolding. There were pictures of snipers in fields of stubble, shooting at broken-down farm dwellings. There were bloodied bodies lying in woodlands, and pictures of solemn Serbian and Croatian women and children with suitcases, filing out of towns and villages. There were tanks rumbling through the settlements we were now cycling through, brutally crushing everything in their wake.

Our Troubles in Northern Ireland paled into insignificance.

*

This was our second day of cycling through Croatia and the story was still the same: the bullet-holed render, the smashed plaster revealing crumbling brick below, the shuttered windows, the cracked panes and the damaged roofs between the new villas. And I wondered how this could still be, so long after the war. In Vukovar, we found a guesthouse smelling of fresh plaster and new furniture – another new building that had risen from the spoils of the war. I asked the Croat owner about the damaged houses we had seen.

'How come it's still like this so long after the war?'

'Pah, our government doesn't care about us – all the money goes straight to Zagreb.'

'But surely there was some kind of compensation after the war – funding set aside for all the war damage?'

'Well, yes, we were given so many metres in compensation, calculated against the destroyed property – but it was grossly underestimated. This property is only a fraction of the place we lost. But, you know, you just get on with it. I moved to the Dalmatian coast, made money in business, then came back and built this place.'

'But the damaged houses in every town and village: why are people still living like this so long after the war?'

'Those houses are mostly owned by Serbs. A lot of them

didn't come back; some of them are occupied, but haven't been repaired. The Serbs are lazy. They don't get on with fixing their properties.'

'I suppose if you are old though, say a widow, you might not have the health or the money to fix your property?' I mused.

He didn't respond, so I asked about the relationship between the Serbs and Croats in Vukovar now that the war was over.

He shrugged. 'We have to work together, do business together, but there's no trust. How could there be? Small children were murdered by the Serbs in the war. I have a son. How do I know they wouldn't do something like this again?'

I nodded, recognising his anger. I'd heard it before. I knew how bombs and bullets and personal loss fed hatred and bitterness.

'What about schools. Are they mixed?' I asked.

'No, outside of everyday business, Croats and Serbs don't mix. Serb and Croatian children go to separate schools, even at secondary level – only at university is education shared.'

It was a story I knew so well from Northern Ireland, but the pain and suffering caused by the war in Slavonia was on a completely different level, although the emotions were just the same. The outward scars of the buildings echoed the inward scars of the Croats and Serbs. It would take a long time for them to heal.

That evening, Jamie and I ate in a fast-food joint opposite a bombed-out building – roofless and pane-less and reduced to bare brick. It was a building like many others in Vukovar – except each window on the top floor was spilling curtains of fresh pink geraniums, clearly tended with care. And in them I recognised a symbol of hope and optimism.

As I paid for our meal, I asked the man behind the counter about the building. He scowled and pretended not to understand my question. I suspected he was a Serb. I would have liked to hear his story – but the expression on his face didn't invite any more questions.

Cycling out of Vukovar the next morning, we stopped at the War Memorial Cemetery on the outskirts of the city. I walked a path that separated rows of white crosses marking 938 graves, which brought home the senselessness of war – row upon row of headstones with pictures of fresh-faced boys and men who had all died within weeks of each other in the autumn and winter of 1991. A little further up the hill, we passed the road that led to Ovčara, a lonely farmstead, where 200 patients and staff had been taken from Vukovar hospital. Many of them had been beaten and shot, then thrown into a mass grave. They were later exhumed by UN forces and reburied at the cemetery we'd just visited.

We continued on to the border past more broken and derelict houses, my heart heavy and yet hopeful at the same time. Jamie had broken a spoke just outside of Vukovar. At the bike shop below the war-damaged water tower, left as a memorial, two youths, too young to remember the war, set to work and fixed the spoke, laughing and joking as they worked, their lives under the bombed-out water tower rooted in the present.

The future lay with them.

*

7. Into Serbia – *Cheers* in Bačka Palanka

From Vukovar the road rises to a plateau high above the Danube and winds through woodland, orchard, vineyard and deep-cut valleys that slice the land all the way to Ilok on the Serbian border. At the base of each valley, houses huddle together as if caught at the bottom of a chute. Our bikes flew down the six to eight per cent gradients to these villages, the speed exhilarating – until we hit the incline on the other side. All morning, I struggled up the hills on the Tank. Still, I was determined to cycle them all, knowing the inclines were short and the pain manageable. At the top of each summit I congratulated myself, while Jamie waited patiently for me at the side of the road.

Outside Ilok, there was one last climb – this one much longer than the short, sharp rises that had gone before. But since I'd cycled the other five, I was damned if I wasn't going to cycle the sixth. Hot and thirsty from the exertion, we stopped at the supermarket in Ilok to buy drinks. I gave away the last of our kuna to the shop assistant and she filled our water bottles in exchange, asking about our Journey.

'You cycled from Rotterdam? You are going to Istanbul! I cannot walk the length of Ilok!'

We said goodbye and shot down to the bridge that crossed into Serbia, the shop assistant's laughter still ringing in my head. I'd seen the best and worst of mankind in this bittersweet region of Croatia. I felt its pain and recognised its wounds. But I'd also seen how humans possess an innate resilience and humour that enables them to pick themselves up and move on from the past. And so, with a sense of sadness and privilege, I crossed the bridge with Jamie and headed for the Serbian border town of Bačka Palanka to look for Sashka, another CouchSurfing host.

*

'Would you like a bottle of water? No? What about a juice?'

I'd only stopped off at the tourist office to find out whether I needed to report our stay in town to the authorities. I'd read conflicting stories on cycling forums. Some cyclists claimed they had been turned back at the border on leaving for not having the correct paperwork. The friendly assistant was not sure either. It was clearly not a common question, so she phoned the police and reported back her findings.

'Yes, you need to report each place you're staying in. It doesn't cost anything, but you will need to buy a stamp book to record your destinations.'

I thanked her and turned to walk out the door.

'Is there anything else I can do to help you?' she asked.

'No, that's it. Thanks.'

'Well, have this leaflet about the Danube *charda* – our famous fish restaurants. And please take these postcards. Oh, and here's a couple of bookmarks. Are you sure you wouldn't like a juice?'

I'd not experienced a welcome quite like this in a tourist information office before. If this was our introduction to Serbia, it looked promising.

Our next stop was Sashka's home. Her mother had prepared a feast with little European flags planted in each of the dishes: a welcome for Jamie and me and a celebration of Danube Day.

Sashka had given up her room for us and we had the whole upper floor to ourselves. Once again, we were overwhelmed by the generosity of strangers. Stuffed to the gills, Sashka drove us to her local hangout, a cave-like bar that was dark and rickety, yet cosy – and packed with Sashka's friends.

'It's a bit like a Bačka Palanka version of the American sitcom *Cheers*,' I laughed.

'Exactly,' said Sashka's friend, Doc, who wasn't really a doctor, but a sports and tourism student.

After our drink, we headed down to the Danube with Bager Lake behind it, a place where locals went to swim, boat, fish, barbecue and camp – or just hang out.

'There are no hotels here. It's not developed, but maybe that's a good thing,' Doc mused as we walked along the river path. Across the Danube, the red roofs of Ilok shone in the evening sun, the light playing on the Danube below it. It was a beautiful place.

Doc pointed over to Croatia. 'The war's over. We've moved on. I've nothing against the Croats. We cross over to Ilok all the time. No point dwelling on the past.'

There was a youthful arrogance to his remarks. I thought of our guesthouse owner back in Vukovar, still angry and hurting from the war. For Doc, dismissal was easy: he hadn't experienced the ethnic cleansing across the border. He'd not seen the children and women lined up to be shot at random. He'd not witnessed the shovelling of Croat bodies into mass graves. He didn't have a daily reminder of the war in the bullet-riddled houses, damaged gables and broken roofs. Here, a few miles away in Serbia, there was no sign of any past conflict. His crass dismissal would have offended many Croats, and yet he was right: the countries of the former Yugoslavia had to put the past behind them and move forward. It was just that forgiveness isn't always easy. I knew that on a personal level.

My parents had fumed at the Peace Agreement in Northern Ireland. Not at the idea of peace, for they were tired of the years of destruction like everyone else, but angry that terrorists were being released from prison as a trade-off in the negotiations.

'How can they?' they raged. 'These prisoners are murderers!'

'I know it's a bitter pill to swallow,' I agreed. 'But it's the only way we can move on from the Troubles and stop the killings.'

My father bristled at my argument. Northern Irish Unionism had been built on principle – or intransigence – and compromise didn't sit easily with its followers. *No surrender* was Paisley's rallying war cry, but even he came to realise that war without end was destroying his much-loved province.

Unionism had always been about supremacy – not unlike the politics of South Africa. The minority group were a threat to be suppressed. If you believed that Catholics and Nationalists were inferior, the task was easier. The narrative of staunch Unionists was always the same: Catholics were lazy and untrustworthy – and murderers – even though they patently weren't. It was the age-old racist (or sectarian) argument: pin the deeds of terrorists on an entire religious or cultural group. Getting beyond that point of view was not easy. I, of course, as a Protestant did not hear the bigotry expressed on the other side.

Sashka, though young, had also been affected by the war. As a small child, she had lived on the Istrian Peninsula on the Mediterranean – an idyllic life by the sea. She had Croatian friends, but with the uncertainty of war, her father had pulled them from their Istrian home and taken them to the Serbian stronghold of Vojvodina.

Now, many former Yugoslavs look back on the Republic with nostalgia, in the same way the East Germans regard the old GDR with affection. Its authoritarian leadership had held its people together. With its collapse, the region had fallen into civil war.

'Under Tito, the country was strong,' one Bosnian pointed out to me. 'Croats, Serbs, Bosnians and Albanians: we all lived side-by-side in harmony. Catholic, Orthodox or Muslim – no one cared – for everyone had a job and security.'

'My neighbours and friends were Muslim and Orthodox,' another Croat told me. 'We were all getting along fine. It was the politicians and generals who divided us.'

*

In the morning, we lingered over breakfast with Sashka and her family as Novi Sad, our goal for the day, was a short twenty-five miles away, along Route 12. When we finally cycled out of town, we found the Novi Sad road busy with lorries. Their drivers had even less regard for cyclists than the Hungarian lorry drivers back on the road to Esztergom. I was relieved when Jamie swung right down a tree-lined road at Čelarevo, happy to be under the shade of the poplars in the rising heat of the morning, and to escape the dust and noise of traffic. We slipped onto the dyke, the path stony and uneven beneath the tyres. I gripped the handlebars, telling myself it was better than facing death-by-lorry on the smooth tarmac of the trunk road.

Here on the riverside, there was little life but for the buzz of insects. The air was humid already. We cycled past a couple of the Danube *charda* fish restaurants the tourist information assistant had recommended. Sashka had told me how the *charda* in Bačka Palanka had prepared the biggest fish stew ever in an outsized vat with 1,700kg of fish in an attempt to enter the *Guinness Book of Records* in 2001. I was sorry not to have experienced the Serbian *charda*, but Jamie hated fish.

By mid-afternoon, we'd reached Novi Sad and found the bungalow apartment we'd booked for the night. With two bedrooms, a kitchen, a terrace and the garden, it wasn't a bad place to be holed up, and even less so when the landlord's wife came home from work, chattering in English while pouring freshly picked raspberries into our hands.

In the morning, we pondered our options. Our Danube bike guide warned against cycling to Belgrade: *Due to the heavy traffic on the exit from Novi Sad and the entry into Belgrade, we suggest taking the train for this last section. Although it is not permitted to take bicycles on the trains, experience suggests that it is possible.* I remembered the thundering lorries on the edge of Bačka Palanka. If the road was dangerous between the two towns, what would it be like cycling into the capital? We decided to risk the train, despite the conflicting information about taking bikes. I didn't like the idea of not cycling part of our route: it seemed a cop-out, but the thought of the monstrous lorries bearing down on us sealed the decision. We headed for the railway station.

*

8. From Belgrade to Bela Crkva

It was just after eight in the morning when we wheeled the bicycles out of the bungalow's garden. It was the first of July. We had been on the road two months exactly and this was our eighth country, not including our coffee break in France. After a few false starts on the Upper Rhine and on the Inn river, summer had finally settled in with a hot, breathy bluster. The heat was intense in the cities, but we were able to cheat the worst of Serbia's fierce summer temperatures on our bikes with the cooling breezes we created.

We pedalled slowly to the city centre. There was no hurry, I imagined. Surely there would be plenty of trains travelling between the two cities, just over fifty miles apart. After weaving through the morning commuters, we pushed our bikes into the cavernous space of the station, our eyes adjusting to the darkness. There were four or five ticket windows in one corner.

I approached one, only to be dismissed 'No English. My colleague speak English.'

I moved into the queue for the next counter and waited. 'No English.'

And from the next, another stony face: 'No English.'

I was surprised after the easy fluency of Sashka, Doc and their friends. You'd think there would be at least one English-speaker in a major railway station. But no. In the end, I grabbed a student and begged her to translate for us. We successfully bought our tickets, only to discover the next train didn't leave until late morning. With hours to fill before our train departure, we found a terrace café on the boulevard and settled down for the long wait.

The next obstacle was getting the bicycles onto the platform. There was a steep flight of stairs and no lift, and when the train arrived we had to manhandle the bikes into the carriage high above the platform. Another student came to our aid, helping us lift the bikes to the back of the carriage, where we stashed them between seats.

Now I knew what the guidebook meant when it said it was 'possible' to take bikes on trains.

When I saw the train attendant approaching, I fretted he would tell us we couldn't take our bikes, not least because they were blocking four passenger seats. But the attendant nodded nonchalantly and produced a ticket with a picture of a large piece of post-war styled luggage, what looked like an oversized woven basket and a heavy sit-up-and beg bicycle exactly like my own. He drew a line through the suitcase and basket and circled the bicycle, then scribbled down the additional cost of the bikes, the equivalent of a few pennies in dinar. So officially it was possible to travel with bikes by train. Practically, it was less than easy.

I settled down on the sticky seat, breathing in stale air laced with the smell of urine and sugary drinks. The train lurched forward then crept out of the station like an injured beast, rolling from side to side. It groaned as it pushed to pick up speed.

The journey felt interminable, and it was a relief when the train's brakes squealed to a halt in Belgrade station. There was no one to help us with the bicycles this time. I lifted mine over the seats and wheeled it to the door, easing it down to the platform a couple of feet below me, but the weight of my bike, combined with gravity, dragged me down with it. A railway official watched on as I tumbled to the track below, the bicycle landing on top of me before he sauntered over to have a closer look. As I picked myself up off the track, knees grazed, I wondered if it would not have been easier to have cycled to Belgrade after all.

*

Belgrade revealed itself as a heaving, cosmopolitan city, its station surrounded by peeling baroque buildings, brutalist high-rises from the Communist era and slick twenty-first-century offices of glass.

We headed up the hill into an up-and-coming bohemian quarter, liberally sprinkled with trendy coffee bars, delicatessens and street cafés. Our B&B was hidden down one of the narrow side streets that criss-crossed this leafy part of the city, set in amongst elegant buildings of decorative arched wrought-iron gates and sculpted masonry. We pushed the gate open to the hotel and restaurant and found ourselves in a cobbled courtyard shaded with fruit trees. There was the hum of quiet voices and clink of glass and cutlery as Belgradians tucked into Parmesan and rocket salads and sipped on cocktails. The restaurant garden was an oasis of calm away from the city noise. Upstairs, the attic rooms had a New England vibe, while the reception rooms downstairs had a retro, vintage look. I flung myself on to the bed, happy we had found this chic little boutique hotel for a handful of euros; happy that we had a day off to explore the city – our first rest day since Budapest.

We spent the next day walking the parks and the historic

quarter, finding our feet again. It was as if we'd been at sea on our bicycles, and it took a while to adjust to our land legs, the pounding of our feet on pavement feeling strangely heavy.

Our bike book tempted us again with the train out of Belgrade, warning of heavy city traffic. But after our experience of the Novi Sad train, I preferred to battle the roads. Jamie plotted a route through back streets until we were forced onto the main artery that led to Pančevački Most – the bridge that would take us out of the city and straight onto quiet dykes on the north bank of the Danube.

The last section of city was surprisingly short. We rode the pavements when they were not busy with pedestrians and delivery vans, and soon came to a large roundabout that swept us onto the dual carriageway and the treacherous bridge. I gritted my teeth and went for it, feeling the suck of air from the lorries that thundered through. On the other side of the bridge, we left the road almost immediately and followed the dirt and gravel path alongside the river – glad that the weather was dry enough to make it passable.

There was little in the way of purpose-made cycle paths on the Serbian section of the Danube Route 6. We had to make do with rough dyke paths, broken asphalt roads and the occasional town cycle path that was often cracked and uneven. In Pančevo the front wheel of my bike almost lunged into a large, uncovered manhole. The open manholes would be a frequent hazard in Serbia. Occasionally someone would have the foresight to stick a tall branch into the hole as a way of warning. We were grateful.

What the route through Serbia lacked in terms of cycle paths was made up for by its signage, which offered words of wisdom and encouragement. It was as if the authorities had come together and said: *Well, we can't afford to build cycle paths, but hell, we'll put all our money into the best signage the entire length of the Danube. The Austrians may have made state-of-the-art mini-roads for bicycles across their country, but we are going to create poetry with our signs.* And so they did.

The signs were fascinating, and, at the same time, frustrating: I wanted to stop at each and every one to read the words of inspiration, but our journey would have been one of stop-starts the width of the country, for the Serbs had not only produced wonderful signs but placed them at every significant junction.

I'd encountered the first sign as we'd crossed over the border from Croatia, consoling those leaving Serbia with the words: *So you are about to leave Serbia. Don't cry because it is over – smile because it happened.* Now, just across the bridge on the outskirts of Belgrade, the sign gifted me Goethe: *We always have enough time, if we use it the right way.* A few miles on, advice was offered from Walter Bagehot, the British businessman and essayist: *The greatest pleasure in life is doing what people say you cannot.*

I smiled at Goethe and saluted Bagehot. I'd taken ownership of my time, ignoring the puzzled frowns when I'd shared my plans – shrugging off the unspoken words that hung in the air, the sharp intakes of breath and the polite smiles that said, *What a strange thing to want to do.*

Just outside of Kovin, the French writer Antoine de Saint-Exupéry asked: *How could drops of water know themselves to be a river? Yet the river flows on.*

It was Saint-Exupéry's question that stayed with me as our bikes trundled downstream with the flowing Danube: *How could drops of water know themselves to be a river?* I was fifty-three

years of age and still working out my place in the world: retracing the route back to the beginning; unfolding the sections of
the map to work out where to go next. I was figuring out the
journey from my sheltered Brethren childhood in the sixties
and seventies to the vast unchartered space of adulthood.

My father was still here with me on this journey, but his
voice, heard in the songbirds, was growing weaker, just as the
cuckoo was fading out with the Serbian summer. His image
was blurry, far away on my northern island – an old man bent
over his walking frame in the care home, his hands covered in
liver spots, looking slightly ridiculous in his hoody and joggers
like a geriatric delinquent. This was my father who had dressed
in a suit and tie for the beach, and carried a large Bible on the
dashboard of his car.

Sometimes I felt that I was travelling away from him, in
order to put distance between us. But, at other times, I was sure
I was travelling towards him – towards some kind of absolution,
towards some kind of acceptance of the past. There was plenty
of time to think on the long days on the bike. And yet, and
yet, there was a still that hardening of heart and that stubborn
set of the jaw that I'd loathed in my father. How much of my
father did I carry within me? The burden weighed me down the
length of the Rhine and now on the Danube. And I realised the
absurdity of the repeated history: I could not forgive my father
any more than he was able to ask my mother for forgiveness that
night so very long ago in our kitchen. And knowing, regardless
of what had happened, that without forgiveness there would be
no peace. I had held on to my own bitterness, my own intran-
sience, which had irretrievably damaged my relationship with
my father. Was he even aware of my coldness towards him in

the dulled, shadowy lands of his depression? It was difficult to know.

But I was still on the journey and there was some way to go; still studying that map; still not sure who I was and what I could be: *the drops of water not yet seen as a river*.

I would carry on.

9. Tarzan on the Serbian Border

'Welcome, welcome, welcome,' the bear of a bartender said, grabbing my panniers with a yank. I watched with dismay as one of the straps partially gave.

'I like Tarzan – not speak much English. Welcome in Bela Crkva. Please! Come!'

Our last night in Serbia would be spent in this ramshackle border town next to a series of flooded gravel pits. The artificial lakes had gleamed a summer blue as we'd cycled towards the town earlier that afternoon and we'd been unable to resist stopping at one of the lakeside cafés for a much-needed drink.

'God's own country,' the waiter said. 'There's nowhere more beautiful on this Earth.'

But the crumbling town centre and the impatient horn blasts from a blocked-in delivery van suggested otherwise. And now, as Tarzan flung open the door to a dusty attic room, I could smell stale cigarettes and mildew. Jamie and I picked at the balls of dust from the bed under the skylight, but on inspecting the bedsheets more closely, decided they were clean. The place would do.

Having settled in, there was an urgent thud on the door. It was Tarzan again.

'Please. Your passports. Give here. I bring police. You need stamp. You need paper from leaving town.'

I handed over our passports, wondering if we would see them again.

Back in Bačka Palanka the police had said we needed a stamp for every town we stayed in. Sashka had consulted a lawyer friend, who told her we didn't need a police report from anywhere we were staying in for less than twenty-four hours. Our landlady in Novi Sad told us the same as she offered us raspberries from her garden. I still wondered about the record book the police said we must buy. Had it just been a money-making scam? Now Tarzan was telling us something different. The conflicting advice was confusing.

I was relieved when Tarzan returned with our passports along with the required papers to leave the country. We could relax. Jamie and I bought dinner at the bar, leaving just enough for a coffee in the morning: we didn't want to fill our panniers with unwanted change.

Returning to the attic room, we settled down for the night, knowing we needed to rise early to tackle the hill that led to the border with Romania before the heat of the day. But just as I closed my eyes, a band struck up on the bar terrace below. At first, there was just the tortured warble of a single voice. Then the accordion player joined in with his own jabbing cascading runs that clashed with the singer's. The guitarist and mandolin players leapt in with their own manic meandering tunes –

adding to the menagerie of sounds, now undercut by the throb of the double bass.

'Klezmer,' Jamie said with a grin, referring to the traditional Jewish music of Eastern Europe.

My sons were talented musicians: Jamie had learned violin, while Patrick had taken up the cello. They were fortunate to have been part of one of the best youth orchestras in the UK. By the time the boys had left school, Patrick had taught himself double bass for the school folk group and Jamie was running scales through the songs, confident enough to play against the main tune of the piece. They'd idly taught themselves the basics of other instruments too: guitar, ukulele and keyboard – and the piano I'd had shipped to England from my parent's house.

Growing up in the Brethren, only sacred songs were heard in my home to begin with – usually my father singing with a forced but tuneful voice. He whistled hymns, too, that cheerfully vibrated around our house. It was the sound of comfort – as much as the smell of my mother's soda-bread charring on the griddle. My father bought a bulky record cabinet and a handful of 78s – again, mostly hymns, but one record intrigued me: a mournful voice singing *Don't Sell Daddy Any More Whiskey*. It was the only secular record I could remember in my father's collection.

My mother would sit at the piano – the one that she would later ship to me – playing badly and singing out of tune. It was painful to listen to and yet it was good to see my mother doing something that didn't involve cooking or cleaning and caring for her children. Although the Brethren assembly hall, with its solemn *a cappella* singing, rarely permitted instruments, my mother felt it important that my father paid for all his daughters (not sons) to learn piano. Perhaps it was something she felt young women should do, like the women in a Jane Austen novel, to entertain guests and visiting preachers. Later, as my older siblings reached adulthood, more secular music entered our house, introducing me to pop music that made my blood pulse with excitement: The Beach Boys and The Beatles. My parents disapproved of the new music. 'Like cats wailing,' my father said disparagingly.

I ran downstairs behind Jamie to see the terrace outside the bar filled with locals, cursing myself for spending all our dinar. I would have loved to sit on the terrace, wrapped in the warm velvet of the night sky while listening to this wild music, with a glass of wine in my hand. Instead I lurked in the shadows as a local woman shouted to the band in a voice that sounded aggressive, not sure if she was hurling abuse or adoration. It appeared to be the latter as she thumped the arm of the man at her side, who threw a dinar note on top of the accordion. As the tune progressed, the woman shouted louder and the music became more demented. The instruments clashed in full battle mode – the runs of voice, guitar, mandolin and accordion weaving through each other furiously.

It was breathless and awful and brilliant.

That evening, the Klezmer music unleashed something in me – despite the lack of wine. Jamie and I talked long into the night, laughing hysterically at our journey along the rivers. 'Do you remember . . . ?' And we'd set off into another round of giggles. Everything about our cycle trip was inexplicably, belly-achingly funny: Asher and his Noah's Ark, The German in his underpants, Iris and Brian's magical Mary Poppins pannier, our torturous coffin tents, Sabine with her cartoon sound effects, the crazy tree-wrapping Bobo, and Tarzan in the bar behind us. But in truth, our hysterical laughter was less to do with the humour of our encounters and more to do with the sheer joy of the journey and the frenzied Klezmer music playing outside the window. Finally, the music died away in the darkness, and our laughter with it, and we fell to sleep with aching mouths and sides.

In the morning, I felt stone-cold sober. Despite our newly acquired paperwork, I worried the border officials would refuse us entry into Romania, turning us back. At customs I nervously handed over our passports with their single stamps from Bela Crkva. The border official took the papers with a curt nod and stared at them for an inconceivably long time – then waved us through. We wheeled the bikes over the line that divided the two countries. I glanced back one last time at Serbia and thought, *I am not crying because it's over, but smiling because it happened.*

ROMANIA AND BULGARIA

200 km

ROMANIA

Bela
Crkva
Orșova
Drobeta-Turnu Severin
Ploiești
Bucharest

1. Pârneaura
2. Câmpia
3. Socol
4. Moldova Veche
5. Coronini
6. Dubova

Gruia
Calafat
Bistret
Corabia
Giurglu
Oltenița
Ostrov
Ion
Corvin
Constanța
Eforie
Nord
Silistri
General
Toshevo
Negru
Vodă
Bechet
Turnu
Măgurele
Zimnichea
Ruse
Cerventi
Dobrich
Nevsha
Vetrino
Provadia
Dalgopol
Asparuhovo
Daskotna
Aytos
Yambol
Karnobat
Plovdiv
Elhovo
Erdine

Danube

SERBIA

Veliko
Tarnovo

Sofia

BULGARIA

North
Macedonia

BLACK
SEA

GREECE

TURKEY

1. Into Romania

Was this the last time I heard my father's voice in the call of the birds with any clarity? I am not sure. Somewhere across Europe the symphony of birdsong, with all its tempos and moods – *largo, lento, adagio, andante, moderato, allegro, vivace* and *presto*, its *staccato* and sustained notes, sweet and rasping, sorrowful and joyous – died away to a single voice. At times, falling into silence.

I think I last heard the cuckoo on the hill out of Bela Crkva – its voice just discernible in the hum of summer air, carried towards me on the surf of the breeze before being snatched away again. I strained my ears to hear its gentle two-note through the rumble of tyre on asphalt. Towards the crest of the hill, the sound of the cuckoo was overtaken by that of the skylark, the song and bird dipping and rising with the undulating meadows of wheat, sunflower and corn. It too faded out, leaving only the sound of my rasping lungs pulling at the air as I struggled up the long hill.

Across the border, we had a decision to make: we could head due south over the Banat Mountains to Pojejena on the Danube, or we could backtrack along the border on the Romanian side, cycling parallel to the road we'd climbed out of Bela Crkva, before heading south to the river and then east again along the Danube. The valley route was more than double the mountain route, but with the slow ascent out of Bela Crkva fresh in our memories, the thought of the mountain climb held little appeal. We chose the flatter route.

At first, the road running along the Nera River valley was flat and pleasantly bucolic. A group of Romanians were camped out on the banks of the river below us, some splashing in the Nera, others sunbathing on its grassy verge. But soon, the patched tarmac began to rise and fall with the contours of the land. We passed through empty villages, each one looking very much like the last with cracked render and exposed brick. Paint was peeling off garage doors and gates, and fences were flaying with rust. Stray dogs lay in the shadows of trees.

Between Párneaura and Câmpia, Jamie pointed to Bela Crkva, just a few miles to the north of us, on the other side of the border. We'd spent a good part of the morning heading east out of Bela Crkva before turning 180° to run parallel to the Serbian road in the opposite direction. I wondered about the wisdom of our decision.

At Socol the road made a wide sweep to the south where it hit the Danube. We stopped our bikes and took in the bulge of the river that opened out a pale blue to the south before continuing its journey east. It was a glorious view. Various signs on a wide, grassy bank at the head of the swollen Danube extolled the virtues of the river and region. It would probably have been covered in picnic tables or a café if it had been in Germany or Austria. Not here though – there was no one except a solitary shepherd on the side of the road, sheltering beneath the sagging thatch of a wattle and daub hut that leaned into the hillside.

Ahead, the road followed the curves of the river, now running parallel to the Neva valley north of us, forming the last loop of our meandering, backward 'S'. By and by, we came to Pojejena, the village that lay at the foot of the mountain road that cut straight south from the border. It was late morning and we'd lost a great deal of time with our snaking route. We needed to push on downstream towards Moldova Veche.

I'd seen on the map the spread of villages along the Danube – Baziaş, Divici, Belobreşca, Şuşca and Măceşti – and imagined there would be plenty of opportunity to stop at shoreline cafés. But there were only fishermen with their folding tables and picnic chairs and lines of rods surrounded by litter, and the odd family emerging from modest single-storied houses to cross the road in swimming costumes and flip-flops. At last in Moldova Veche we found a cafe blasting out dance music with a brashness and volume that we would soon learn was typical of Romania. The idyll of the Nera valley seemed far away. We negotiated the unmade roads and begging Roma children at the south end of the village and peddled on to Coronini, our goal for the day.

*

As we cycled on through the country, I was taken by surprise: no one had prepared us for the beauty of the Romanian Danube. On the Rhine, we had been told of the delights of the German Danube awaiting us, *more spectacular than the Mittelrhein*. On the German Danube, we were told the Austrian section of the river was even more beautiful. In Austria, Sabine's eyes had shone with passion as she'd spoken about Slovakia's Bratislava and Hungary's Budapest. But no one mentioned Romania – including its Serbian neighbours. Even the Romanians seemed to have turned their backs on the beauty of their own stretch of Danube (a third of the entire river's length), preferring the concrete-covered Black Sea and the mountains of Transylvania.

And so we pedalled on along the near-empty Danube byway with little in the way of settlement or traffic, even though the road was surely one of Europe's most beautiful. Back in the day, someone must have seen something of the river's potential: picnic tables and benches, some with thatched shades, had been placed along the banks of the river. But they were now lying rotten with neglect, the ground around them scattered with rubbish and faeces.

Beyond the laybys with their rubbish-strewn, rank-smelling picnic areas, the hills of Serbia on the opposite bank folded and enfolded into themselves in shades of grey-blue and green, like a Japanese watercolour, fading away to a block of cloudless sky. Occasionally, the river spread itself out into glassy bays, the sweep of watery curve smudging the steep-sided woodlands in its reflection. At other times, the Danube squeezed through the karst rock of the Carpathian Mountains, the road clinging so close to the water's edge, it felt as if we were sailing the river.

While the road surface had been improved in sections, and the eroding rockfaces stabilised, in other places it became increasingly churned up. Where rockfall had blocked one side of the road, the authorities simply left it, placing barriers and diversion signs around the obstruction. I prayed we wouldn't find ourselves in the wrong place at the wrong time: I didn't want to join the copious roadkill. Our scrap of metal and bike helmets gave us little protection. On the other hand, the variable road conditions meant we almost had the Romanian Danube to ourselves.

At Cozia, we passed by the blackened shell of a factory, one of Ceaușescu's ghosts. Weeds and trees were growing out of the cracked concrete, empty windows and broken rooftop. It was a strange sight in this isolated section of the Danube, where even villages had become an infrequent sight. It seemed a fitting image for Ceauşescu's utopian dream turned dystopian – gone, yet ever present, like a gaping wound that wouldn't heal.

In the fjord-like bay at Dubova we rented a wooden cabin. It was late afternoon and a group of noisy youths were horse-playing in the swimming pool of the holiday home over the fence, their dance music pounding the air and bouncing off the bay. Ceauşescu would have turned in his grave at their hedonism. It was deafening. As the manager showed us the cabin, I pointed to the group and held my hands over my ears. The woman, speaking little English, said, 'It okay. Not stop eleven, police come.'

But the woman was long gone by eleven and the music continued until daylight. I didn't sleep.

At dawn, we wheeled our bikes to the gate. It was locked. I was furious: furious with lack of sleep; furious that we had been imprisoned in this sleep-deprivation torture chamber, somewhat ironically in the quiet beauty of this Danube bay; but most of all, furious at the woman's lies. Then, I realised, if we wheeled the bikes around the back, the rough ground stretched to the road without fence or gate. As we took off down the road, the green of the bay glinted in the early morning light. It was hard to remain foul-tempered when cradled by hill and cliff and water, and embalmed by the soft light of the new day.

Beyond the bay, the Danube narrowed again, forcing its path through the Carpathian cliffs. It felt as though I could reach out and touch the limestone on the opposite bank in Serbia, the rock taking on a pinkish hue with the rising sun. I could see the road on the other side also clung to the side of the Danube but dropped and fell with the contours of the hillside before plunging into countless tunnels. Our side remained level at the water's edge: I was glad we had chosen to ride on the Romanian bank and through the Iron Gates Natural Park.

When we turned a corner to see an onion-domed church teetering on the water's edge, its white walls glowing in the sunlight, the sleepless night was forgotten. Just a little further on, we crossed a bridge where a Carpathian spring seeped into the Danube, to find a rock ogre with bulging squirrel-cheeks and a stock of electrified hair standing 140 feet high over the inlet. This was Decebalus, the last king of Dacia (though more comical than regal in appearance) who had fought off two Roman emperors to protect his country's independence – the equivalent of modern-day Romania. It had taken a decade, from 1994 to 2004, for a Romanian industrialist to realise his larger-than-life vision of Decebalus Rex – from designing the rock sculpture, to blasting the rock and carving out the detail. However odd the king's appearance, you couldn't fail to be impressed with his magnitude on the hillside.

Now, in the early morning with the roadside stalls shuttered and the laybys empty, we had Decebalus to ourselves and he looked across the inlet at us with pupil-less stony eyes, as if rolling them heavenward. His tight-lipped grimace seemed to say, *Why have they turned me into a pillar of stone in this backwater of the Danube?*

As we rode on, the road remained quiet. The only burst of activity was at a roadside fountain, where men and boys filled up plastic containers of mountain water – moving aside to allow us foreigners to jump the queue. I drank the ice-cold water with appreciation. Here on the Romanian Danube, it was the simplest of pleasures that made me grateful.

At Eşelniţa, we made the long hard climb over the pass to Orşova, enjoying the equally long freewheel down into town, where we bought some supplies and ice cream as a reward for making it over the lip of the Carpathians. Ahead of us was a short, sharp cycle through heavy traffic to Drobeta-Turnu Severin, but we were on the home run with a rest day ahead. We'd be in Drobeta by early afternoon. We were feeling good as we pushed off out of town when we heard a sound we'd not heard since Vukovar in Croatia: a quiet ping.

2. Spokes and Spirits

If a spoke had to break, this was the place. Having cycled through the Iron Gates Natural Park with few villages or hamlets, never mind bicycle workshops, we had been fortunate: this large town would surely have a bike shop. I asked one man, then another, for help. They offered us Italian and French, but no English. On my third attempt I found a man who spoke German and offered to show us a place.

And he turned his bicycle around and led us back up the hill from where we'd come. He stopped and pointed to a ramshackle building where deep-cut steps led into a long corridor lined with stalls and clothes that disappeared into the darkness. It didn't seem very promising.

Jamie hauled his bicycle up the steps, while I searched the indoor market for the elusive bicycle shop. There wasn't one.

No one spoke English or German, but eventually, after some wild gesticulation, a young girl led us through the stalls to a clothes shop. Just as I was beginning to despair, I noticed a stack of bicycle tyres in among the racks of jeans and T-shirts. Perhaps, just perhaps, the broken spoke could be fixed here.

'Broken. *Kaput*,' I said to the middle-aged shopkeeper, pointing to the spoke.

'*Da, da*.'

She didn't look like a bike mechanic, with her coiffured hair and painted nails. At first she thought there was a problem with the tyre, but then she understood and went away and returned with pliers. She bent down . . .

'No, please don't cut the spoke,' I pleaded. I didn't like the way she was wielding the pliers. It looked like she might cut more than one spoke. And it certainly didn't look as if she had either spokes or a tool to fix it.

Jamie and I made our escape, wheeling our bikes down to the shore of the Danube, where we tried a hotel. But no one spoke English there either. I drew a rather pathetic picture of a bicycle wheel with a broken spoke and it was finally established there was no repair shop in town. Jamie shrugged his shoulders and unclipped his back brake. He would have to cycle the last fifteen miles to Drobeta with just his front brake and hope for the best. It wasn't a great option as we were about to face our most dangerous road of the journey so far.

*

Across the Danube promenade, we found ourselves swallowed up by the E70 – a dual carriageway thundering with lorries all the way to Drobeta-Turnu Severin. Our bike book had solemnly declared the road unsuitable for bicycles, then announced – without a trace of irony – that it wasn't possible to take a train. There was nothing for it but to put our faith in the lorry drivers and hope they would spare us.

The road into the city made the Esztergom trunk road in Hungary look like a quiet backwater. There was no hard shoulder here, and the articulated lorries passed by with inches to spare, almost sucking us under their wheels with the draw of air they created. Leone's advice back in Hungary – to move out into the road and pull in when the lorries were parallel – was of little use: the two lanes were bumper-to-bumper with speeding traffic. Yet more frightening were the bridges that narrowed the road, forcing us even closer to the lorries. But the danger on the bridges paled into insignificance compared to the half dozen tunnels or so. We put on our reflective jackets and clipped on our cheap bike lights but were still barely visible in the tunnel. One lorry driver, not noticing my bike in the blackness of the tunnel, only became aware of my presence in the last minute as he bore down on me. The tunnel exploded with the sound of horn, almost causing me to fall off my bicycle.

For fifteen miles the road continued with bridges and tunnels and the squeeze of verge-less carriageway. At last, we reached the outskirts of Drobeta-Turnu Severin and collapsed into the seats of a taverna, where we quenched our thirst and calmed our nerves with long, cold sugary drinks. In Drobeta we found a guesthouse that offered us a suite of rooms and a little balcony for the price of a standard room. The woman on the desk located a bicycle shop for Jamie and a hairdresser for me.

The middle-aged man in the bicycle shop didn't inspire

confidence: he didn't seem to know one end of a bicycle from the other, but he promised that the spoke would be repaired by the end of the next day. It was fortuitous we had planned in a rest day. We rescued the bicycle from the repair shop just before closing, repaired and ticketed. I still wasn't convinced that the staff were competent mechanics – and my fears would later be justified. The boys in the bike shop back in Vukavor had done a decent job; Jamie's mended spoke had lasted 300 miles. I wondered how far we'd get on this latest repair.

Before leaving town, we consulted our bike book again. It warned us the next available accommodation after Drobeta-Turnu Severin was at Calafat, over eighty miles away. It seemed a stretch in the summer heat, but then, when checking the route on Google Maps, I spotted Pensiunea Gruia tucked between a lake and the Danube just outside a village of the same name. I found the website: photographs showed an Alpine-chic building of stone and wood in Danube sunsets and a swimming pool of clear-blue water surrounded by sun loungers. More than that, it was cheap. We'd aim for Gruia.

At first, the way out of Drobeta was easy, the road smoothly surfaced and even. The character of the Romanian Danube valley changed again, spreading out across wide flat plains to meander in a stately manner through shrubland and cultivated fields. The road hugged the river until Batoți where we took the 56B, which hung back from the Danube. After Țigănași, Jamie ignored the bike book map and took us onto an island that lay between the main waterway and one of its branches. It was a pleasant diversion, but when we crossed back over a narrow bridge, the road turned into loose rubble so bad we were forced off our bikes to walk the unmade road back to the

Danube bike route. On track again, we climbed a hill until we were high above the Danube, the river appearing from time to time as a flash of silver.

In the village of Gruia, we found the road that dropped steeply off sandy cliffs to the lakes and wetlands of our guesthouse. I spotted a pink villa at the bottom that looked imposing enough to be a *pensiunea*. We pushed off and careered down the cliff, past a shelter painted with two antlered stags sharing a branch under a bright blue sky. Roma boys, gathered round its fountain, shouted greetings and waved as we flew past, our wheels still spinning furiously as we hit the watery plains.

The pink villa was guarded by fierce-barking Alsatians, discouraging us from entering through the gate. I tried calling, but there was no reply. Beyond, the lane, cracked and pot-holed, disappeared into woods, with no indication there was a guesthouse on the other side. I looked at a clump of trees on raised ground and wondered about the possibility of wild camping, then saw some fishermen had already set up camp.

It was an eerie place at the base of the cliff, with the wind moaning and the sound of waders drifting through the air. I thought I heard the call of a common tern somewhere beyond the clump of trees with the fishermen's camp, the two-toned trill a familiar sound from Lough Neagh. My father and I had watched the terns with their long, forked tails, aptly nicknamed sea swallows, from one of the bird hides, raising our necks to follow the birds surf on a thermal above the Oxford Island peninsula, graceful and light of wing. They hovered over the water, as if weightless, before plunging for fish. We knew summer was on its way when they flew in from East Africa in April, taking up temporary residence on nameless Lough Neagh islands to raise their young; and that winter would soon be upon us when they departed in August.

We cycled up and down the road looking for the *pensiunea* until Jamie insisted the house had to be on the other side of the trees. He was right. But when we reached the Alpine-style chalet, it didn't look anything like the website pictures. The gate and fencing were broken, the pool drained and grubby, the plastic loungers cracked and its wooden sign peeling. Jamie and I scouted around but couldn't find a way in. I went around the back to find a couple of men drinking beer on a wooden balcony, looking a little worse for wear. I called to them and they directed me round to the front of the building again, where at last we found the entrance.

Inside, the house creaked like a shored-up schooner, its rooms encased in dark wood like the hull of a ship. There was no one around but us and the proprietors. The man and his wife prepared us drinks then offered a meal. They emerged from the kitchen with great bowls of beef-tomato salad, followed by chicken broth and plates of bony stew. We sat in the shadowy light of the narrow dining room listening to the clink of our cutlery and the windblown creak of floorboard. It felt as if we'd been abandoned on the *Mary Celeste*, the owners now having disappeared into the bowels of the house. Upstairs, our room was snug as a cabin, the wind wittering through gaps in the dark-wood panelling. The whole place felt haunted. I pulled open the door that led onto the balcony and watched the sun bleed into the Danube, lulled by the long, low call of a curlew.

That night, I lay awake and listened to the building as it sighed and whispered as if in conversation with itself. Just before daylight, I heard movement: footsteps on the floorboards and the deep, low rumble of male voices. Were they the voices of the men we'd seen on the balcony earlier swigging beer? Perhaps they were fishermen, as elusive as their avian counterparts – the kingfishers that hid on the banks of rivers.

Perhaps they were the ghosts of the Danube.

3. Troubles in Dolj County

Gruia will always stay with me. There are places on the journey – long stretches of empty road lined with crop or weedy shrubland – that have become blind spots in my memory, and there are others where the detail remains as sharp and defined as the day we cycled through. Gruia is one of them.

As we pushed our bicycles up the cliffside in the bluish light of early morning, we could see a stick of a woman far below us, striding across the wetlands in a tangle of aprons and skirts whilst jabbing the ground with a crook. Her voice rang out across the valley as she berated an errant heifer, words tumbling out like staccato notes before being snatched away by the river breeze.

I thought of my father with his wayward cattle, dancing around them with outstretched arms: 'Huh-ah, huh-ah.'

The further east we cycled through rural Romania, the greater the sense we were cycling into the past. Men in black with collarless shirts sat outside shops on half-broken plastic seats, leaning over their sticks. Girls crouched on grassy verges with gaggles of geese. Once, a couple of escapee horses galloped down the road towards us, their chains rattling behind them. We passed women walking the roads with hessian sacks overflowing with flowering herbs, and we saw youths on rusting bikes, sometimes loaded with kindling or farm machinery. Tractors and trailers and the hitherto perpetual white van were replaced by horses and carts – whole households out on the road along with the family dog.

It reminded me of the Ireland I had grown up in, particularly the countryside where my father drove his grocery van. One of his customers was a bachelor farmer who lived in a tumbledown cottage along one of the high-hedged lanes beyond my town. We'd push through the overgrown garden to the open door of his cottage, the old boy calling us in, to stand among half-broken furniture. He smelt of wood-smoke and unwashed body and his trousers were held up with twine. My father liked to tell tales about the farmer, who was unbothered by society's niceties. Once Johnny had taken a fallen tree trunk from his farmstead and trailed it through the door to the open fire. Too lazy to chop it up, he shoved it further into the grate as the fire devoured it. My father tittered with laughter as he told this story. Only later had I asked myself why the fire had not spread down the trunk and set the house on fire. Perhaps the wood was too wet. Unseasoned, there would have been more smoke than fire, which explained the pungent smell off Johnny – like an old smoked kipper.

My father, who had begun to fade out through Serbia and Romania with the dying birdsong, returned to me again in this quiet hinterland of the Danube; a place where time seemed to have stopped. This part of Romania – despite Ceauşescu's efforts to obliterate country settlements and create an urban, industrialised country fitting of a communist state – echoed the simplicity of rural Ireland during my sixties' childhood; a world my father had clung to with his little garage grocery shop and delivery van.

We cycled on through this bucolic corner of Romania, with its linear villages of low-lying cottages, communal squares, fountains and little shops stocked with staples and a self-service coffee machine. These small settlements contrasted with the bigger towns, where Ceauşescu had torn down streets of cottages and replaced them with multi-storied blocks of brutal concrete. I could see they had been flung up in haste – the balconies now crumbling, the lines not quite straight. I'd read somewhere the individual flats had been built without kitchens in order to force the residents to eat communally in a large dining hall in the basement or ground floor. It was less to do with fostering a community spirit and more to do with Ceauşescu's paranoia: the community dining rooms had spies; private kitchens allowed private conversations.

Ceauşescu reconstructed towns and cities across the whole of Romania in the same fashion, wiping out entire communities of centuries-old houses to replace them with apartment blocks set around grid systems, the grey symmetry only broken up by the softer green of the public park. Each large town or city had an official state hotel, sometimes the only accommodation option. These Communist-era hotels still exist and continue to be run in the old Communist way. Prices and menus are set – *and please don't make individual requests*; customer service is seen as something for soft-headed capitalists.

Panoramic Hotel in Calafat was our first experience of one of these Communist state hotels. As we checked in, we were instructed to take the lift to the thirteenth floor. The metal box, barely big enough for two, shuddered its way past the first eleven floors then came to an abrupt stop somewhere between the twelfth and thirteenth. We opened the door to a concrete wall and a gaping hole that dropped all the way back down to reception. Hastily, Jamie pressed the button for the thirteenth floor again. Nothing happened. He jabbed the button again and again. Still nothing. We waited for a few minutes then pressed the help button. Silence. We stood in the stuffy lift and wondered if we would die from suffocation or thirst. What an irony that would be after surviving the lorries across Eastern Europe. I could see the newspaper headline: *Cyclists die in hotel lift after riding across Europe*. The thought made me giggle, not without a hint of hysteria.

Jamie tried the button again. There was no movement. In desperation, he pressed the ground floor button and the lift shot down at speed. Jamie and I emerged from the lift, back at our starting point, laughing hysterically and feeling shaken. Then we ran for the stairs. Who cared if we had multiple flights of steps to climb: we might be exhausted by the time we reached the top, but we'd still be alive.

Our room hadn't been renovated since the seventies. There *was* air-con, but no remote to switch it on. There was a fridge that didn't work and a shower that gave us lukewarm water. The balcony had just enough space for the air-con condenser – but if you squeezed past, you could just make out the hotel's claim to panoramic views of the Danube.

That evening we ate in the hotel dining room with its long rows of tables and chairs of pink nylon tied with bows. We were the only guests. So, in the morning, we were surprised to see the dining hall busy. It could have been a scene from Monty

Python. It was a set breakfast and the diners were handed trays with identical plates – with a cup of tea *and* coffee. This was Communist efficiency in the modern world. If some guests insisted on breakfast coffee while others only drank tea, then a tray of both beverages meant they could continue their conveyer belt system without having to talk to anyone. It was as comical as it was ingenious.

So when I returned my coffee because it was cold, I caused pandemonium. The server frowned, nodded then promptly ignored me. I returned again. Finally, a hot cup of coffee arrived, just as I was swallowing the last mouthful of my breakfast. We left the Panoramic Hotel feeling bemused. Bizarrely, we'd enjoyed our time there – it was worth every leu of our money.

*

Our bike book was at it again – urging us to take the train from Calafat to Corabia over 100 miles away. Why write a bike book that discourages cyclists from riding their bikes? This time, it wasn't to do with the weight of traffic (we were truly in the sticks) but rather the lack of accommodation between the two towns.

Jamie and I still had our tents, which hadn't seen a campsite since Austria. Hotels and guesthouses from Slovakia onwards were often cheaper than the Austrian and German campsites, and a comfortable bed at night after a long day on the bike was a temptation too great to resist. There had been no campsites along this part of the Danube anyway – and I still had an irrational fear of wild camping.

Then Jamie found Zavāl Camping on Google Maps, about halfway to Corabia. It was the only campsite we'd spotted since

Austria. There was little information on the place, other than the fact that there were a few ramshackle cabins. And while it looked to be set in an idyllic spot on the Jiu, with riverside swimming (which our bike book did mention), I discovered a couple of touring cyclist blogs that alluded to strange goings-on in the night: our campsite seemed to be a kind of camping brothel. Still, we would investigate.

We arrived at the campsite mid-afternoon, hot and tired. The riverside site was filled with motorbikes and men in black leather striding around with tins of lager in their hands. I asked an expressionless girl if we could have a pitch for the night.

'No place,' she said in a flat, bored voice.

We bought soft drinks at the bar and pondered our options. Tired, I was loath to cycle on. Some of the bikers came over to chat.

'Yeah, you can stay. You'll be safe with us.'

'Look, I leave my money lying around without worrying,' said another, and he flung his wallet on the bar with a flourish, as if to demonstrate his point. 'No one will take your things – but it will be noisy. We'll be partying all night, but if you pitch back there in the trees, it might not be too bad.'

It was tempting to stay. Tiredness was overriding common sense. Then Jamie stepped in. 'I think we should go on. I think we can find something further along the road in Bechet.' Google Maps hadn't indicated any accommodation in Bechet, and I dragged my bike back onto the road reluctantly, but I knew deep down that Jamie had made the right decision.

For the first time, I thought we might have to wild camp. As we rode along the road that sliced through a forest, I peered into the trees, trying to imagine what it would be like to camp there, the ground uneven and covered in broken branches and low-lying vegetation. I could see mosquitoes circling the birch and ash. It wasn't an enticing option.

Then I heard that noise again: ping. It was worrying that the spokes on Jamie's bike were breaking with increasing frequency – especially now we were cycling through this rural part of the Danube. And here we were just outside Bechet, a long way from the nearest town of Turnu Măgurele. What would be the chance of finding a bike shop here? Once more, Jamie unclipped the back brake and we rode into the village looking simultaneously for a bicycle shop and somewhere to sleep.

We found accommodation almost straight away on the main road – a large, modern building with the letter 's' squeezed in brackets between the 'o' and 't', as if it couldn't decide to be a hotel or a hostel.

'We're almost full,' said the girl at the hotel-cum-hostel entrance. 'We have a school party tonight, but we can squeeze both of you into a single room if you want. Let me show you the room and you can decide.'

As expected, there wasn't a bicycle shop in Bechet, but the girl phoned a friend who arrived a short time later. He rummaged around a storehouse at the side of the hotel until he found a bike with a wheel the same size as Jamie's. 'Okay,' he said. 'I can use a spoke from this old bike. Leave it with me. I'll have your bike sorted in no time.'

While he fixed the bike, the girl led us along corridors of Persian rugs and leafy plants to the single bedroom. It was still big enough for a double bed.

'We can get you another mattress. Hold on.' And her friend returned with a brand-new mattress, still wrapped in plastic.

'Your bike's fixed,' he told us.

'How much do I owe you?' I asked.

'Oh, nothing.'

That evening we feasted on a jug of the hotel's homemade wine and a plate piled high with food. The family invited us to join them at their table to share a watermelon. Later, we discovered that somewhere between the storehouse and the hotel, Jamie's water bottles had gone missing. 'No worries,' said the son, 'We'll check the CCTV footage,' and he sat with Jamie, scouring through reams of CCTV footage for about an hour – all in vain. The mystery remained unresolved, but we didn't mind: we had a bed for the night, a mended bike and a belly full of food and wine – and all for eighteen pounds. The following morning, as we cycled out of Bechet, I thought of Ingrid's redstarts way back in the German vineyards, bringing good luck. The redstarts were evidently still with us.

4. High-fives, Horse Carts and Touring Cyclists

'Bună, bună!'

'Alo!'

'Salut!'

'Servus!'

'Ciao!'

As we cycled from village to village across the Romanian plains, children lined the main streets, arms outstretched and palms held up in anticipation. When three tiny, sweet-looking girls almost knocked me off my bike with the force of their high-fives, I pointed to Jamie behind. I didn't want to re-break my recently smashed wrist (held together with a metal rod and nine pins) in the backwaters of Romania and have our trip come to an abrupt end just short of the Black Sea.

Our bike book had dropped any positive spin when it came to the Romanian plains, bluntly calling them 'monotonous' and reiterating its advice to jump on a train. I was glad now we'd paid no heed, as the richness of our encounters with the Romanian people more than made up for the lack of geographical diversity.

Across the flatlands of the Danube valley each village seemed to have its preferred choice of greeting, and everyone everywhere called out and waved at us as we cycled through. The passengers of the ubiquitous horse and cart would sit bolt upright, their faces breaking into wide grins as we passed. Back in Hungary, the Syrian refugees were not being made so welcome. Prime Minister Orbán had started to erect the 'wall' Eszter had talked about, a razor-wire fence along the border with Serbia. I read my newsfeed with a saddened heart as we sailed through borders. Despite all the warnings regarding Eastern Europe, the further east we travelled the bigger the welcome. Here, almost every village had its own *magazin*, an old-fashioned grocery store with outside seating, serving coffee, beer and spirits. No hour was deemed too early for the male villagers to congregate at the store for a beer or a swig of homemade *rakia* straight from the hipflask. The men would try to engage with us as we sipped on our coffee, dredging up any word we might recognise – 'Chelsea', or once, to my surprise, 'Margaret Thatcher'. Sitting with our hot drinks, we watched the village world wander in and out of our line of vision: scarved and aproned women carrying sacks of greens and youths balancing gas canisters on ancient bicycles.

I saw these villages were poor in material wealth but rich in community life. The predominance of horse and cart, bicycle and walker meant that people stopped frequently to talk to each other, and I realised the car back home had broken down communities. In the UK, people lived behind walls and stepped straight from the front door to their vehicle – brick, stone and metal separating them from the outside world.

During two sub-zero winters in the Peak District, the snow had lain so deep in my adopted town we had to abandon our cars for days on end. Suddenly the streets were filled with people lugging heavy bags of shopping along icy roads. I talked to more of my neighbours in those wintery weeks than I had the rest of the year. I thought of my mother, setting off to walk into our town with her cloth bags, my hand in hers. Returning home was a test of endurance for a small child, not much interested in tittle-tattle as my mother stopped to talk to neighbours and acquaintances. I hopped from foot to foot while the women stood deep in conversation. From town to home, she not only collected bundles of shopping tied up in string, but armfuls of gossip and neighbourly connection. My father's grocery business was also a point of contact for country folk living in isolated country cottages and farmsteads: the delivered goods exchanged with cups of tea, garden produce and a lingering chat.

Romania was a window into our loss.

*

On the edge of one of these villages I saw two cyclists far ahead of us. I peered into the heat haze, wondering if it were possible that they could be tourers, as we had not seen any long-distance cyclists since Serbia.

'Jamie, I think they are touring cyclists!' It was as if I'd spotted a rare and endangered species. 'Yes! I think I see panniers!'

Jamie smiled at my excitement.

I quickened the crank of my pedals until I'd caught up with the couple ahead – an American called Tom and his Dutch girlfriend, Cindy. I cycled alongside the bear-like American for a while as he told me his story. Tom was one of the United States' top climate-change scientists who'd gone into semi-retirement and had cycled across the world and criss-crossed North America in all seasons. He didn't think anything of cycling in deep snow. Once he caused a major incident when he chained his expensive bike bag to a rack outside a New England airport – he had no room for it in his panniers and cycled away, oddly expecting to find it still there on his return. The airport authorities, fearing a terrorist incident, blew the bag up. When a lorry crushed him and his bicycle, causing multiple injuries that nearly killed him, Tom got back on his bike, relearning to ride a bicycle with debilitating injuries. On top of that he had Huntington's disease.

Cindy was also a fearless cyclist, who was conquering the world country by country with her bike. Now, she and Tom were doing a 'soft' trip across Europe – not too far from her parents who needed her support. She stopped frequently to photograph the street urchins who lined the road: small faces smeared with dirt; slight girls in thin summer dresses and flip-

flops; boys in ragged shorts and ill-fitting T-shirts – all with
cheeky grins and sun-darkened arms from outdoor living. One
boy on a scrappy bicycle, several sizes too big for him, began
to tailgate Jamie. Jamie raced away from the boy but he was no
match for the Romanian child who slammed his front wheel
into the back of Jamie's bike. Jamie skidded to a halt: he'd had
enough. But Tom raced off instead, glancing back at the boy
in invitation. The two sped away until they were specks at the
other end of the village.

I thought of my bike book and its disparaging 'monotonous'
and smiled: there was more to a bike trip than a landscape.

The touring cyclists were important to me. It was not that
I didn't enjoy mingling with local people –they were a deeply
enriching part of our journey – but it is natural also to search
out like-minded people, our 'own kind'. It is as if they give us
validation of who we are.

In Eastern Europe we were meeting people who had cycled
around the world and looked on a trip along the Danube as a
short hop across Europe. I realised that we were meeting a new
breed of long-distance cyclist, and it made me feel somewhat
inadequate. From Rotterdam to Budapest we'd primarily met
leisure tourers, usually individuals who had taken a few weeks
off from work to cycle the Rhine or a section of the Danube.
The cyclists east of Budapest were hardcore. We crossed paths
with a father and son from Newcastle who were packing in
100 to 150 miles a day across Europe. I felt like a dawdler in
comparison. They paused to speak to us before speeding off on
their bikes, still fifty miles or so in front of them even though it
was late afternoon.

One pair we met – a Londoner and his French companion

– were cycling in the opposite direction to us. While Jamie and I had been pushed along by the eastbound Danube winds, these two were struggling west and north, and despite their extended cycle through far-flung countries such as India, they seemed, like us, to be struggling with the heat. As we did, they rose at dawn to catch the cool of the day, but unlike us, they set up camp by the banks of the river – when the sun was at its highest – to sleep away the heat of the day, setting out again in the coolness of early evening. They thought nothing of wild camping, and were living on around five euros a day.

'What about the mosquitoes when you're camping by the river?' I asked.

'Ha, I'm the world's greatest mosquito killer,' the Brit said, pulling a fly-basher from his pannier and manically thrashing the air.

My fellow Brit seemed to have a cycling disease common to many long-distance bicyclists. Unable to settle in one place, he was already planning his next cycling trip before he'd even reached the threshold of his London home. It was difficult for me to imagine living out of panniers for years, but I understood why touring cyclists found it hard to stop: the freedom of the road, the open air, the soothing rhythm of turning wheels, the anticipation of something new every day.

At the hotel-cum-hostel in Bechet, we'd spent the evening with an Englishman, Graham, and his German companion, Stefan. Jamie and I continued to bump into the Anglo-German duo: we found them in one of the villages, taking a large bag of ripened beef tomatoes from a man who'd emerged from his garden to offer his gift – because he had grown more than he could use, and no he didn't want any money for them.

We caught up with them again in Turnu Măgurele, where they were hunting down a place for the night like us. We had already tried the one Communist-era hotel in town, where a hatched-faced woman at the reception desk had refused to haggle. In fact, she'd looked decidedly unhappy at the mere suggestion. Finally, she'd offered me a tiny reduction on the room price, but would drop no further. At that point I'd walked out, determined to find somewhere else – not knowing it was the only accommodation option in town. No wonder she'd smiled to herself as I left: she knew we'd be back.

'No worries,' said Stefan when I told him about the overpriced hotel. 'I'll bargain her down. You stay here – it's better that way. I'll deal with her.'

He came out of the hotel with a large smile spread across his face. 'I told her there were four of us and got us a great deal.'

I didn't have the heart to tell Stefan she'd made us exactly the same offer an hour earlier.

That night the four of us dined in the empty hotel restaurant. Our voices echoed around the room, and Graham, angry when the hotel only offered expensive beers rather than the local brew as advertised on the menu, fumed with barely contained anger. The waiter brought Stefan, Jamie and I our dishes – leaving Graham still waiting long after we'd finished. No longer able to contain his fury, he'd gone to the kitchen to shout at the chef. It was an uncomfortable evening – far removed from the pleasant tale-swapping in the courtyard of the Bechet ho(s)tel the evening before – and I felt on edge by the violent undercurrent that filled the room, and the surly waiter who hovered nervously at our table.

By the time Jamie and I approached Giurgiu, we'd had

enough of the Communist-style hotels. We crossed the bridge into Bulgaria for just two nights, to escape the similar hotels of Romania, and booked ourselves into a small boutique hotel with a little courtyard that served good food. We were due another rest day.

5. To the Black Sea

After our sojourn into Bulgaria, we returned over the border to Romania. The character of the land changed again after Giurgiu as we climbed into the hills high above the Danube. The road was punctuated with villages and hamlets – Pietrele, Puleni, Prundu – the names and settlements interchangeable. Soon fields of crops, shrubland and sandy cliffs gave way to vineyards that striped the hillsides like an egg slicer. We were cycling the roof of Giurgiu County.

I focused on climbing each rise in the heat, enjoying the fan of air as we freewheeled down the other side. Between the climbs on the long straight roads across the plateau, Jamie and I began to dream about our two weeks in Turkey after reaching Istanbul. There'd be sleep-ins and long leisurely breakfasts – and even longer lunches of olives, juicy tomatoes and freshly baked bread with Tom and Patrick and my sister, Maggie, and her husband. In the heat we dreamed of the clear, cool water of the Turkish Mediterranean. We would cycle nowhere.

And now the end point was tangible. We sensed the Black

Sea was within our reach: less than 180 miles away. I could almost smell the ozone of ocean in my nostrils, taste sea-salt on my tongue, feel the sea breeze on my skin.

Just one month today and we will be welcoming you in Istanbul, my sister wrote. She had been following our route closely in her atlas. *On the page with the Black Sea now*, she added. *Getting there!* And my heart flip-flopped.

The feeling of progress was heady as we ate the miles from Olteniţa through the ribbon villages of Ulmeni, Spanţov and Chiselet. But as we reached the end of Mănăstirea village we heard a bang. Jamie's bike did a sort of horse shudder, almost throwing him off. It lurched forward as the front wheel sank into the ground. This time it wasn't a spoke, but a shredded tyre. We looked at the rubber – scarred and sliced as if Jamie had ridden over spiked metal. The tear was too deep for the slime to do its job. We would need a new tyre.

Once again, I asked myself where we'd find a bike shop: we'd seen plenty of little grocery stores in the villages we'd just cycled through, but nothing resembling a bicycle store. We sat down on the steps that led down to Galatui reservoir and tried to work out our options.

'We just cycled past a garage,' said Jamie. 'It had lots of car tyres out the front. Maybe they have bicycle tyres as well.' He took the wheel off his bike and we headed back to the garage. The mechanic shook his head when I asked him if he had any bike tyres. But he told me in basic English where I could find one.

'Hurry – I shut two. I go home and eat.'

While Jamie stayed at the garage, I cycled around the village, the old tyre slung over my shoulder, trying to find the elusive shop selling tyres. At last, I found it, but the tyres were all too small for his wheel.

'There is another place,' the shopkeeper said, and he gave me instructions on how to get there.

Frantically, I cycled around the village again in search of the second store, all too aware that 2pm was fast approaching. In the end, a youth cycled to the shop with me. I was in luck: the shopkeeper had a tyre big enough for Jamie's large bike frame.

A new tyre on the bicycle – albeit a road tyre that was narrower than the original hybrid one – we headed for the reservoir again. The heat of the day had built up to an oppressive soupy thickness of air. Down in the dip of the dam head, I could see a Roma woman sheltering from the glare of the sun under a piece of faded canvas, held aloft by four sticks. She lay on a mattress, surrounded by her possessions – pots and pans, a gas cylinder and a pile of clothing – while a couple of goats nibbled on yellowed grass behind the tent.

That evening, we holed up in our last Romanian Communist-era concrete tower. In the morning, we would cross the river by ferry, leaving the Danube behind for good to cut across the hills to Constanţa – and the Black Sea.

*

At the ferry terminal we fell into conversation with two local men. I chatted enthusiastically about the friendliness of the people in Romania, the strength of the communities. But the men were more critical.

'We have real problems with alcohol here. A lot of men start drinking from early morning.'

I couldn't argue with that; Jamie and I had seen it for ourselves in *magazin* after *magazin*. Unemployment was a problem.
We had cycled through enough towns with streets scarred by
Ceaușescu's industrial ruins, the blackened factories quietly
returning to nature. *Stillgelegt* is the German word – disused,
closed down. There is something of eerie abandonment captured in the German that's not expressed in English – a sense
of silence and stillness, even ghostliness.

In contrast, the village communities we had ridden through
were vibrant, the streets filled with playing children and gossiping neighbours: women exchanging vegetables over garden
walls; old men huddled in groups outside a shop; a horse
and cart driver halting to speak to a friend on the roadside;
cyclists stopping to shout across the road at each other. And
almost every house had a bench outside the garden fence in the
main street, where the owners would sit in the coolness of the
evening, catching up with passing neighbours.

On the other side of the Danube, our tyres rumbled over
cobbled-stoned streets as we climbed out of the valley, the river
now on our left. The land stretched out in waves of wheat,
orchard and vine to a powder-blue sky. We had a hawk's view
of the silver snake Danube – the flash of shimmer appearing
and disappearing with the curves of the road. I felt a heaviness,
knowing the river would soon disappear from sight. It was
like leaving a lover. We had stayed faithfully with the Danube
from her beginnings at Donaueschingen way back in May.
Now, almost two months later, the river was turning northeast
towards the Danube delta while our road swung southeast then
straight across the hills to the sea.

Ahead, we could see the asphalt rising sharply, the metallic domes of Dervent Monastery flashing in the sunlight near the crest of the hill. The road sign warned of a seven per cent gradient, and we rasped our way to the monastic complex, dismounted from our bikes and entered the garden. Through the shadows of one of the buildings, I could see a black-robed monk polishing candles, the glint of gold catching the shafts of light in the entrance. Overhead a bird of prey hovered on the wing before curving off to ascend the skies. A kestrel?

As with songbirds, my father was fascinated by raptors, recording numerous sightings in his diary: *First time I've seen a hawk killing a bird at Wood Lane; back lawn*, he squeezed into the tiny space of his diary allotted to 14 August. There was only room for an asterisk to express his thrill at the killing in his own garden. He recorded other sightings of hawks later that year: at Kilmore, his townland of birth, no doubt while out in his grocery van; and in County Londonderry while visiting my brother. He also recorded sightings of kestrels: a single bird in one October and a pair a few weeks later. My father, when bright and interested, would have mourned the decline of the kestrel, so common in our Ulster landscape in the late eighties when he was writing his condensed entries.

The kestrel, which Gerard Manley Hopkins called the 'windhover', was just as much my father as the heron: keen-eyed and able to home in on those who preyed on his mind with a ruthless, sharp-tongued killing. But he also had a kestrel's stillness: watching quietly, at one with his own company, forever patient. The peace of his faith and love of nature gifted him quiet serenity in the outdoors, where he contemplated the world with love and devotion – *in the country with my God*, as he had written in his diary. Before the shutdown of his depression.

I wandered through the garden of the monastery, enjoying the stillness of this place, my father by my side again. The birdsong had all but disappeared in the heat of the Romanian summer, apart from the waders at Gruia, but my father's avian presence was with me again, circling the sky above my head.

Below the raptor and the monastery, the land dropped away to the Danube on one side and Lake Bugeacului on the other. Dervent means 'beyond the creek', a place of tranquillity caught between the waters, a perfect spot for the monks' quiet devotion. The monastery had been built just before World War Two, only to be closed down by the Communists a couple of decades later. It was taken over by a farming co-operative before the monks returned to restore the order in 1990. The sick and maimed come here to look for cures – and the touring cyclists, like us, in need of a rest before tackling the rest of the hill.

We left the monastery garden and fetched our bikes. Jamie checked the bike book for the next stage of our journey across Constanța County. While the Bible was my father's road map, the bike books were our guide across Europe – a cartographical bible, pointing the way ahead. From Rotterdam, we had worked our way through two Rhine books, five Danube books and hundreds of maps. The information we sought from the maps was always the same: How many miles were we cycling that day? What condition were the roads in? What was the weight of traffic? Where were the settlements? Did they have shops or cafés? Where could we find somewhere to sleep? And were there any significant hills?

Here in Constanța County, Jamie and I didn't have to worry about the roads: they were in good condition, yet almost devoid of traffic. Neither did we have to worry about finding food – every village had at least one *magazin*, sometimes more. Accommodation was another matter. Our last book told us there was nowhere until the city of Constanţa on the coast, a distance of almost 100 miles. Could we cover that distance in one day? The answer was no – not least because we were about to face the biggest hills of our journey yet. Could I steady my nerves then, and my fear of wild animals and imagined hatchet-wielding men, to camp out wild in the woods? Well, if I had no other choice . . . Then we heard from Stefan, several days ahead of us, who'd found a place on the edge of Ion Corvin. The day was saved by our German scout.

Other than my preoccupation with finding somewhere to sleep, my biggest map obsession was those insignificant-looking arrows on the roads. Those tiny little arrowheads meant big hills – and Jamie and I counted thirteen on the way to Ion Corvin. But somehow we made it to the *pensiunea*. Shattered, I crashed down on the bed and consulted the map for the next day ahead. There were fifty miles to conquer and the same number of arrows – only this time some of the arrows were double-headed and in heavy black. We had, in my mind, mountains to climb.

That evening, we pulled out our little camping stove to cook pasta on the veranda of the motel-style rooms. The owners knew they had a monopoly out here in this Romanian hinterland – and dared to suggest prices for food and drinks that Romanians would have laughed at, knowing the tired and hungry Western Europeans would agree to whatever they asked. There was no interest in the foreign cyclists, no connection. We were just leu signs on a piece of wheeled metal.

The next day was a helter-skelter of hills and valleys, of sweeping curves and rolling plateaus and painful ascents through crumbling limestone banks and shrub-covered slopes. On top of Constanţa County, the open spaces were intoxicating – a patchwork blanket of land that spread out in folds of faded summer colour to big skies. We followed the lines of the contours, circling ploughed fields of brown corduroy, ink-green squares of woodland and the paler ribbed-greens of crop that lay between the spread of buttery grasslands.

Then the downhills: the long curves, folding this way and that, the wind in our face, our bikes leaning into the land. But each new hill rose higher and more steeply than the one before. We pushed our bikes up through villages perched on escarpments, only stopping to buy chilled water and ice-lollies when the heat became too much. Once we paused to watch children gathered round a fountain, splashing through muddy puddles in bare feet. 'Drink! Drink! Water very good. Very good!' And they formed a ring round us in order to watch us fill our bottles as if we were some alien species.

Between the open land and ribbon villages, the road was swallowed by chestnut trees, their bases painted white against bugs and disease. Sporadic red and white road markers on the verges told us we still had far to go. Towards the end of the afternoon we crossed the motorway and dropped down to the coastal plain where the road followed the edge of the woods in a ruler straight line. We were cycling through a buffer zone between deepest rural Romania and the coastal city. Young women teetered in high heels on the kerbside between forest and road, skirts and tops barely covering their breasts and bottoms. They were the ladies of the night, touting for business in broad daylight, and their brothel was the woodland.

From the junction at Murfatlar, we crept through suburbia,

the noise of the trunk road into the city disconcerting after the quiet of the countryside, the fumes and weight of traffic unpleasant. Traffic lights, roundabouts, multi-lanes, slip roads, bridges, tower blocks, cranes all spun around me in a confusing mess. I was struggling to deal with the sensory overload.

Then in the distance I saw the Black Sea – the colour somewhere between charcoal and blue rather than black – and I realised we'd made it. Just to the south of us was Istanbul and Asia. I felt my eyes prickle and wasn't sure if it was the city dust, petrol fumes, exhaustion or joy. Perhaps it was a mix of all four.

We would have a rest in Constanța and then leave the waterways and sea behind for a while to head into the interior of Bulgaria and Turkey. But, for now, we would dip our feet in the ocean.

6. Into Bulgaria

The Black Sea was an important milestone, a body of water surrounded by lands exotic and unknown: Ukraine, Georgia and Turkey. It was the buffer zone between East and West, and between ancient and modern. In my mind, the Black Sea symbolised the merging worlds of Europe and the Orient. From here we'd cross the Balkan Mountains and it would be downhill all the way to the Sea of Marmara and Istanbul. I was wrong.

That night we slept on the outer edges of Constanța – the sea still several miles away. With anticipation we rode our bikes down to the ocean the next morning, landing at an old casino that jutted out on a promontory like an encrusted limpet on the shore. At first sight, it was an impressive building of magnificent proportions on the skyline, all arches and balustrades and massive shell-shaped windows, a mix of unrestrained baroque and the simpler curves of art nouveau. But, on drawing closer, I could see some windows boarded up, rusting ironwork and the detail in the masonry crumbling away.

Later, I found out it had been commissioned by King Carol I in Constanţa's heyday at the turn of the twentieth century, when royals and nobles would travel across Europe to stay at the fashionable seaside resort. It was to be a symbol of the city's wealth and prosperity – no expense spared. Now, the Romanian government finds it too expensive to maintain and has left it to the rats and pigeons, and the stray cats that feed off them. Photos show a place of abandoned glamour and beauty – of intricate wall murals, stained-glass windows and art deco railings. Broken glass and fallen masonry lie on the floors beneath great chandeliers. It is achingly tragic to see so much art and beauty left to collapse and decay.

I took a photo of Jamie in front of the casino before we turned around to look for a promenade café to order a celebration breakfast. We stretched out our legs under the table and enjoyed the sunshine, happy in the knowledge that we wouldn't be cycling anywhere for a while. We moved down the coast to Eforie Nord and booked ourselves into a boutique hotel for a few days. There was no hurry – we weren't due to cross into Turkey until the beginning of August and it was only 20 July.

The Black Sea was not as I had imagined in my daydreams as we'd crossed Constanţa County. The bay was filled with noisy speedboats and plastic debris, the air heavy with the smell of diesel fumes and the fat and sugar of doughnuts. The sand was all but obscured beneath the rows of deckchairs. We could have been sitting on concrete, for all I knew. Beyond the strands, the coastline was indeed covered in concrete: hotels, restaurants and souvenir shops. Jamie and I briefly swam in the syrupy water before picking our way through the blubbery bodies of Romanians and Russians – leather-faced women with rolls of fat hanging over bikini bottoms and men with swollen bellies obscuring tiny Speedos – back to the quiet sanity of our air-conditioned room. There was a sense of decay here that reminded me of Thomas Mann's *Death in Venice*.

'I think I'll die if I stay here any longer,' I said to Jamie.

'Let's go, then.'

So we packed our panniers and rode out of town, following the long, straight E675 inland and across the plains to the Bulgarian border.

*

As I'd cycled further east and south through Europe, the sense of displacement had grown. In Germany, Switzerland and Austria, the familiarity of language and culture and old friendships were the stitches holding past and present together. Those familiar places and faces along the way reminded me of who I was and where I'd come from. And so I never truly felt any sense of alienation until we reached Bratislava. In Hungary, Tom and Patrick had dropped back into our lives like a calendar reminder of a forgotten appointment as wife, mother and home-contributor. My completed family reminded me they were the fabric of my life – the warp and weft that wove us together, sewn imperfectly into a family unit, making the person I had become, at least in part. In Hungary and Serbia, after Tom and Patrick had departed, kind hosts had beckoned Jamie and me into their homes and communities, and allowed us to fix a few more stitches in the fabric of our journey.

In Romania, that essential sense of shared humanity – the tacks that held this part of the journey together – felt more fleeting and fragile: the smiling faces on horse carts as we cycled by; the children stretching out grubby hands in villages; the man reaching out with the beef tomatoes from his garden, a holding of gaze and a nod of silent communication that connected us as humans. There were other brief encounters in shops, cafés, hotels and guesthouses: a brush of skin when money and goods were exchanged, a moment's eye contact and a smattering of essential words that linked us briefly to strangers – *salut*, *mulţumesc*, *mersi*. Without them, we didn't exist.

In the end it hadn't been the dogs or the Roma or even fear of sickness or accident that had caused anxiety – but the sense of disorientation. I began to wonder if I was travelling to find myself or to lose myself, to lose my father or to find him again. I realised that tuning into the sights, sounds and smells of the journey gave me a peace my father had also found in nature. But I was also slowly coming to the realisation that living in the moment was only a solution so long as I was locked into my surroundings, engaging all my senses. At other times as I cycled along, I found myself slipping into the past, my childhood memories threading through the present journey. My father was present, first in the birds, and then in the time-frozen countryside. But still I locked down on the darker memories and thoughts, as if unlocking that door would release something unbearable. I would have to work through the past, I acknowledged, with all its light and shade, and come to the peace of acceptance – accepting others for what they were and accepting myself too. It was a revelation. Now I just needed the courage to reject that stubborn part of my brain that wouldn't let go of something that had happened a long time ago and forgive.

*

In the border town of Negru Vodă we lingered for a while. I climbed chipped concrete steps to the bank to exchange the last of my leu for Bulgarian lev, but the bank teller laughed at me as if I had asked for Mongolian tögrög rather than the currency of a place that lay a couple of miles away.

Negru Vodă had nothing going for it, just a few high-rise flats in a state of disrepair, the bank and a couple of mini-markets. It was a hick town that came to a full stop on the border. I bought some food for a picnic lunch and went outside to discover a group of Roma children circling Jamie in the hope of a few coins. We made our escape.

Apart from the twist in the road at Negru Vodă, the straight diagonal artery slashed across Romania to the border and continued on in the same fashion through Bulgaria to Dobrich. There was an inevitable pattern to the ride: fields of sunflowers followed by fields of crops and weedy burdock, followed by weedy village. At the Romanian border town, we'd still only completed the first half of our day's journey. We aimed to cycle on to the large town of Dobrich before stopping – another thirty miles ahead – but the heat was bearing down on us, making cycling exhausting.

At the border, I looked back at Romania one last time.

It had taken us two weeks to cross the country. Romania, I thought, had been like the plucking of a daisy: I love you; I love you not. I'd liked Romania as soon as we'd entered the tranquil Nera Valley, but my positive feelings had turned to horror when I saw the rubbish-lined Danube. I'd loved the unexpected beauty of the fjord-like Iron Gates, but not the stuck-in-the-past, 'do-as-we-bid' Communist tourist hotels of the Danube towns. I loved the exuberant horse-cart owners and ragamuffin kids who made us feel like royalty; the small villages alive with community, and the haystacks and brightly coloured beehives; the painted flowers and patterns of Romanian folk-art that adorned the woodwork of doors and fountains. I didn't love the gaudy Black Sea resort with its dance music pounding from showy cars and fast-food joints. My feelings shifted by the day, sometimes by the hour. But ultimately, I left Romania with warmth and affection.

In General Toshevo, we found a bank to change our leu and lingered on to eat our picnic on a park bench.

'Where are you heading?' An old man with a stick stopped shuffling along the pavement and looked from us to our laden-down bicycles with open curiosity.

'Istanbul.'

With the Turkish border less than 250 miles away now, my answer didn't seem quite as ridiculous as it had back in the Netherlands and Germany.

'Don't take the road to Dobrich. It's not interesting. Take the left turn to the Black Sea and follow the coast into Turkey. It's very nice.'

I smiled and nodded. It was too complicated to explain we had sought out the flattest route into Turkey. True, most cycling tourists stayed with the Black Sea, just as our helpful stranger was suggesting, but after Eforie I wasn't sure I would miss the coast buried under tower-block hotels and tarmac roads, no doubt jammed with Ladas, Fiats and Moskvitches and their pot-bellied owners, or new-money sports cars driven by peroxide blondes and muscle-and-medallion-bound men. I knew the coast road rose and fell with too much regularity before rising steeply to the Balkan Mountains. We'd puzzled for long enough over the problem of how to get the Tank through these mountains and we agreed that the pass between Asparuhovo and Aytos was by far the flattest route to the other side.

Now the Balkans were drawing close. General Toshevo was one of the last level towns we would cycle through before climbing into the rolling foothills and mountains. As the administrative centre of the area, it had an air of prosperity with its scrubbed-down and freshly painted offices that lay behind neat, tree-lined verges dotted with planted flowers and tidy box-hedges.

Just fifteen miles on, Dobrich was another matter. It was a city of brutalist high-rises, pushing up from the cracked concrete of roads and plazas, like straggly weeds trying to find daylight. The buildings – both futuristic and in a Cold War time warp – were squeezed into the confines of a ring-road; although 'ring-road' is too grand a name, really, for this potholed, patched lane that rose and dipped with the undulating landscape. From the bypass, minor roads climbed into the city. Hot and tired, I wondered when we would finally take one of them. At last, Jamie stopped, consulted his map, then took us up to a hotel sitting in the green of a park. I marvelled at the cheap room he had found for us with its balcony overlooking spreading trees and colourful flowerbeds. Below, we could see a swimming pool spanned by a little wooden bridge and a waterside restaurant. We had arrived in paradise. We decided to stay a second night in this oasis among the high-rises, but the hotel had other plans: it was fully booked for a wedding. There was nothing for it but to move on, deeper into the Bulgarian interior.

7. House Martins

They say that travelling broadens the mind, but in some ways the opposite is true. Travelling, by the very nature of its transience, narrows perceptions. It's looking at unfamiliar places through the confines of a lens. True, our bikes slowed us down so that we could savour it more fully, but for all of that, we were always moving on, never stopping for long, not really getting to grips with a place. At best, we were gathering ephemeral, half-formed impressions and picking up fragments along the way: a field of waving corn, bright sunflower heads, a half smile in a shadowy doorway, a blur of bicycle, the clip-clop of hoof, the taste of wood smoke, the chirrup of cricket, the thrump of wood pigeon on the wing, or the fading out of birdsong. Our view of a country was formed by the thin strip of road that led through it, by the places we chose to pause in and by the strangers who wandered in and out of our line of vision.

Travel is a fleeting response to fleeting moments. It's not only a narrow lens, but also a filter. For me the Netherlands was orange-bright; Germany, a pastel rainbow; Switzerland, silver mists; Austria, gold; Slovakia, beige speckled with child-bold primaries; Hungary, paprika-red; Croatia, the colour of pain; Serbia, the yellow of heat; and Romania, the moss-green of folk-art and haycarts. Bulgaria was grey.

Perhaps if we had taken a different route, travelled through at a different time of year, or stopped in a different place, the colour chosen for Bulgaria would have been brighter. As it was, Bulgaria had the same crumbling towns of grey concrete as Romania, with villages of rusting wrought-iron fencing and peeling paint. But here there were no waving horse-and-cart drivers, no grinning children lining rural streets, no villagers gathered round squares and greens or in front of shop windows. Even Dobrich was a ghost-city, with its higgledy-piggledy offices and shops that seemed to stagger on the hill with us, as we cranked our knees into action in the hazy start-of-day light.

The ripples that had ebbed out across the land from Eforie on the Black Sea towards Dobrich became waves as we headed deeper into rural Bulgaria. There were long downhills and knee-twinging, lung-sanding uphills. There were villages of strangely empty streets. I thought it must be a Sunday, but then remembered it was Saturday. Where was everyone?

The heat was thickening. Just outside Dolina, Jamie dropped a large bottle of water, spilling half its contents. Further on, feeling dehydrated, he flung his bicycle to the ground and flopped down under a tree on a scrubby piece of no man's land at the edge of Cerventi. I fed him biscuits until his head stopped reeling and we could carry on to the village shop. We bought supplies and sat down next to a large concrete building that also seemed to function as some kind of Communist-era municipal hall. At another village we rested outside a municipal building that was a clone of the one in Cervenți – with the same large windows upstairs, presumably serving as a function room. Male youths loitered round the shop, looking bored: unemployment was high in this part of Bulgaria.

With relief we reached the town of Vetrino, where there was a bank in the dug-up square – we were almost out of cash. Every village or town in Bulgaria seemed to have a square that, like the municipal halls, had a disproportionate sense of importance in an otherwise ramshackle settlement. We lingered for fridge-cold drinks and ice cream. I didn't have the energy to cycle any further, but there was no accommodation here, so we pushed on to higher ground where we knew there was a guesthouse in the village of Nevsha, stuffed into the hole of a hillside. It didn't matter that it was eight miles off our route, and that we'd have to cycle up into the hills, it was still preferable to wild camping.

Jamie took a left turn onto a narrow lane that climbed stead-ily, table-top escarpments stepping the plains in the distance. Beyond, the land fell away to Varna and the Black Sea. As the sun dropped through the sky, its low-level rays washing the countryside in a dusty grey-white, we followed the road along the base of the hillside, asphalt giving way to the scrubby fields below. There was no sound as we pedalled other than the rustle of vegetation. It felt as if we had left civilisation far behind – until we heard the hum of traffic and crossed the A2 motorway leading to the coast. Finally, the road curved and dropped steeply to reveal Nevsha.

There was nothing to indicate a guesthouse – just a few houses hidden behind high walls and single-storied houses of exposed brick and breeze block and sagging roofs, mingling with more pristine paint-fresh homes. We asked a couple where the guesthouse was. The man searched in his mobile and shook his head. We continued steeply downhill into an increasingly dilapidated village devoid of life. Some buildings were collapsing into the earth, while others lay shuttered, or half-abandoned, roof tiles gathered at their feet like a discarded slip. 'Are you sure it was this village?' I asked Jamie. It was beginning to look like we'd have to find a sheltered spot on the hillside.

We turned our bikes and climbed back up through the upper part of the village. A man appeared from a house further up the hill and pointed to a high wall near the crest of the hill. We weren't hopeful, but when we reached the wall and pushed open a door and shouted hello, a small rounded woman with raven hair bounded out of the outdoor kitchen terrace, closely followed by a Labrador with matching black coat. She strode across the lawn of the garden, wiping her hands on her sides before stretching out a hand. 'Welcome. Yes indeed, this is Villa Elma. Yes, we have rooms free. Please, sit down. Have a drink first and we'll show you the rooms.'

I sat down at the table under the covered terrace and breathed out.

*

'You have to come and look,' said Martin, our Dutch landlord and a farmer who owned the guesthouse with his Bulgarian partner, Amelia. 'He just left everything behind. Everything!'

Martin limped across the lawn, slightly bent despite his strong build, one shoulder ahead of the other as if he'd lifted one too many potato sacks in his life. He moved with an impressive pace and energy in spite of it. Martin had a finger in all sorts of agricultural business pies (or fields), including a farm in Zeeland, as well as consultancy and investment work. He had lived in Bulgaria for years, working with various ex-Soviet countries in farming, and he spoke Russian. Martin met Amelia through an online dating agency and they were well matched, for she was also a successful businesswoman and accountant. The guesthouse property in Nevsha had been another invest-ment. They'd bought the house, built by an Englishman, and the grounds that came with it, in order to build a larger villa alongside the original house. Martin and Amelia lived in the Englishman's house and rented out the tastefully furnished rooms in the new villa.

'This way,' Martin said, leading me past the swimming pool and into the older house. He beckoned me into the living room and swept his arm around the room. 'All of this belonged to the Englishman. Every piece of furniture, even the contents of the drinks cabinet here.' He opened it up to show me the rows of spirits and pulled out a bottle of brandy. 'Would you like it?'

I wondered if Martin offered all his guests a gift from the previous owner.

He opened a drawer in the dated wall cabinet. 'Look, here. All these CDs are his! He didn't even take his music collection.'

'Why did he leave so suddenly?'

'I think he was ill. He just left with two suitcases and the clothes on his back. Maybe there's more to it. Perhaps he'd been unlucky in love. Who knows.' Martin closed the drawer again. 'I contacted him to ask if he wanted any of his stuff. He wrote back and said he had no need for any of it – that I could do with it as I wanted.' Martin grinned. 'So we just live with all of the

Englishman's belongings. It's like living in someone else's house ... or in a museum.'

*

Jamie and I spent a second day in the villa. Even at this higher altitude, the heat was intense. I sat on a sun lounger and watched house martins glide over the surface of the swimming pool, searching for insects. They swooped low over the water, both precision-bombers and ballerinas of the sky. Their wings, feet and beaks barely disturbed the surface, only occasionally causing a delicate ripple as they snatched at the flies hovering over the pool.

Observing the birds, I recalled the house martins at Oxford Island beside Lough Neagh. I'd gone there with my father just after the chironomid flies had hatched in their thousands, maybe millions. The midges were notorious around the Lough. In the breeding season, they swarmed the shores of the water, driving the Lough folk insane. I'd run through the insects screaming, causing them to rise up in a cloud of dizzy black. I learned to shut my mouth after swallowing a mouthful of the tiny creatures. They were harmless though, for the unfortunate mouthless insects could neither bite nor feed and were doomed to a handful of mating days before perishing.

On that visit with my father, there had been an infestation of the midges. I had never seen anything like it: the sky was black, while the surfaces of information boards and bird hides were covered in the writhing insects. The air was thick with house martins, too, swooping and bombing – a flash of black, a swipe of underbelly white. What a banquet for the house martins – more food than they could ever gorge on. Later, I'd returned there with Tom, the eaves of the newly built Kinnego Discovery Centre drooping nests made from mud pellets and compacted together with grass, hair and feather found by the industrious house martins.

After my father had moved into the care home, I'd taken him back to the Lough. 'What's that bird?' I'd asked him, wanting to rouse him from his inner world. He shifted his head slowly as if the weight of his thoughts were too heavy for his body and answered in a flat monotone voice before retreating again. Not long after, the psychiatrist called me into his office.

'It's not looking good for your father. There are some quite serious issues here.' He pushed a piece of paper over to me. 'Look at this clock I asked him to draw for me. The numbers are muddled – back to front, mixed up. This should be a simple exercise.'

I recognised the light, economical pen marks as my father's. He'd drawn pictures for me when I was small: sketchy, three-dimensional houses, birds and animals. Cats. He had the makings of an artist, but he never did much more than doodle. After his depression set in, I gave him paints and an art pad for Christmas, hoping they would help to bring him back to life. But they sat on the living room sideboard untouched. I felt angry he had chosen to leave us, despite all our efforts. As if there had been a choice for him – I, of all people should have understood this.

'It's not safe for him to be at home,' the psychiatrist had said. 'There are parts of the brain that are damaged beyond repair, dead.' He spoke with a clinical precision, his voice cold. 'Some of his behaviour is bizarre, anti-social – that part of the brain is badly damaged. He needs to be in permanent care.'

Now, here at Nevsha, the house martins skimmed elegantly over the water. My father would have enjoyed these streamlined birds when he was still strong and bright and flawed and human – before he began to fade in and out, becoming increasingly distant. We first lost him the year Tom and I got married, when depression shut him down completely. The hospital staff told us the shock treatment would jumpstart him back to life. It didn't work, although they promised us it would; promised us that even though it was an extreme treatment, *and yes, seems cruel,* it would bring him back to us.

They were wrong.

My father came and went like the martins, communicating less and less as the years went on, becoming as dull as tarnished silver. Once, quite unexpectedly, he'd said, 'That shock treatment: I shouldn't have had it. My brain doesn't work properly any more. It's made me stupid.'

All afternoon I sat by the pool, watching the house martins flittering in and out of my vision. I had experienced my father's depression. I could see what it does to a person. I still had to fight the shadows. When I was outside, the darkness slipped away. My depression was diagnosed as moderate, downgraded to mild (by my own reassessment). Now it was barely detectable – but always lurking in the background, threatening to creep up from behind when I thought it gone for good. I'd thrown the pills away and allowed the outdoors to heal me. But I couldn't spend the rest of my life on the road, could I?

While the open road was my saviour, my father turned his back on the outside world and his birds. He sat in the shadows, even clothed himself in them. He stopped going out. But it wasn't a choice. I saw that now. Severe depression is a much greater beast to fight. My father, the man who hated hospitals, realised how desperate things were when he checked himself in. There was nowhere else to go.

As the sun dropped through the Bulgarian summer sky, I idly wondered what Jamie was doing. I imagined he was indoors, crouched over his phone, lost in his own electronic world. Jamie, my constant companion for this entire spring and summer, would soon be going off to university. When this trip was over, he would dip in and out of my life like the martins by the pool. I had lost my father bit by bit, and I would lose Jamie too. But that was okay. He would migrate south with the house martins, albeit only as far as Wales, not Africa. Life is coming and going, ephemeral and transient. Nothing remains the same. And I knew now I was wrong to reduce my father to one dreadful night in our kitchen that had taken place so long ago.

8. Stranded in the Balkan Mountains

The sun was a blood-orange segment on the crest of the hill as we cycled out of Nevsha; its rays a blush spreading out across the curve of the hill as it welcomed another day. At the junction of the slip road it was tempting to drop onto the A2 motorway. After all, the sign forbad tractors, not bicycles, and it would cut down the distance to Provadia. There wouldn't be much traffic at six in the morning and we could cycle on the hard shoulder. I hesitated, then cycled on, my law-abiding self resisting the temptation.

In the early morning half-light, we stopped at a village fountain to fill up our water bottles, slyly observed by an elderly man in black trousers and a grey-washed, collarless shirt. He leaned casually against a stone wall, watching us with a mixture of curiosity and wariness, his small eyes almost lost in the bulge of skin above his cheekbones and a half-smile playing across his face. He didn't speak – and neither did we. It was as if the stillness of dawn demanded the reverential quiet of a dimly lit church.

As we cycled towards Provadia I was lost in the rhythm of the horse-pulling cart ahead of us when I heard a sharp, metallic clatter that echoed round the hillside. A man flew down the hill, shuddering on a clapped-out bike.

'Did you see that?' Jamie said, looking after the cyclist in astonishment.

'See what?'

'There were no tyres on his bicycle! He was riding on the metal wheel rim!'

We settled into a topographic pattern: rise, plateau and drop. The downhills were ecstasy, a respite from the heat – a flow of oxygen that cut through the thick treacle of hot air. And on the plateaus, we could spin the wheels hard enough to at least agitate the atmosphere. But the long slow inclines pushed our body temperatures up, and my face turned an inelegant scarlet.

We stopped in a layby near Komarevo to eat crisps, replenishing the salt we had lost sweating up the hill, gratefully resting in the shade from the pines at the side of the road. As we stood on the melting tarmac, a puppy emerged from the trees, followed by a second. Then a kitten slipped out from the undergrowth, and another and another, until we were surrounded by skinny cats and the two dogs. The cats meowed and sniffed around the crumbs of crisps that had fallen from our shared bag, disdainful of our unintentional offerings in spite of their hunger. I looked around but could see no buildings – just woodland and fields. Was there a farmhouse hidden from sight? Had the animals been dumped here, unwanted? We would never know.

I remembered how my father had taken a sack of newborn kittens to the stream at the bottom of the field nearby, grimly pushing the writhing creatures under the water until their mewing ceased. At home, the mother had roamed from room to room, crying in distress as she searched for her babies. I too had felt distressed. 'Why?' I had asked my father, but he hadn't answered. And I'd puzzled over his cruelty, knowing his love for animals. It was the first crack in the harmony of my childhood.

At the crest of the hill, we stopped on the sweep of a bend to take in the meadow and dark copses that dropped away to Tsonevo Reservoir in the distant haze. The pale body of water curled through the hills, our end-point for the day. We could see our route mapped out in front of us in three dimensions. If we had been birds, we could have swooped down in minutes – or so it felt. As it was, we flew down the hill on our bicycles and on into Dalgopol.

It seemed nothing could stop us that day as the wheels of our bikes spun through the hills in spite of the heat, but just as we were approaching the reservoir, we heard a sound we knew only too well: the quiet, high-pitched ping of a broken spoke. We thought of returning to Dalgopol to look for a bike shop but our hotel was tantalisingly close. Alternatively, we could forge on through the Balkan Mountains to the town on the other side, less than thirty miles away. After all, Jamie had cycled a good distance with a broken spoke in Romania. Plus, there was a better chance of finding a bike workshop in the bigger town of Aytos. Since it was unlikely there'd be a bicycle repair store in the handful of mountain villages we were cycling through, it would be a risk. Nonetheless we decided to cycle on.

It was a foolish decision.

*

The two sisters at the reservoir hotel filled our palms with fruit from the garden – plums, peaches and pears.

'For you and your son,' the older sister said.

'For the journey through the mountains,' the younger sister said, tipping more fruit into our hands. A darker, sharper, stick-like version of her plump sister, she darted around us in tiny birdlike movements, watching to ensure we did not bruise the fruits as we packed them into the panniers of our bicycles.

Beyond the garden, splashed with blood-red oleander, the early-morning milk of the Tsonevo Reservoir glowed pale in the hills. And, on the skyline, a buttery dawn spread across the Stara Planina, the Old Mountain – the first of the Bulgarian Balkans, where we were heading. As we prepared to leave, the stillness of the waterside garden was only broken by the zing of mosquito and the murmur of distant Bulgarian. Not many passed this way, just a handful of travellers and the occasional fisherman who preyed on the bream, perch and catfish lurking in the depths of the Tsonevo.

With the panniers secured, the sisters took it in turn to have their photograph taken with us, then clutched our hands like a pair of fussing grandmothers. They were still shouting their good wishes for the journey as we wheeled our bikes up the stony lane and out of sight.

On the main road, Jamie nursed his bike around the pot-holes that pocked the tarmac, the wheel delicate and slightly wobbly. To make matters worse, my brake had started to rub against the front wheel. I unclipped it: somehow, I'd manage with just the back brake. I'd have to go easy on the downhills – unfortunate, as there was the long, steep descent into Aytos. To compound all this, I discovered my lowest gear wasn't work-ing, not great either for the biggest climb of our journey since leaving Rotterdam.

A defective wheel, brake and gear: it wasn't the best time to be heading into the Luda Kamchia Gorge and over the Aytos Pass, a wilderness broken only by a handful of scruffy mountain villages. Our mechanical problems, however, were quickly for-gotten as we crossed the causeway that sliced above the Tsonevo Reservoir. The sun had just broken the crest of the mountain ridge, flood-lighting the limestone that flanked the reservoir. Beneath us, the banks of the Tsonevo cut a line of symmetry, inverting the sun-warmed limestone in a glassy film of water. The shadows lay deep, the light sharp.

We cycled on, the loftier railway bridge on the right drew a parallel line with our road, while on the left, chalk-white columns of limestone rose from the far bank of the Tsonevo like giant stalagmites. The ascent was still easy, the air holding onto the moisture from last night's rainstorm. Thick vegetation dripped dewdrops. I felt the mountains drawing me on, even as I feared the ascent with the Tank.

My love of high places had started as a young child when I'd stared out of my bedroom window to the Dromara Hills. In the fields beyond my house, I'd catch glimpses of the Mournes on clear days, higher, more majestic. They begged to be climbed. Later, my brothers would take me with them to scale the peaks along the Mourne Wall – the rocky-topped Binnian and Bearnagh – and traverse the paths that criss-crossed the range. They had strange and romantic names, such as the Brandy Pad and the Devil's Coach Road. There were other landmarks that paid homage to fowl and bird: Pigeon Rock, Buzzard's Roast and the Cock and Hen. On top of Slieve Donard, the highest mountain in Northern Ireland, I saw yet more mountains that called to me across the Irish Sea to the Isle of Man, the Lake District and Wales. A wider world was reaching out to me.

Once, I'd set out with my father from Newcastle to climb up through forest and glen to the mountain valley that rises up to the saddle between Commedagh and Donard. My father had looked at his shiny dress shoes and the rough track beyond the gate that headed up the valley and hesitated.

'Let's go on,' I pleaded with him.

I could see in his eyes that he too was drawn to the mountains in front of us. Then he gazed at the wall of scree and rock below the saddle and shook his head. 'Best get back.'

I'd thought him timid and unadventurous back then, but he must also have thought of my mother, down in the town, waiting for us in his cousin's house. My father's horizons were pulled in again.

*

Jamie and I carried on along the Kamchiya Valley, listening to the tinkle of water and feeling the dampness of mountain dew on our skin – just as I'd experienced on the River Glen below

Donard with my father. Then it happened again: another ping –
a second spoke. I looked ahead at the road as it headed up into
the mountains. How would Jamie's bicycle bear up with two
broken spokes and the stress on the back wheel as we climbed?
We cycled on in troubled silence, no longer appreciating the
song of the river or the cooling balm of mountain air.

And the ping came again: a third spoke. I sighed. To cycle
on three broken spokes would put too much stress on the
wheel. Jamie and I dismounted from our bikes and contemplated the long walk to Aytos, still twenty miles on the other
side of the pass. I opened my pannier, to get the map and
figure out our options, and found the hoteliers' fruit. Biting
into a peach, the sweet juice hit my tastebuds in a burst of
flavour. Above us, the hillside bounced with the call of a
shepherd. I lay down on the grass verge and closed my eyes,
forgetting the broken spokes for a moment, just savouring the
soft flesh of the fruit, our gift from the Bulgarian sisters.

'What shall we do?' Jamie was asking.

'Let's walk up to the next village and see if we can get help.'

What sort of help, I wasn't sure. The road that had been
devoid of traffic at dawn was now slowly filling up with traffic,
mainly white vans. I looked at the back doors and thought how
easy it would be to slip in two bicycles. Could we thumb a lift
with two bicycles? Would anyone stop? Was it wise anyway?

So we continued on, my eye on the buildings tumbling off
the hillside, the village appearing and disappearing with the
twists and turns of the road until, at last, we reached Daskotna.
We found a typical Balkan village store and I started to tell the
shopkeeper about our problem, but then noticed his eyes were
uncomprehending. He didn't speak English.

I made circular movements with my fists to indicate pedalling. The shopkeeper frowned. I touched the wire of a vegetable rack then drew the shape of a wheel in the air, spokes radiating from the centre, saying 'ping, ping, ping' as I pushed finger and thumb apart. The shopkeeper looked from me to the door as if hoping someone would come and rescue him from the mad foreigner.

Then a look of comprehension, followed by, '*Ah, ah, ah. Da.*'

Somehow, he'd understood my desperate sign language and he followed me outside to see the 'air wheel' in reality. He held up his finger in a 'wait' motion and waved a mobile with his other hand. He spoke at length into the phone then handed it over.

'You are with my uncle. You have a broken bicycle?'

'Yes.'

'Please, don't worry. The minibus can take your bicycle. It will come at twelve-thirty.'

'Twelve-thirty!' It wasn't even nine in the morning. We settled down for the long wait on the outside bench when the shopkeeper reappeared. He handed the phone to me again.

'Hello?'

'I'm sorry the minibus is too small for two bicycles. It can't take you to Aytos.'

These were the kind of obstacles that filled my mind with worry before we'd left England. But here on the road, I was learning that with every obstacle there is a solution. The shopkeeper's nephew phoned back.

'My uncle has organised someone to take you to Aytos. You pay him thirty lev. Okay?'

I imagined one of the white transit vans that were so

plentiful on the road, but when our skinny rescuer in frayed shirt and ripped trousers arrived, he had a clapped-out estate covered in boils of rust. He grabbed the bikes and slung them into the boot, indicating that I should squeeze into the small space beside the bikes and panniers. I refused and climbed into the front with Jamie. The driver shrugged, running dirt-ingrained fingertips through a tangle of woolly hair. He jumped into the driver's seat and turned the key in the ignition. The car shuddered to life and the stench of exhaust fumes filled the vehicle. He offered us cigarettes, then chewing gun, before shooting off at speed, dust flying up from the unmade road.

The estate ate up the miles at a ridiculous pace after the months of leisurely cycling – buildings and landmarks shooting by in a fuzzy blur. Then our driver slammed on the brakes.

'*Politsai!*'

He did a quick U-turn on the road and drove into a petrol station, indicating again that I should go into the boot. There was no arguing this time. I squeezed under the bikes, and we set off once more, past the policemen who, seemingly concerned about three in the front, were less troubled by the lack of seatbelts or the exhaust smoke that would have had the car impounded in most other places.

From now on, my view was of sky, ridge and treetop. I could sense gravity pulling the car down to Aytos – until we came to a sudden halt outside a small bike shop in a side street. The shop owner and his wife pulled our bikes out of the car and onto the pavement, where they started to check them over.

'Come back two hours. All done.'

Jamie and I found a square and sat down on a bench to

eat our rolls. I watched two toddlers play with their toy cars on a low wall beside a fountain while their mothers gossiped with friends among the prams. I tried to imagine an alternative existence in this Balkan town caught in the shadows of the mountains, but couldn't.

When we returned to the bike shop, the bicycles were ready as promised: six spokes and a tyre replaced on Jamie's bike; my brake and gear sorted.

'Old tyre not good,' said the shop owner with a disapproving frown. 'From India. Bad. Dangerous.'

I nodded contritely.

'Where you buy it?'

'Romania.'

'Romanian bike shops no good.'

It was too complicated to explain how I'd searched for a tyre in a small Romanian village, grateful for any tyre that would fit, so I smiled my agreement.

'All good,' the owner's wife said. 'Here, for you.' She handed us a set of lights.

I was grateful for their thorough service and repairs, and for the gift.

'Strong spokes now – but bags too heavy.'

In retrospect, we should have bought front as well as back panniers. Too late now: we'd continue on and hope for the best. Cycling out of Aytos, we were relieved to be back on the bikes. Ahead, the road climbed with the thermostat. The temperature was pushing forty degrees, the yellow sun sickening. We stopped at a roadside taverna, packed with locals eating stew. I wondered how they could eat the steaming food in the heat of the afternoon sun. We managed ice cream, pushing our bodies against the eaves of the building on the outside terrace, trying to catch the thin strip of shade.

On the bikes again, the hill ahead went on forever. My head began to fuzz. It was a gradual incline, long and shallow, yet my legs felt like they were pushing wheels of concrete.

'I've got to get off the bike,' I said to Jamie, and crawled into the vegetation on the roadside, trying to find its shade. Now it was Jamie's turn to feed me biscuits, along with sun-warmed water.

Somehow, I made it to Karnobat and our park-side hotel. I ordered a bottle of wine on the terrace and waited for the sun's clawing heat to retreat. Tomorrow was my birthday. We would have a day off and finish the wine. We would ward off the evil eye of the sun in the cave of our air-conditioned room. We'd come out in the evening, like vampires when the shadows were falling.

9. Birthday Blues

The nausea began late in the morning of my birthday, building up in waves like the Bulgarian landscape. My stomach fisted into a ball of pain and I retched and retched, my body heaving, but nothing. Then relief as I brought up the contents of my stomach. Before the process started all over again.

Happy birthday: the messages rolled in on my mobile, but I felt miserable. By evening, I was still retching, although there was nothing left to bring up but water and saliva.

The next morning, Jamie brought me dry toast from the hotel kitchen. I sent him down again to book another night and curled up in bed, weak and full of self-pity. For the first time, I wanted to go home. Sofia was just over three hours away by coach. The temptation to abandon the bikes and fly back to England was hard to push away. I drifted in and out of sleep, only to get up once in a while to retch over the toilet bowl yet again. Outside, I could hear children playing in the park, giggles and cries just audible over the hum of the air-conditioning, their shouts of delight mixed with the conspiratorial soft voices that children use to invent worlds.

And in those fitful dreams, where reality and fantasy and past and present blur, I too was a child again, back in my lumpen bed with some childhood illness – chickenpox or measles, perhaps – and my father standing over me with a bottle of Lucozade, speaking softly. He'd pour me a glass and pass it to me. My father's concern, the sound of fizz, the sharp burst of sweet, sticky foam on my hot tongue – that combination was the best medicine. My mother, in comparison, had little patience for sick children who got in the way of her daily cleaning, but she would come in to my room to remake the bed, roughly pulling the sheet and blankets tight around my body until I felt I was encased in a cool cocoon. There were cold mornings of illness, when I could see my hot breath steaming against the chilled air, my bedroom scraping together just a few degrees in the single-glazed room without heating.

'Turn the air-con off,' I muttered to Jamie, shivering under the duvet as the children's voices outside the hotel window faded away.

In those winter days of childhood illness, there would be silence, except for the distant hum of the Hoover and the sombre song of a solitary robin somewhere. There were summer illnesses, too, when the room was filled with the blackbirds' sweet melody or the neighbour's homing pigeons rhythmically cooing like a soft heartbeat.

My parents never said they loved me, but their love for me was present in the everyday: in the proffered Lucozade and remade bed; my mother clothing me with her own knitted and sewn creations and feeding me up with her rounds of Friday baking. It was there in woodland and field walks with my father, foraging and flower-picking, cricket games on the beach and the shared bags of chips on the way home. And when my father waited for me in his green grocery van outside the school gates on wet days. It was a mutual love. What went wrong? My heart running cold? *That night*, unspoken of in my family, but always with me – a hammer blow. What had happened that night I had carried with me into adulthood, the darkness and heaviness of my knowledge weighing me down. My siblings had responded differently. They'd rewritten the narrative of that evening into something more palatable, I sensed, something that fitted with their romanticised view of our childhood. Who could blame them? Isn't that what we humans do? Rewrite the narratives of our lives to create a world we want to present to others and wish for ourselves? Isn't it how we protect ourselves from pain? But I, I had to be out of step, disrupting the equilibrium of our family, brutally honest with myself and others – no matter how much pain it caused.

*

On 31 July, I woke up having had enough of hotel walls.

'I think I can continue,' I said to Jamie. 'I think I can make it to Yambol. It's just over thirty miles. What do you think?'

We crept out of the hotel at dawn and reclaimed our bicycles beside the rubbish bins at the back of the building. I still felt wobbly and was thankful for the long, straight road that led, mostly level, alongside vineyards, where bags and coats were slung surreally over posts on the edges of fields. Large signs rose from the bushes announcing Chardonnays and Muscats with pictures of bunched grapes and slender bottles of wine.

On the edge of Yambol, we cycled past rickety buildings with windows covered in plastic sheeting, while on the other side of the road, shacks of corrugated tin and wood lay low in the ground alongside the pavement verges, the makeshift homes not much more luxurious than a pig house. Further in, there was a mix of dilapidated concrete blocks and broken pavements. I was shocked to see this level of poverty in a European country.

We reached our hotel by ten-thirty and spent the first part of the morning on the terrace before booking in. I still felt weak and had no appetite, but I was determined not to take any more public transport. Besides, Elhovo, the border town with Turkey, was tantalisingly close – a mere twenty-three miles away. I could manage that.

In Elhovo, our accommodation was located above a DIY shop and we booked in at a counter stacked with cables and work tools. That evening, we ate in one of the restaurants – my first meal since the eve of my birthday. After days of only hearing Bulgarian, I was surprised when two Englishmen sat down at one of the tables. They had just arrived in Elhovo after driving across the continent over four days.

'Four days!' I exclaimed. 'It has taken us three months to cycle here!'

The men laughed.

'And why here?' I asked.

'We found a house we liked on the internet. Elhovo is cheap. The weather's good, and we could buy a house for a few thousand pounds.'

I couldn't imagine anyone wanting to live in this quiet border town with Yambol as its nearest point of civilisation. Even the Black Sea and Burgas were over an hour away by car. 'Have you spent time in Bulgaria before?'

'No, never. We hadn't even seen the house until today.'

'So, you've been learning Bulgarian, I guess?'

'We were going to learn the language but we're discovering everyone seems to speak English.'

I pondered this. It hadn't been our experience. English was rudimentary, even in the hotels and restaurants. I wondered how the men would integrate into the community when the level of spoken English covered the weather and the most basic of everyday platitudes.

'Well,' I said doubtfully, 'I suppose you could always go back home if you don't like it.'

'Oh no, that's not possible. I've sold my house there – I can't afford to go back,' one of the men said.

It was an astonishing act of abandonment and I wondered how they would find this small border town in the depths of the harsh Balkan winter.

Back in our room, we discovered the fridge didn't work and we had to down our yoghurt drinks that were meant for breakfast. Worse, the light didn't work, meaning we had to grope around in the dark, using the torchlight on our mobiles. We managed to pack up in the darkness of the pre-dawn. This was our habit now: slipping onto the road before the heat of the day.

Just a few miles out of town, we saw our first sign for Istanbul – our endpoint there in blue and white. Even closer was the border with Turkey, a handful of miles away now. Our eleventh and final country, excluding our coffee stop in France, was within reach.

We climbed the summit of the last Bulgarian hill and turned a corner to see the Turkish flag flapping in the breeze high above the queues of lorries, petrol stations and shops. Jamie and I stopped to message Tom with the news we had made it to the Turkish border.

The way through Bulgaria had remained stubbornly grey through my filtered lens: the grey of concrete; the grey of expressionless faces in restaurants and hotels. But there had been splashes of colour: the blood-orange sun of Nevsha and the bright Dutch farmer; the deep-pink hues of fuchsia and oleander and the warm smiles of the sisters in the Tsonevo Reservoir garden; the fresh wet green of the Kamchiya Valley.

At the border controls, I fetched out the Turkish visas that had lain at the bottom of my pannier since Rotterdam at the beginning of May. It was the second of August.

TURKEY

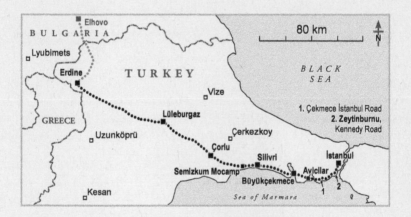

1. Into Turkey

It was the colour after the grey, so bright it dazzled
Tangy orange
Avocado green
Tomato red
Midnight blue
Sunflower yellow

It reminded me of a time long ago when I'd spent a winter in the Swiss Alps, the luminous green of the spring-melt had dazzled my eyes after months of monochrome snow and sky.

While my father hadn't wanted me to leave for Switzerland, he'd accepted my decision. The week before I left, he'd asked me if I would drive to Clare Glen with him. We'd walked along the banks of the River Cusher, dark with hazel, oak and ash, the steep ground beneath the trees covered in bluebells and wood anemone, both of us aware that I would probably never return home. As we followed the river, we listened to the fresh spring song of dunnock filling the air, my head light with thoughts of new beginnings, my father's head bowed with the weight of my departure.

How many miles had we walked side by side before our paths diverged? My father, unable or unwilling to move from the place he'd taken up residence inside his head; me, to travel to far-flung places.

Now I was edging towards Asia.

At first, the changes between Bulgaria and Turkey were almost imperceptible. Topography and geology don't always recognise borders: there was the same scrubbed, whitened land, the same rolling hills and fields of sun-dried crops. The colour would come later.

We pushed up the wide four-lane carriageway away from the border and past a ribbon-town of articulated lorries parked up on the roadside. Despite the waves of land rolling across to Edirne, riding the rises along the D535 was easy in the partial cloud. For the first time since Karnobat, I was experiencing the joy of cycling again, and I felt physically strong and psychologically in the right headspace. I reflected back on my fears at the beginning of the journey: would I be fit enough? How would I cope with aching limbs? Now cycling had become such an established part of my everyday routine I hadn't thought about the effect it was having on my body, but here on the D535 I realised there were no sore limbs, not even an aching bottom (as a friend had teased me about). Cycling, unlike walking, is kind to muscles and joints. I had lost weight, too, although I wasn't sure if it was because of the exercise or because of the fierce heat that suppressed my appetite. Spending long days in the fresh air, strengthening muscles and breathing deeply on the inclines, had made me fit and healthy. And I was walnut-brown from spending so much time in the sun.

As we turned a corner I saw two women on the bend of the road, dressed in niqabs and long black robes, dark among the pale fields of wheat: this was Turkey, not Bulgaria. But it was the colour of Edirne's cityscape after the grey of Bulgaria that made me feel as if I was emerging from the shadows into bright sunlight. First the apartment blocks on the town's skyline, followed by the shopping streets and the wares spilled out onto the pavements. And, finally, the people. All filled with colour.

We dropped off the plateau, the hillside town tipping us down through chaotic streets towards the river valley. The smell of lemons filled the air, along with the aroma of koftas cooking and spicy aubergine. We sped past stores selling everything from shoes and fabric to magazines and tobacco, leather-faced, hawk-eyed owners eyeing the town from child-sized wooden seats on the pavement.

We found our hostel down a quiet side street, the city noise reduced to a murmur, only interrupted by the cries of a fruit vendor as he wheeled his barrow past us, piled high with watermelons. We chained our bicycles up in the hostel's little courtyard and went in search of food, finding a side street of restaurants that sold nothing but deep-fried battered liver and hot chillies and plates of beef tomatoes.

Edirne was a messy, chaotic city. Hens negotiated tourists and townspeople in the pedestrianised thoroughfare, while skinny cats fought for scraps under tables and chairs so tiny they looked as if they came from a children's nursery. Along the streets, the burble of street fountains mingled with the hum of human voices and meows of kittens. Shop fronts lining the cobbled precinct were topped with structures of wood – a strange muddle of steeply sloping, carved and balconied mountain huts in the sky. In amongst the jumble of streets, the needles of minarets punctured the burnt blue sky, the curve of mosque domes soft against the sharp elbows of buildings. We took refuge from the midday sun in the Selimiye Mosque, the swirling patterns of carpet and tile and painted ceiling in among the white stone reflecting the colour and chaos of the town.

At dawn the next day we unchained our bikes in the court-yard and wheeled them out onto the empty side street, the town still asleep. With trepidation, I followed Jamie on to the wide carriageway of the D100. I'd read of the horrors of this main artery feeding into Istanbul – a monster of a road choked with aggressive traffic that smoked and fumed and spat at cyclists.

*

'Hang on. I'm coming over!'

The Romanian had been cycling in the opposite direction, northwest from Istanbul. He'd stopped on the far side of the carriageway and shouted over the four lanes of traffic, his words almost swallowed up by the rumble of wheel and throb of engine. He stood on the hard shoulder, his thick neck protrud-ing like a turtle as he scanned the road for a space in the steady stream of articulated lorries and vans speeding past. Then he ran, springing lightly over the central divide with thin, sinewy legs.

'Where are you guys going? And where have you been?'

He seemed as excited to see us as I was to see him – for we'd not encountered a single touring cyclist on the road since Constanţa County in Romania.

'Istanbul.' With every month, week and day, the word sounded less ridiculous.

'Istanbul . . . I'd think carefully about cycling into the city. It's dangerous. A tourist cyclist was killed on the D100 close to the city centre just the other week. It's better to take the bus.'

I relayed the cyclist's warning to Tom over the phone that evening.

'Take the bus? You can't do that! You can't cycle all the way across Europe then take the bus into Istanbul. What an anti-climax that would be.'

I listened, understanding the sense of his words, yet un-believing that my cautious, risk-adverse husband was willing to throw us to the lions – or the infamous Istanbul traffic. I teased him that he was trying to get rid of Jamie and me.

In truth, the D100 was not as horrific at this point as I'd imagined. The road was wide, the hard shoulder generous, the traffic still moderate and the articulated lorries slow enough that I didn't have the sensation that I was going to be sucked under their wheels, unlike the road feeding into Drobeta-Turnu Severin. Perhaps the Romanian cyclist had been exaggerating the dangers.

As we cycled on, the residue of night-time cooling quickly surrendered to the heat of the sun. The heat haze shimmered on the road ahead of us and the troughs and crests rose and fell with increasing frequency, the tidal wave of tarmac threatening to exhaust me. Outside Lüleburgaz, the D100 rose yet higher, the wall of road climbing to the sky. I slipped off my bike and pushed it up the hill – before remounting to tumble headfirst down into the city – and to our final CouchSurfing host, Ayhan, who was waiting for us.

*

2. The Turkish Twins

I'd written to Ayhan way back in Constanţa, Romania, asking him if he had a couch going at the beginning of August. Ayhan gave a tentative yes to my request so far ahead of our arrival date, and confirmed a spot on his sofas for Jamie and me when we were in Yambol. I was looking forward to experiencing a slice of real Turkish life beyond the hostels, hotels and camp-sites we'd booked along the D100.

Ayhan's instructions led us round the edge of the town, where the rectangular plots of new-builds bumped against the rectangular patches of field and farm. In this place, the tradi-tional and modern came together – a suitable location for the farmer's son turned agricultural salesman, who liked all the comforts of modern living.

Our thoughtful Turk was waiting for us by the entrance of his apartment complex as we scrunched through the gravel of the newly created road towards him. He'd waited to make sure we didn't get lost in the fresh mushrooming of apartment blocks in Lüleburgaz. Ayhan led us to the lift and up into his flat – a chic, contemporary bachelor apartment with black leather sofas and crate coffee tables. While I washed off the dust from the D100, Ayhan headed for the kitchen to make coffee.

'How about a swim?' he asked as we downed our drinks, and the three of us spent the late afternoon by one of the pools in the complex, Ayhan on his mobile phone most of the time, deciding whether to go self-employed or find another company now that he'd given up his old sales job.

Ayhan was born in Bulgaria, but had left when he was just three, though his parents had held on to their land in the area, still returning on occasion to visit the family they'd left behind.

'So, why did your family leave?' I asked.

'Well, the Turks were persecuted during the Cold War in Bulgaria. Any citizen found speaking Turkish in the street, for example, was heavily fined. A lot of Bulgarian Turks returned to Turkey during that time.'

Ayhan had held on to his Bulgarian citizenship, his EU passport giving him visa-free access to much of Europe and with his dual citizenship, he'd travelled all over North America and much of Europe.

At the poolside, I flicked through the newsfeed on my mobile and saw that Bulgaria, following in Hungary's footsteps, was building a final section of razor-wire fencing that would completely seal their border off from Turkey. The Syrian refugees would now have to find another route through Europe: further north, colder, wetter. Time was not on their side as summer slipped away.

When we returned to the flat, Ayhan's twin, Nurhan, appeared. The two brothers had points of similarity, but in many ways, were as different as salt and pepper. While Ayhan spoke English fluently, Nurhan didn't speak any. Ayhan was the more confident twin, secure in his pale good looks, his blond-brown hair and light green eyes. Nurhan had the same pale eyes, but with darker hair and ears that curled out. He was small and sinewy with a sweet smile and an easy, natural charm. Both brothers liked adventure, but while Ayhan sought out the bright spots of far-flung cities and exotic locations, Nurhan roamed his own country on his racing bicycle.

While Ayhan put together a makeshift meal, Nurhan showed me pictures of himself cycling through a winter Turkey of moss-covered canyons, snow-covered mountain passes, plunging waterfalls and dripping pine forests. It was a far cry from the dusty D100. Despite Nurhan's lack of English, we managed to communicate. I asked him about the dangers of the D100, Ayhan shouting a translation from the kitchen. Nurhan found Google Maps on his mobile and traced the route with his finger from Lüleburgaz to Beylikdüzü followed by a thumb's up. Then he traced the road from Beylikdüzü to Istanbul and gave a thumb's down.

'Bad.'

Ayhan returned from the kitchen with a small plate of stuffed vines and egg and urged us to eat up as he'd arranged for us to meet his friends in town. In the café, we sat surrounded by agricultural graduates as they talked tractors and farm machinery, or so I imagined. As I listened to their gravelly Turkish, I felt bemused to find myself, a middle-aged British woman, surrounded by muscly, moustachioed and bearded Turks who politely answered my questions while daintily drinking tea from tall thin glasses on saucers. I tried to imagine agricultural students at home spending a night on the town, soberly drinking tea, and the thought made me smile to myself.

'So, did you all grow up in farming families?' I said as we stood up to leave. The men grinned a yes then held out strong farming hands to wish us all the best for the remainder of our journey.

I thought of my mother's farming family, out in the fields

that lay in the drumlins of County Down. We'd spent Saturday evenings visiting my mother's birthplace, her parent's farm at Ballycross. I'd fed my grandmother's orphaned lambs with bottled milk (kept warm in the plate-warming cupboard of her Aga). I'd climbed onto the shed roof in the corner of the front field to gather conkers and grazed my grandmother's kitchen garden for bitter gooseberries and plums. My mother's brothers were tough men who spent long days in the fields and Sundays in the meeting house. They were teetotal too.

At first, my father had loved Ballycross, envying the days his brothers-in-laws spent in the open. But his feelings towards them slowly soured after he married. His tongue grew sharper with the years and my mother had taken his criticisms of her family badly. In bed, I listened to my parents argue, my mother's voice raised in hurt; my father's cold and angry as he tore into her family, kestrel-vicious with his harsh words. My heart hammered in fear and helplessness, wishing they would stop. The idyllic world of my childhood was falling apart and the harshness of real life was a shock.

Back at Ayhan's flat, we said our goodnights to Ayhan and Nurhan and slunk off to our sofas, exhausted from the fifty-mile dual carriageway cycle in the heat, while Ayhan went off to party with neighbours by the pool, no doubt with a cup of tea in his hand.

*

3. The Sea of Marmara

Leaving Ayhan and Nurhan, our journey ahead to Çorlu was only thirty-three miles, and we were glad of it: by 10am, the heat was already fierce. The D100 was still quiet and its hard shoulder continued to provide a reassuring amount of space between our bikes and the lorries. It had a now familiar smell of diesel, oil and exhaust fumes, dust, dry earth and stagnating vegetation. We cycled in silence, concentrating on each rise and enjoying the freewheels to the next dip. The fields of crops stretched out on either side of the road, interspersed with petrol stations and glassy salesrooms. I'd asked Ayhan about the new roads and buildings we'd seen everywhere in Turkey and he'd rolled his eyes: 'Built with borrowed money.' As for us, we were glad of the shiny new garages that served up free tea in little side-rooms. One petrol pump attendant had laughed at Jamie's height, and indicated with his hands that he thought him too skinny. After the sobriety of the Bulgarians, I was enjoying the gregariousness of the Turks and their banter.

We were now seeing road signs for Istanbul with increasing frequency. I longed to see Tom and Patrick. August was marching on. We'd last seen them in June and they were fading from memory like the sun-washed landscape that surrounded me. But the Sea of Marmara was only fifty-odd miles away, and the stretch to Istanbul beyond that along the coast, even less. In theory, we could be there in two or three days, but Tom and

Patrick were not arriving for another ten days and we had no choice but to dawdle.

We arrived in Çorlu in the early afternoon, weaving through a maze of narrow streets and blocks of peeling apartments. Our flat overlooked a large square dotted with plane trees that were circled by old men in shirts and nylon trousers, squeezed together on wraparound benches, leaf-deep in gossip. The women, in contrast, hurried by, swinging bags of shopping. Children ran up and down the steps of the plaza or played hide-and-seek behind the trees and the little clock tower. We booked the apartment for a second night and spent our rest day wandering through the shopping streets and spreading out in the coolness of the flat. I watched the pigeons waddle across the square before flapping noisily up into the branches of the plane trees. Cats threaded themselves through the plane trees, rubbing skinny bodies against trunks and human legs.

Strings of cats had threaded themselves through my childhood too: black and white cats, striped tabbies, the gingers belonging to my grandmother. With more than idle interest our cats watched the homing pigeon hut that backed on to our garden. One evening, we heard the crack of a shotgun. The sound ricocheted around the garden, the sudden explosion making my heart pound. Our cat was not seen again after that day. My father marched round to the neighbour, accusing him of killing the cat.

'I didn't kill your cat, but if I find it after my pigeons again, I will shoot it.'

My father contained his anger, but his ice-cold voice sliced the air like the cheese cutter in his shop.

My father, loving, caring and sometimes warm as a summer

breeze, also had a heart that blew as cold as a blast of winter Arctic. The nights spent tearing into my mother's family, with the viciousness of our cat torturing a trapped bird, continued through summer and on into winter. I buried my head under the blankets of my bed and held my ears, but I could still hear their voices, filled with anger and hurt, ricocheting around the room like our neighbour's bullet. One night, my mother came down the stairs and started to pour painkillers down her throat. I sat in my nightie in the cold kitchen, hugging my knees. My father's shoulders stiffened in mental lockdown, his eyes hardened, his jaw set.

'Just say sorry,' my eldest sister pleaded with my father, but he stood there silently, then turned and went back to bed, leaving my sister to fish the pills from my mother's mouth.

The warmth of my childhood home had become an uninhabitable place of winter.

*

On the morning of 6 August, we carried our bikes down the stairs, ready to face the D100 for one last time before the Sea of Marmara.

We stopped at a ramshackle building on the side of the road, half-obscured by rows of football-sized melons, and climbed the steps in search of coffee.

'*Deutsch? Ja, ja, Ich spreche Deutsch!*' the farmer and café owner said. '*Willkommen bei mein Café.*'

German was becoming extremely useful in this country, for Turks were the biggest non-German ethnic group residing in Germany. Some Turks returned home in retirement. Others divided their time between the two countries. Many

German-Turks had businesses or second homes in the old homeland. Now I was finding that if someone didn't speak English, there was a good chance we could communicate in German.

The proprietor led us into a small courtyard behind the shop, where a group of burly Turkish men bent over dainty glasses of tea with gold handles served on patterned saucers of dusty pinks, blues and greens.

'I lived in Germany for years. Managed businesses there. Did really well. There was good money to be made then. Now it's not so easy, so I came back.'

'You can make good money from the shop and café here on the D100?'

'Well, yes, but I also grow melons. All those fields behind are mine. Yes, it was a good move coming back.'

Our friendly melon grower offered us tea on the house, but much as we wanted to linger under the shade of the fig trees, we sensed the Sea of Marmara was not far off.

After more than 100 miles of the D100, I yearned to leave it behind for a while – the boredom on the dual carriageway was hard to bear. I longed for the back roads of Romania with their friendly cart drivers and settlements of waving villagers. I thought back to the spring in Germany and Austria and the near-empty bike paths along the Rhine and Danube, the woodlands filled with birdsong. It seemed so long ago now, setting out on the journey with a sense of nervousness, excitement and adventure. Everything was new: the cycling, the fresh green of leaf, the call of recently arrived birds in search of a mate, the bud of spring flower. Here, the land stretched out treeless and bird-less and yellowed with sun-dried crops and stubble: it was the dustiness and exhaustion of late summer. And I realised I felt weary.

I slumped over the handlebars of my bike as the dual carriageway swept a corner – and there in front of us was a ribbon of blue: the Sea of Marmara. The thin line of blue, buffered up against a paler sky, had the same impact as a shot of caffeine. My head cleared and I sat up straight on my bike and yelled, 'Yahoo!' The road curved around again to follow the line of the coast, the ribbon of blue fanning out like a celebratory flag in front of us.

We left the D100 at the first opportunity and followed a narrow lane through coastal housing, white-washed villas jostling for a sea view between scrubland awaiting development. The way twisted left and right. Jamie stopped here and there to check his mobile until, at last, he made a sharp turn down a sandy track that led to Semizkum, by the ocean. We'd reached another long-awaited landmark.

*

The campsite manager shook his head, looking bemused. 'Not possible. Our price is our price.'

We still had our tents mouldering on the back of the bikes, not once removed since we had camped in a damp Tulln with Brian and Iris. But the hard earth and the lack of shade didn't make it an attractive option. Plus the cabins – or cottages, as the campsite called them – didn't cost much more. Still, I persisted, haggling him down a few lira. I thought I had the sharp edge of a businesswoman until I realised I'd save us pennies, not pounds.

'Cottage' was a glorified name for a garden shed: the interior of the hut was kitted out with beds, nothing more. Outside there was a veranda, an American-style fridge, a plastic garden table and two chairs. We had our little gas stove. Everything we needed. And the sea was just yards away.

This is what we had dreamed of back in Romania: *Nichtstun*, as the Germans say – 'doing nothing', compressed into one sweet noun. In the morning we wouldn't have to pedal anywhere, wouldn't have to bear down on the D100. We wouldn't have to rise at dawn to cheat the heat for a couple of hours.

We changed into swimwear and headed down to the shore. The sea was warm and cooling at the same time. I found a sun lounger and settled down under a palm shade, wriggling myself into the role of holidaymaker. It felt strange, an indulgence. Children played in the sand, and a group of older women floated out from the sea edge, their brightly coloured beach hijabs billowing out in the water, looking strangely like jellyfish from a distance.

But it wasn't long before I began to feel restless. We wandered up to the campsite store and bought bread, beef tomatoes and olives. It was the food of the gods as we'd discovered back in Çorlu. The loaves were soft and light and doughy with a crisp crust, the olives salty and full of oily flavour and the tomatoes so sweet I could finally understand why they were categorised as fruit.

In the evening, we wandered through the caravans that lined the seafront. These were no ordinary caravans, but miniature homes that spilled over onto sandy grass. There were carved tables and chairs, linen tablecloths and candelabras, Turkish carpets and tilly lamps, and the omnipresent *çaydanlık* – the two-tiered teapot that boils water from the bottom while the tea draws at the top. With Istanbul a mere fifty miles away, these caravans were homes from homes, an escape from the airless city heat. Entire families decamped to Semizkum for the summer season.

By the second day, we were bored of sitting by the sea. It felt as if my legs were still rotating. It was as if I couldn't stop spinning. This dream of *Nichtstun* didn't match my physiology any more than my psychology.

Restless, Jamie and I walked the beach to Altinorak Sitesei and found a small grocery store where we stocked up on the essential bread, tomatoes and olives as well as pasta and a tin of tuna for our one-pot evening meal over our camping stove. We asked the shop assistant for coffee and settled down on an outside seat with our bags of groceries, but when I went to pay, he shook his head. I asked him why and he typed the Turkish word into his mobile to show me the English translation: hospitality. It was an aspect of Balkan life that extended through Turkey and the Middle East, often forgotten in the west.

By the fourth day, Jamie and I agreed we'd rather creep along the Marmara coastline than spend another day in *Nichtstun* with our overheated garden shed. We packed our panniers and wheeled our bikes up the sandy lane again.

*

'You crrrazy, you. Crrazy wo-man.'

We'd cycled an absurd half-dozen miles from the campsite to the town of Silivri, finding the back roads off the D100, lingering over coffees in seaside town squares and on the shoreline. But we were moving again. We'd found a cheap hotel room with air-conditioning and I'd gone out to find a hairdresser – my hair as faded and dry as the sun-drenched Turkish fields.

The hairdresser held the comb suspended in the air. Mamma manager, who'd been swishing around the room in her long skirt barking out orders from under her headscarf, stopped now to stare at me while her teenage assistants in their knee-slashed skinny jeans giggled into their hands.

'You come all way from Eng-e-land?'

'Yes.'

'To Istanbul?'

'Yes.'

'On a bee-ce-clette?'

'Yes.' I reeled off the countries: 'Netherlands, Germany, Switzerland, Austria, Slovakia, Hungary, Croatia, Serbia, Romania, Bulgaria and Turkey.'

The hairdresser shook her head, uncomprehending. 'When you start?'

'On the first of May.'

'How long you on bike?'

'Almost four months.'

'Four days in car!'

'Plane, four hours,' one of the assistants laughed.

'Crrrazy.'

'Crrrazy wo-man,' another one said.

That evening, we walked past fish restaurants to sit on the shoreline, watching dogs canter through the shallow waters as the sun spread gold across the bay. I wondered if our hairdressers *saw* what lay beyond the shop door. The foreignness of a place gives the unfamiliar a sharpness, like wiping condensation from a window. The world from my bicycle was a place of brilliant intensity and colour.

*

4. Into the Megalopolis

We stood before an ancient crossing: the Kanuni Sultan Süleyman Bridge. It unfurled a stony streamer across the shallow waters of Büyükçekmece Bay, a remnant of the Ottoman Empire in among the highways and high-rises, the factories and refineries. Jamie had guided us here through the chaos of lanes spilling over with rubbish and tyres.

'Let's get away from the D100,' he'd said to my relief, and we'd slammed down the narrows chutes of streets crowding the hillsides above the Sea of Marmara. Now and again, we caught glimpses of sky and sea between the gaps of buildings. In this industrial hinterland of Tepecik, the air was filled with fumes and the insect hum of traffic from the motorway was always in the background. As we twisted this way and that through the back streets of Istanbul's suburbs, it was hard to believe these roads could lead to anywhere but a dead-end, and I grew less sure of Jamie's rerouting.

Then this.

The buildings gave way to wasteland, and beyond that a pale sheet of water stretched out to the hills and an expansive sky. Our destination lay on the horizon, in among the skyscrapers and the satellite tower with its wraparound bubble building, like a spaceship that had collided with the construction and skewered itself onto its needle.

Across the bay, Kanuni Sultan Süleyman Bridge rose and fell in waves of stone, echoing the topography of the land around it. No motorised vehicle had ever crossed this bridge, although this sixteenth-century construction was as broad as a highway. The roughly hewn stones were too uneven for any modern vehicle, even our bicycles. We dismounted and pushed them over to the other side.

The bridge was built by Mimar Sinan between 1566 and 1567 and named after Suleiman the Magnificent, the longest reigning Ottoman sultan, who expanded the empire across Europe into Serbia, then Hungary, only to be halted at the gates of Vienna. It's said the water in the shallows were pumped out to make way for the building of the three island supports for the bridge, and some 40,000 cubic metres of stone were used in the construction – a magnificent feat of engineering for the magnificent Sultan.

We set off across the bridge, with its twenty-eight arches, feeling the privilege of passing over this foot-worn crossing, footsteps on footsteps through the centuries. For a moment, the advance of civilisation was halted, and there was just us, the rolling Ottoman bridge and the cry of the gulls above our heads.

On the other side, we stepped back into the twenty-first century with its colourful wall murals and quirky plastic statues dotting a leafy park. We climbed up to Büyükçekmece, the steepness of the streets forcing us off our bikes and onto our tiptoes, until at last we met the D100 again, now merged with the E5 motorway. The traffic was thickening, along with the fumes and smog. We cycled on into the heat of the day, our bodies sagging over our bikes in the endless rise of road, until, at last, we saw a restaurant, emerging like a mirage from the heat haze. We stopped to rehydrate and reboot our energy levels with chilled, sugar-loaded drinks. On the edge of the terraced garden, Istanbul's suburbs fell away to the sea, with soil and grass giving way to concrete. It covered the hills along the coast as far as the eye could see in both directions, a mangle of chalky buildings that tottered drunkenly on the coastal hills.

Here in the shaded garden, sounds were muted and the glare of sunlight dimmed by the shade of plane trees. As I closed my eyes in appreciation of the breeze and quietness, a burst of noise broke from a nearby minaret speaker: the call to prayer. Then wave upon wave of undulating voice echoed from mosques across the hillsides as if in discordant conversation until they found a fragile harmony.

We continued up the hill, the satellite needle growing before us, until at last we reached the summit. The E5 at this point was a knot of roads curling under and over each other. Across the multiple lanes was our eleventh-floor refuge in the sky. Fortunately, there was a footbridge and a lift at either end of it, just big enough to take our bikes – if we took them one at a time. On the other side, in amongst the shops and skyscrapers, sat KAT11, our home for the night. We just didn't know where. We skirted the block, looking for the name without success. We asked in stores, but the shopkeepers shook their heads. Then, a moment of enlightenment: KAT11 simply meant floor 11. The hotel was secreted away, high above Büyükçekmece in the skyscraper next to us.

Ahmed, the hotel manager, was concerned that we had left our bicycles in the underfloor garage. He wrung his hands. 'It's not safe. They could be stolen. They should go in the underground office with the security men. Go down and ask them to keep them for you.'

Jamie and I took the lift down to the garage, but the office was locked and there was no sign of the security men. We reported back to Ahmed, who nodded with worried eyes. Later, without telling us, Ahmed had gone down by himself and had somehow managed to manoeuvre the chained-together bikes into the office.

In our nest in the heavens, we had a view of the metropolis that spread for miles, the concrete disappearing into a million lights when darkness fell. Neon lights flashed in jelly-pinks and electric-blues with the names of big brands: Nike, Mercedes-Benz, Shell. I edged to the window, unused to being so high and feeling dizzied by the drop beneath me.

It was a world far removed from the rural Northern Ireland I had grown up in. Looking out of the window at the high-rises and lights stretching out towards the centre of Istanbul, my thoughts returned to that night at Wood Lane when my mother had cried out for help with a bottle of sleeping pills – threatening to sleep forever.

I'd allowed my father's inability to seek forgiveness to destroy me too. I'd played this scene over and over in my mind over the years. A single event; a hardened heart. An abandonment. Now I realised I had a choice: I could give in to my bitterness and the sense of betrayal, or I could come to terms with the past and move on. I needed to accept it was a moment in time: a failing of character made manifest on that terrible night. This was not the sum total of my father, just a part of him.

My father, now ninety-two, was a husk of his former self. His pride had long ebbed away. His thoughts and hopes and disappointments, unspoken. There was no outlet for his experiences during those war years – or for his past with his own father, who he'd revered, yet who had beaten my father into adulthood. Life was never simple. There were all those nuances of grey.

As I gazed down at the ocean of Istanbul lights, I knew it was time to move on and put the past behind me. Tomorrow, we'd cycle into the urban concrete with courage. We'd not look back.

*

'Ride defensively.'

'Ride decisively.'

'Expect the unexpected.'

Nurhan hadn't been the only one to warn us about the highway from Büyükçekmece into Istanbul with a thumb turned down. One Turk told us it would be better not to take to the roads – even he found it stressful and he was used to the unpredictability of Turkish drivers: 'They're insane.' And there was the Romanian cyclist south of Edirne who had begged us to take the bus. Good luck messages and words of advice came in from worried friends.

Even though I'd studied the maps with Jamie again and again, there was no real alternative to the D100/E5 around Büyükçekmece. We had, however, noticed there was a service road on either side of the motorway. A quieter option, surely. But, if anything, the service road proved to be even more dangerous, with parked vans pulling out unexpectedly and cars driving at speed on and off the many slip lanes. Their drivers seemed to suffer from bicycle blindness – or perhaps it was 'kill a cyclist day'.

Jamie rode in front, with me following closely behind. We hadn't been on the road long when a driver pulled out directly into Jamie's path from one of the slip roads. There was no time to brake. Jamie swerved violently, all too aware of the stream of traffic on his left side.

Time slowed down. I watched Jamie move out into the speeding traffic, while the car from the slip lane careered blindly towards him, his wheels now inches from the thin frame of Jamie's bike. I watched Jamie caught in the squeeze of traffic, his lean body no match for the speeding cars. *If he is killed now, it will be my fault and all because of my hare-brained scheme to cycle a continent.*

Jamie – this child I had waited an agonising five months for, whose life was announced by a thin line of blue on a pregnancy stick – was now dicing with death. Tom and I had watched him grow from the size of a pomegranate seed to a cherry, then from a lime to a butternut squash and watermelon. We'd laughed at the pregnancy book comparisons to fruit, but I'd watched my stomach swell with pride and anticipation. I waited with increasing impatience as his due date came and went – first by one week, then by two, and finally three.

Now, on this Istanbul highway, the moment that could have been Jamie's end had passed. Somehow, he'd slipped between the cars and carried on. I breathed out and the world began to spin again. But minutes later, a second car drove out from another slip road straight into Jamie's path. Jamie slammed on his brakes this time, wobbling briefly before coming to a halt.

While he'd been reluctant to enter the world, he was not ready to leave either. All those years ago, when I was finally taken into hospital to be induced, Jamie was still loath to make an appearance. My labour lasted a day and night and by the next morning there was still no sign of my child. Tom watched the anxious faces of the midwives as they gathered around the monitor showing Jamie's dipping heartbeat, while I lay there exhausted, unaware of what was happening. There was nothing for it, but the operating table, and so Jamie was pulled into the world on someone else's time, not his.

Friends had told me how incredible birth would be: the deep, unconditional love a mother feels as soon as their child is placed in their arms, but I'd felt empty inside that day, with no emotion for this long, bloodied baby. My love would come slowly over the months and years, but it would come. But the guilt at my lack of connection for my longed-for baby stayed with me for a long time. No one had spotted I was suffering from postnatal depression, least of all me.

I dragged my bicycle onto the pavement, thinking I'd rather walk the rest of the way to Istanbul than kill my son. Mothers were supposed to protect their children, not put their lives on the line. Jamie followed.

*

After Avcilar, we found a route through a series of waterside parks that greened the edges of the Sea of Marmara. The parks should have been a pleasant diversion, but the paths were littered with broken glass and the lawns lined with rubbish and the sleeping bodies of the homeless. Still, it was infinitely better than the suicidal service road.

Where the E5 curved north away from the coast, we continued south and east along the shore and on to Çekmece Istanbul Road. The road was pleasant and cool, shaded by the spruces that lined the pavements. Then to my delight, Jamie found a cycle path that ran alongside the seafront. We skirted the airport, the planes flying low, their wheels almost touching our heads, or so it seemed. My sister Maggie and husband Andy were possibly nearby, having spent the night in an airport hotel, and Tom and Patrick would be arriving soon.

All those weeks and months I had been cycling away from them, riding thousands of miles across a continent, and now they were tantalisingly close. But it still felt unreal. I couldn't imagine the end-point, when my wheels would stop turning. For good. Now cycling along the Sea of Marmara, the grimness of the D100 behind us, my head felt fuzzy. There was a strange numbness, and for once I felt strangely removed from my surroundings. But it was a pleasant feeling, like the sensation of floating after coming around from a general anaesthetic.

Rauf Orbay Avenue became Kennedy Avenue and from there we slipped into another strip of green. The park path led on to a promenade that curled between road and shore. We dodged families with toddlers and youths on skateboards. We passed bottles lined up on the rocks of the shoreline defences and rows of pink balloons – an improvised shooting range for the city strollers. I wanted to cry and I wanted to laugh. I wanted to shout out 'I'm going home', or rather, 'I'm *coming* home' – because home was the place where my family was complete. But I didn't. Instead I cycled on, my head as light as the balloons.

By the time we arrived in Zeytinburnu we were just seven miles from Sultanahmet and the other half of my family, but we were under strict instructions from Tom not to arrive until the next day. We pulled our bikes over the footbridge that crossed the dual carriageway and found beds for the night. And so we sat it out on the fringes of the city centre like the great grey tankers anchored on the Sea of Marmara, waiting for the signal to continue to the Bosporus.

5. Between Sea and Sky

I had brought Tom to Istanbul for his fiftieth birthday. We had come to this city that teeters on the edge of Europe and Asia, one foot in, one foot out – like a teenager loitering in the entrance of a night club. We'd stayed in a little hotel run by two brothers below the Blue Mosque and explored the city that freezing Easter. I remember how we'd picked our way through the fishermen on the Galata Bridge, their fishing rods dangling off the rails, and on to the quayside, where men in gilded boats were grilling mackerel on great skillets. I remember the reek of smoking fish, and how, unable to resist the smell, we'd squeezed in apologetically between women in brightly patterned head-scarves and their more sombre-clothed, moustachioed menfolk, to order fish sandwiches. We'd devoured the fresh catch in the crusty bread, olive oil dribbling down our chins as black-eyed gulls wheeled overhead, angling for titbits. The city had glowed in the gathering darkness and I'd felt mesmerised by this place with its mix of ramshackle dwellings, glassy towers, Ottoman palaces and golden mosques, calls to prayer ringing out across the water in fugue-like waves, rising and falling before fading away. As we'd headed back alongside the port, the calls to prayer had been replaced with the rough cries of the ferrymen touting for business, their calls carried by the wind above the cry of gull and lap of shore: *Bospor, Bospor, Bospor.*

Little did I know I would come back a few years later, only instead of flying through the sky in a fistful of hours, Jamie and I would cycle in slow motion through days, weeks and months to this very spot by the Galata Bridge. Along the way, we'd experienced the gradual transition from Europe to Asia: the low-lying cottages on the Austrian border with Slovakia heralding the Balkans; the onion domes of Hungary; the men gathered outside cafés in Croatia; the Klezmer music in Serbia, so Middle-Eastern in sound; the echoes of the Ottoman Empire in Romania and Bulgaria. It had eased us gently into this exotic place straddling East and West.

Jamie and I woke up early on our last morning of cycling, although we were less than an hour away from our arranged meeting point. Tom, Patrick, Maggie and Andy had agreed to meet us at 10am. We wheeled our bikes out of the hotel into the early morning rush hour and cycled between a squeeze of concrete and corrugated metal barriers, trying not to skin our knuckles on the metal.

Relieved to get off the road, Jamie and I peddled on through Sahil Park, the Sea of Marmara below us the colour of pale pewter. We passed a lighthouse and the towers of the old city wall. Ahead, I caught glimpses of the Bosporus suspension bridge stretching out across the waterway that connected the Sea of Marmara and the Black Sea – those waters beyond waters that linked Europe and Asia. All around us were the places I'd visited with Tom in the April rain and sleet: the Blue Mosque, Topkapi Palace and Hagia Sophia.

Tom was less than a mile away – but we were still too early.

We found a café above the city wall and lingered there. 'It's like Christmas morning when Dad made us wait outside the living room door until we were all ready,' Jamie laughed.

As our meet-up time approached, we headed on to Sirkeci ferry terminal. A cycle path on the promenade took us away from Kennedy Avenue, now choked with rush-hour traffic. The air was thick with exhaust fumes and the sound of manic horns, but it didn't matter: we were almost there. The road bent sharply left and rose steeply one last time before dropping down to the ferry terminal.

Somewhere in the crowds were Tom and Patrick.

Then I saw them, Tom tall among the tourists with his russet-grey hair, and Patrick beside him, his hair still the colour of bright autumn – a younger, slimmer Tom. And my sister and her husband too. Tom had his back to us. I shouted out. He turned around in surprise.

'You're too early,' he spluttered, groping in his pocket for his 'finishing line' streamer.

Jamie looked at me and laughed: 'Christmas morning.'

But I didn't care. My face was already against Tom's, the bristles on his face prickling my cheeks; his smell, familiar and strange; the contours of his body locking mine like shoreline and sea. Then Patrick, the son I'd abandoned for three and a half months. But he was grinning, pleased for us, pleased we were all together again. I turned to Jamie and hugged him too. Gone was the closely cropped hair and the pale, clean-shaven face he had left Rotterdam with. Now his hair was long and unkempt, his face weathered and browned by weeks and months in the open air, and a patchy beard covered his chin and jawline. I craned my neck to try and read the expression on his face. I thought I read relief. I thought I saw pride, but there was definitely a shine in his eyes. I still didn't know what this trip meant to him. One day, I would sit down and ask him, but for the moment I was just glad we had done this journey together.

As for me, I realised, it was not just the rivers and hills and the open roads that had healed me, but the people along the way that had taken us into their homes. I thought of my old friends: Marcella, Andrea, Manuela and Maria. Then the strangers who'd opened up their home to us: Asher, Petra, Hans, Klaus, Kat, Eszter, Zita, Sashka and Ayhan. They'd all taught me what generosity and openness meant. They had restored my faith in human nature and made me a better human being.

We wheeled our bikes onto the boat to cross over to the Asian side to celebrate in Turkish style, with glasses of chai. As the little ferry chugged across the water, the realisation came on slowly: there was nowhere left to cycle. The wheels could stop spinning. I had come home.

*

My father lived somewhere between sea and sky. The birds were his songbook along with his Brethren hymnals. Finches and tits, waders and warblers, his God in the heavens – he knew them all. The fields and the woods were his earthly home and the country lanes that stretched out in invitation. We drove and drove to find the ocean. Nowhere was too far within a day's reach: County Down, the Antrim Coast, Donegal, Galway, Claire, Dublin and Kildare. What was it that called him?

The smell of the sea? The slap of wind in his face? The taste of its salt on his lips? The damp of sand between his toes as he walked the shoreline in his solemn suit? His jacket slung over an arm, braces tangled on his white shirt. He'd roll up his suit trouser legs, revealing shins of creamy white, and paddle through the Irish Sea or the Atlantic. Perhaps he liked the open horizons, the waves that rolled in from other countries, even continents. They were all beyond his reach. His world was limited in thought and physicality. He lived in the straitjacket of his Brethren suit. But it didn't stop him dreaming.

The sea and its waterways had called me too. I'd followed the Rhine from the North Sea to the edge of the Swiss Alps, and the Danube to the Black Sea. In the stifling heat of the Bulgarian and Turkish interior, I'd missed the waterways in the waves of yellowed corn, until we'd reached the ocean again at the Sea of Marmara.

My father was now lost in the corridors of broken neurological pathways and the corridors of the care home, his breathing growing shallower with each passing year, his mind vague as twilight. Visits with him were like reaching into the gloaming: there were moments of clarity, bright enquires after Tom and the boys, until he withdrew into the shadows again. When I returned home, I would tell him about my journey along Europe's waterways and beside Europe's seas. I would tell him about the cuckoo that travelled with us through May and June; the storks that lined the chimney pots of the Upper Rhine and Danube villages; the summer swallows and the house martins on the water. Who knew, maybe he would respond.

'Where do you want to go?' I'd asked him on that last visit before the cycle.

'Dromore.'

'Dromore?' I'd echoed in wonder. Not Tyrella, or Newcastle, or Greencastle by the sea, or even the lough on the edge of our town. I'd taken him to Dromore as he'd requested, to the inland market town with its motte and bailey, firmly wedged in solid land between lake and ocean. And I was puzzled. The next day, back at the care home, he requested to visit Dromore again. Now I saw why: Dromore was my mother's hometown. And I realised that in spite of his silence after her death, as though she had never existed, he'd loved her in his own way. He just didn't know how to express it.

Now, sitting in Atatürk Airport, our bicycles stowed away in cardboard boxes, a message pinged up on my mobile from my sister back home: *It's not looking good for dad. His heart is failing and breathing laboured.*

When exactly had the birds stopped singing? Or had I just stopped listening? And I realised, sitting in the noise of the airport waiting for our flight to be called, I had removed myself so completely from my father, it was difficult to reconnect with him emotionally. I thought of my father, quick to take offence, slow to forgive, dwelling on slights, intolerant of human failings. Hadn't I been just the same? I'd held on to that night in the kitchen so long ago and hardened my heart – feeling only coldness towards him. I'd felt anger at his withdrawal from the world, from me and my mother. Now my father's journey was coming to an end, and so was mine. But as the journey of my life continued, my ties to him could not be severed. I would start out on a new path of acceptance – not just of him, but of me and who I was and what I had become – and in doing so would be freed.

The birds would sing again. The waterways and pathways would draw me once more.

These were his gifts.

Epilogue – What If?

There is a window and a city of red-tiled roofs and skyscrapers beyond it. There are needles of minarets and discs of gold. There are seas of navy and a river striped with bridges. There are swabs of clouds that float suspended in the blue-washed sky. I twist my neck to see the world beneath me. Squinting in the sunlight, I look out over the silver thread of rivers, the peaks of dusty rock and the dark stain of forest. The only sound is the hum of the plane's engine. There is no birdsong, no scent of flower or bread – just the odourless cabin. Turkey, Bulgaria, Romania, Serbia, Hungary, Austria, Germany and the Netherlands disappear in minutes and hours – not weeks and months, as it should be.

In less than an afternoon, I reach the English Channel and the clouds part to reveal the light playing off the ocean below – slate grey to petrol blue, olive green to steel. Beyond the plane, there is the curved thread of horizon between sea and sky. Somewhere out in the greys tinged with colour, there are birds taking wing. I feel the pull of the line between the visible and invisible. And I think, *What if?*

This is the end. As I remember it.

It is also the beginning.

Acknowledgements

Many thanks to my husband, Tom, for his unfailing support throughout the writing of this book, and on a more practical level, for providing a keen eye as proofreader. Thanks to my sons, Jamie and Patrick, for giving me permission to tell my – and their – stories.

Deep gratitude goes to the members of my writing group for their advice and support: Moira Ashley, Stephen Fabes, Elizabeth Gowing, Paola Fornari Hanna, Suzy Pope and Marie Kreft. And to Gillian Shimwell, whose gentle encouragement and wisdom helped me to find the narrative for the book.

To everyone at Saraband: Sara Hunt for her support and guidance; Craig Hillsley, who edited the book with such care and attention, and likewise to Maddie Pollard and Elizabeth Beck for additional proofreading. Thanks to Don Shewan for his excellent cartography.

This book is for all those who've been part of my journey through life and on the cycle. To my siblings for their continued love and support. To friendships across Europe that have endured across the years, sometimes decades. To the Klein and Willms families in the Eifel, Germany, Manuela Gaggiotti and her family in Switzerland and Maria Ives-Strasser and Chris Ives in Austria. Thanks go to Derbyshire friends Chris and Richard Powley, who generously offered their home in Ungstein. My gratitude also goes to the strangers across Europe who welcomed me into their homes and communities. Because of them I was able to experience a slice of real European life, and in doing so they helped me understand my continent and history a little better.

HELEN MOAT

A TIME OF BIRDS

Reflections on cycling across Europe

Saraband

Published by Saraband,
Digital World Centre,
1 Lowry Plaza,
The Quays, Salford, M50 3UB

www.saraband.net

ISBN: 9781912235704
ebook: 9781912235711

Designed and typeset by EM&EN
Printed and bound in Great Britain by Clays Ltd, Elcograf S.p.A.

MIX
Paper from
responsible sources
FSC® C018072

10 9 8 7 6 5 4 3 2 1